FACTORY GIRLS

FACTORY GIRLS

WOMEN IN THE THREAD MILLS
OF MEIJI JAPAN

E. Patricia Tsurumi

PRINCETON UNIVERSITY PRESS   PRINCETON, NEW JERSEY

Library of Congress Cataloging-in-Publication Data

Tsurumi, E. Patricia, 1938–
Factory girls : women in the thread mills of Meiji Japan /
E. Patricia Tsurumi.
p.   cm.
Includes bibliographical references.
ISBN 0-691-03138-X (alk. paper)
1. Women textile workers—Japan—History. 2. Silk industry—Japan—
Employees—History. 3. Cotton industry—Japan—Employees—
History. 4. Japan—Industries—History. I. Title.
HD6073.T42J38   1990
331.4'877'00952—dc20   89-24325   CIP

This book has been composed in Linotron Sabon

Princeton University Press books are printed on acid-free paper,
and meet the guidelines for permanence and durability of the
Committee on Production Guidelines for Book Longevity of the
Council on Library Resources

Printed in the United States of America by Princeton University Press,
Princeton, New Jersey
10 9 8 7 6 5 4 3 2 1

For Maia ————————————————————————————

Contents

Tables

Acknowledgments

THIS book owes a great deal to the Japanese social historians hailed in the introduction and to other scholars whose names also appear in the footnotes. The research required a number of visits of varying lengths to Japan, and each time I visited that country I became more deeply indebted to Professor Motoyama Yukihiko of Kyoto. Again and again the boundless generosity of Professor Motoyama provided me with excellent facilities to carry out my work. From his knowledge and his example I learned so much about Meiji history, I can never thank him enough. My thanks also go to the Faculty of Education of the University of Kyoto for hosting my research sojourns in Kyoto. I am grateful to Ms. Nishikawa Yaeko of Kyoto for introducing me to silk workers of Kyoto's Nishijin district who kindly permitted me to observe them producing the famous Nishijin products and answered my questions about the past as well as the present. In Japan I also owe special thanks to Fukasaku Mitsusada, Fukasaku Sumire, Hoshino Kazumasa, Hoshino Shigeko, Komatsu Machiko, Komatsu Joe, Komatsu Junji, and the five friends who became seven and then eight friends.

I accumulated debts in North America too. Encouragement and help with translations came from W. Donald Burton, Yasuko France, Yori Oda, and Susan Phillips although they bear no responsibility for any final version of a translation. (Unless otherwise indicated, translations in the book are mine.) W. Donald Burton, Brian W. Dippie, and Christine St. Peter read the entire manuscript critically and provided invaluable advice. Tsuneharu Gonnami of the University of British Columbia Asian Studies Library was helpful in many different ways. The Social Sciences and Humanities Research Council of Canada (SSHRCC), the Japan Society for the Promotion of Science (JSPS), and the University of Victoria provided financial support for the research. June Bull, Dinah Dickie, and Gloria Orr valiantly typed the manuscript. Midge Ayukawa, Michael Nardi, and Lois Vickery read proofs. Christine Godfrey compiled the index. Ron made tea. Constant support came from my daughter, Maia.

FACTORY GIRLS

Introduction

MUCH has been written about "the Meiji miracle": those astonishing feats of nation building during the Meiji era from 1868 to 1912 that produced Japan's modern military and industrial establishments and their sustaining infrastructures. While many studies of governmental, industrial, social, and cultural leadership have been completed, much less has been published—especially in English-language books or periodicals—about the large numbers of very ordinary people who made these feats possible. This book is about some of these people. It is about the women and girls whose working lives in the silk- and cotton-thread factories produced so much of the profit that built the "Meiji miracle."

During Meiji the numbers of Japan's first industrial workers rapidly multiplied, but throughout the era they remained a small minority in a laboring population heavily engaged in the occupations of a predominantly agricultural country. Before Japan's industrial revolution was fully launched during the 1880s, 78 to 80 percent of those gainfully employed were in agricultural occupations.[1] By 1902, with the first wave of industrialization cresting dramatically and those gainfully employed amounting to appoximately 24.6 million, 67.2 percent of those working were in agriculture.[2] During that year about 499,000 of all persons employed were industrial workers, and about 269,000 of the 499,000 were working in textile—mainly silk- and cotton-thread—factories.[3] Ten years later about 863,000 of a total working population of approximately 25.8 million were industrial workers, more than half of them textile—mostly female—operatives.[4]

The importance to the national economy of the Meiji *kōjo* or "factory girls" in cotton spinning and silk reeling was much greater than their numbers. From the earliest days of the new era, silk thread was a valuable export earning foreign exchange for the country's costly nation-building enterprises. Cotton spun on machines in Japanese factories had first to combat

#1

---

[1] Robert E. Cole and Ken'ichi Tominaga, "Japan's Changing Occupational Structure and Its Significance," in *Japanese Industrialization and Its Social Consequences*, ed. Hugh Patrick (Berkeley, 1976), 58. See also William W. Lockwood, *The Economic Development of Japan: Growth and Structural Change* (Princeton, 1968), 462–63.

[2] Ibid.

[3] Sheldon Garon, *The State and Labor in Modern Japan* (Berkeley, 1987), 13. The figures for industrial workers given in this introduction are for workers in factories with ten or more workers.

[4] Cole and Tominaga, "Japan's Changing Occupational Structure," 58; Ōkōchi Kazuo, *Reimei ki no Nihon rōdō undō* (The dawn of the Japanese labor movement) (Tokyo, 1952), 205.

the cheap thread from Manchester and elsewhere, which flooded local markets under the terms of the one-sided treaties that were part of the Western
powers' "gunboat diplomacy" before the Meiji Restoration of 1868. But
by 1897 cotton-thread exports were more than twice the amount of cotton
thread imported.[5] Until long past the Meiji era, the performance of the
women and girls in the mills was a key factor in such textile profitability.
And while the female troops in Japan's first industrial army were pioneers
in the new machine age toward which Japan's rulers were rushing the
country, the silk and cotton kōjo also sustained the old agrarian world of
lord and peasant where most of Japan's population still dwelt. On the one
hand, the textile kōjo were—as they described themselves in their songs—
"creators of profits" for factory owners and their class allies directing the
Meiji state. On the other, they enabled their tenant-farming families to
continue paying high rent to rural landlords, who, in turn, invested some
of the countryside's surpluses (which they still monopolized) in the nation's modernizing efforts. As we shall see, the collective and individual
costs of the kōjo's double contribution to Japan's transformation into
modern nation-statehood were very high. Comparisons of these costs with
those borne by other daughters of the poor, those who stayed home in
their villages or "went out to work" (*dekasegi*) in weaving sheds or brothels
instead of thread factories, offer clues regarding how the subjects of this
study and their contemporaries regarded these costs.

As every textbook of modern Japanese history reminds us, it was the
Meiji government that took the initiative to lay the foundations for modern industry. And even after private industrialists appeared on the scene,
the government, committed to *shokusan kōgyō* (encouraging industry), continued to provide direct and indirect financial assistance as well as technical
and other kinds of aid. Government and private management often worked
closely together, sharing goals and aspirations.[6] This was particularly true
for the silk- and cotton-thread industries.

Modern silk reeling began with government mills and expanded with
support to operators of private filatures. The girls and women, mainly from

---

[5] Nakamura Masanori, *Rōdōsha to nōmin* (Laborer and peasant), vol. 29 of *Nihon no rekishi*
(History of Japan) (Tokyo, 1976), 157.

[6] Between the Meiji government and the business community of the era were many close
associations. Garon, *State and Labor*, notes some examples: "The Tokyo Chamber [of Com-
merce] was directed by the influential entrepreneurs Shibusawa Eichi and Mitsui's Matsuda
Takashi, both of whom left the Finance Ministry in the early 1870s. Inoue Kaoru was perhaps
the best-known example of a retired official who moved between the two worlds with ease.
Frequently a minister of state, he headed several government agencies between 1878 and
1898, while serving as director of some of the nation's biggest companies. By the 1890s, the
interests of certain cabinet ministers had become so closely intertwined with those of the mine
owner Furukawa Ichibei that it took years before the government ordered his company to
cease dumping highly toxic wastes at the Ashio Copper Mine" (19).

samurai or well-to-do peasant homes, who were persuaded to work in national, prefectural, or private filatures during the 1870s were urged by government and private managers alike to "reel for the nation." By the twentieth century, when the industry had been thoroughly in private hands for
a decade or two and most of those at the machines were daughters of the
poor, employers still urged their hands to reel "for the sake of the nation."
In the handful of small, mostly government-owned cotton-spinning mills
that existed before 1883, female and male workers from poor samurai families patriotically served their public and private employers much as pre-
Restoration samurai had once served their lords. After the proliferation of
large-scale cotton-spinning works that quickly followed the Osaka Cotton-
Spinning Company's establishment in 1883, the cotton-spinning operatives came from poor, mostly commoner families too. At first they included
both males and females from urban slums or suburban villages, but by
1900 almost 80 percent of them were girls or women, most of whom came
from struggling tenant farmers' homes in faraway villages. These daughters
of the poor were also urged by their employers to work to meet national
goals.

Government and employers' urgings were one thing; responses of silk
and cotton kōjo were often another. In this study we discover that, although the samurai daughters of the 1870s seem to have shared the aspirations of the ruling class, when a new class of worker flocked to the mills,
these factory girls from poor, rural homes had different goals and loyalties.
Molded by unprecedented experiences as Japanese factory workers, the kōjo's own goals and loyalties helped shape their growing view of themselves
as a distinct group with a distinct identity. The emergence of that identity
is an important part of the history of the Japanese working class.

Among the major sources from which this story has been unraveled are
firsthand accounts of life as a kōjo. These include autobiographical mem-
oirs like *Tomioka Diary* (Tomioka nikki), the famous recollection of work
and life during the 1870s at the government's model Tomioka filature and
Rokkōsha filature of Nagano prefecture, written by Wada Ei, one of the
first young women to go to "reel for the nation." Wada may have been able
to draw upon short daily entries from the 1870s when she wrote *Tomioka
Diary* more than three decades later, but its somewhat nostalgic descriptions warn the researcher to study this and other memories of former kōjo
critically. Still, while it is important to check their contents against other
kinds of sources, memories of elderly, retired mill workers—like the oral
histories of former thread-factory women collected by Yamamoto Shigemi
and others—have important things to tell us. Essential in this study too are
the words of silk- and cotton-thread operatives spoken at a time when they
were working in or running away from the Meiji mills. We have such records because at the turn of the century government investigators who

interviewed these kōjo wrote down without alteration the stories they heard. Other words directly from the mouths of Meiji kōjo are in the songs about their working lives that factory women sang. Although these too must be approached with caution, they can be a rich source.[7] I emphatically agree with Yamamoto Shigemi that for those seeking to document the lives of factory girls who "wrote neither letters nor diaries" the work songs are vital historical records.[8] I am grateful to the investigators of the Meiji era and of our own time who recorded the songs they heard factory girls and ex-factory girls singing, including the anonymous lyrics in their reports and published works.

Governmental and nongovernmental reports of factory workers' conditions provide other sources, especially for the last half of the Meiji period. Government reports came out of a series of investigations into conditions existing in factories and mines, investigations that were begun in the 1890s by a handful of reform-minded bureaucrats in the Home Ministry and the Ministry of Agriculture and Commerce. Their major interest in pushing for legislation to improve conditions in the factories was in healthy industries, not healthy workers. Yet unlike other state officials and most of the business community, they believed that short-run profits gained from hazardous working conditions would in the long run cost the nation too much in diminished efficiency on the part of weakened workers, who might also produce sickly offspring.[9] The main thrust of the inquiries they initiated culminated in a number of detailed reports in 1902 and 1903. For bureaucrats trying to convince colleagues, superiors, and industrialists of a need for health and safety standards in the factories, as well as for later researchers, the most important of these was and is the detailed study of factory workers' conditions entitled *Shokkō jijō* (Factory workers' conditions), published as three reports and two appendixes in 1903. Two of the three deal with silk- and cotton-plant operatives, and one of the appendixes carries the interviews during which attentive listeners copied down the factory girls' stories. It is hard to imagine Meiji bureaucrats doing this—and indeed they did not. The factory-survey office established in the Ministry of Agriculture and Commerce was a temporary agency, and most of its work, especially in the field, was done by temporarily hired personnel, not career

[7] Ensuring that a song from earlier times is placed in its proper context can be problematic, but the rewards are so rich they are worth the risks. For productive examination of songs in two very different historical contexts, see Lawrence W. Levine, "Slave Songs and Slave Consciousness," in *Anonymous Americans: Explorations in Nineteenth-Century Social History*, ed. Tamara K. Hareven (Englewood Cliffs, N.J., 1971), 99–126, and Vic Gammon, "Folk Song Collecting in Sussex and Surrey, 1843–1914," *History Workshop* 10 (Autumn 1980): 61–89.

[8] Yamamoto Shigemi, *Aa nomugi tōge* (Ah! The Nomugi Pass) (Tokyo, 1977), 169.

[9] Garon, *State and Labor*, 18–29; Byron K. Marshall, *Capitalism and Nationalism in Prewar Japan: The Ideology of the Business Elite, 1868–1941* (Stanford, Calif., 1967), 77–93.

bureaucrats. Yokoyama Gen'nosuke, the dedicated journalist who had already published his own reports on conditions in factories and slums, was one of those temporary employees of the temporary survey office. Circumstantial evidence suggests that he may have conducted interviews with female textile workers.[10]

The other set of valuable data collected by government investigators comes from the government surveys of health and sanitation in the factories from 1906 to 1910. Beginning in 1909, the young medical doctor Ishihara Osamu played a central part in these, concentrating much of the sophisticated investigations he directed upon problems of female textile workers. With a substantial staff (twenty-three individuals had been assigned to his project), he studied the effects of factory life on the health of kōjo, not only while they were working in the factories, but afterward, too, when they had returned to their homes in the countryside.

Surveys taken by nongovernmental bodies were also motivated by concerns other than the welfare of workers. Private organizations like the Sanitation Society of Osaka (Ōsaka shiritsu eisei kai) were worried about public health. At its annual general meeting in the autumn of 1894, this group authorized a survey that two years later produced a report entitled *Shokkō nenrei oyobi rōdō jikan chōsa* (A survey of factory workers' ages and laboring hours). The extensive survey of operatives in cotton-spinning mills, undertaken for management purposes by the national cotton-spinning employers' association in 1897, has proven to be an especially valuable source.

Another important set of sources is the writings of individuals whom I think of as friends of the kōjo. These individuals were either interested in social reform or filled with sympathy for and solidarity with the poor they visited in the slums, workshops, and factories of Meiji Japan. Several of them were professional journalists who brought a trained and objective eye to what they saw, and they published their findings in books as well as the daily papers. (Contemporary articles in a newspaper that served as a mouthpiece of the business community contain similar information from another point of view.) Among these accounts the most durable are the excellent work of Yokoyama Gen'nosuke, who died of tuberculosis at age forty-five in as wretched living quarters as many he had written about. Another friend of the factory girls of Meiji and of the decade that followed was Hosoi Wakizō, himself a cotton-spinning mill hand from the age of thirteen until his death in 1925. His *Jokō aishi* (The pitiful history of female factory workers), much of which is an eyewitness account, documents lives

---

[10] Portions of the interviews are similar to but more extensive than in Yokoyama's *Nihon no kasō shakai* (The lower classes of Japan) (Tokyo, 1949), first published in 1898. I am indebted to Yutani Eiji, " 'Nihon no Kasō Shakai' of Gennosuke Yokoyama, Translated and with an Introduction" (Ph.D. diss., University of California, Berkeley, 1985), 6, for bringing this to my attention.

of cotton-spinning women from the 1880s to the early 1920s. The title of this classic has entered the Japanese language as a phrase used to describe deplorable working conditions for women.

In addition, this study has been inspired and aided by the committed scholarship of Nakamura Masanori, Sakura Takuji, Sanpei Kōko, Sumiya Mikio, and Yamamoto Shigemi. To these giants of our own day as well as to Yokoyama, Hosoi, and their comrades in earlier times I owe a special debt of gratitude.

Since most of the Meiji factory girls came from rural homes where for centuries family survival had depended heavily upon the work of female as well as male family members, chapter 1 sketches the pre-Meiji background of women in such families. It discusses "women's work" during the last centuries of feudal Japan and describes the challenges that families faced with the opening of the country to foreign trade in the late 1850s and the Meiji Restoration of 1868. Chapter 2 traces the beginning of Japan's modern silk-reeling and cotton-spinning industries during the early years of the new age and the part female workers played in these industries.

Chapters 3 through 8 examine continuities and changes in the working lives of silk and cotton kōjo from 1872 to 1912. For many of the first machine silk reelers, the 1870s was an optimistic time, but after the Matsukata deflation policies began in 1881, increasingly harsh conditions marked the lives of female factory hands in both silk and cotton industries. In these six chapters, recruitment, relationships with families back home, employers' attempts to control female operatives, working environments, dormitory life, sexual harassment, industrial protests, and attitudes toward employers are investigated. As much as possible, the story is told in the words of the working women and girls; sometimes it is told in the lyrics of the songs they sang about their lives in the mills.

Chapter 9 looks at the Meiji textile operatives' life in a comparative light. How did it differ from the experiences of sisters and cousins back home in the villages? Were the health risks of factory girls greater than those suffered by country girls? Were the problems facing Meiji cotton and silk kōjo shared by factory women in industrializing settings elsewhere? Chapter 10 continues the comparative probe with portraits of two other common occupations for daughters of the poor in Meiji Japan: weaving and prostitution. Meiji women in these two trades endured exploitation familiar to female textile workers of their day. This exploitation belongs not only to the early industrializing past; today in Japan the circumstances of some working women are disturbingly similar to those experienced by textile operatives during Meiji. One hopes that the comparisons will help us to place the working lives of Meiji silk and cotton operatives within the larger context of their society. Perhaps they can tell us something as well about the heritage bequeathed to the Japan of our own time by the kōjo's treatment in the thread mills of Meiji Japan.

1

The Background

In 1868 the most urgent concern of Japan's new rulers was resistance to the Western encroachment that had already ensnared their country in a web of unequal treaties.[1] Resistance required, they had quickly learned, rapid industrialization and modern armaments. During the new era, the Meiji period of 1868 to 1912, strategic industry related directly to military considerations was established first, but it was soon joined by production of consumer goods, the most important of which were textiles.[2] Begun initially as largely government enterprises that received government support and encouragement after they were in private hands, the machine silk-reeling and cotton-spinning industries of Meiji were the first in Japan to develop extensive factory production. Their work forces, heavily female, formed a large proportion of the labor force during the first period of Japan's industrialization.[3] This pattern would remain long after the Meiji era had ended.

Although throughout the Meiji period some cotton-mill hands came from urban homes, the vast majority of the silk-reeling and cotton-spinning operatives were women and girls from a rural background. During the first decade of the new era, daughters of debt-free and even well-to-do farming families went to work in the new silk mills, but thereafter the female workers in both silk and cotton plants tended to be from poor peasant

[1] See Jon Halliday, *A Political History of Japanese Capitalism* (New York, 1975), esp. 60–61, and Thomas C. Smith, *Political Change and Industrial Development in Japan: Government Enterprise, 1868–1880* (Stanford, Calif., 1955).

[2] Long ago E. Herbert Norman suggested that light industries such as textiles were also "strategic industries" "because of their importance in export industries intended to compete against foreign products and hence requiring subsidy and protection." E. Herbert Norman, *Japan's Emergence as a Modern State* (New York, 1940), 117.

[3] In 1882, when the government had just begun to sell its major enterprises to private industrialists, textile mills, which accounted for one-half of all private factories, employed three-quarters of all factory workers in the country. Sumiya Mikio, *Nihon chinrōdō shi ron: Meiji zenki ni okeru rōdōsha kaikyū no keisei* (A history of wage Labor in Japan: The formation of the laboring class in early Meiji) (Tokyo, 1955), 114. In 1900, female workers made up 62 percent of the labor force in private factories, and ten years later women and girls were 71 percent of the workers in private plants. Inoue Kiyoshi, *Nihon josei shi* (A history of Japanese women) (Tokyo, 1967), 212. See also Ushiyama Keiji, "Nihon shihonshugi kakuritsu ki" (The period of establishment of Japanese capitalism), in *Nihon nōgyō shi: shihonshugi no tenkai to nōgyō mondai* (History of Japanese agriculture: Development of capitalism and agricultural problems), ed. Teruoka Shūzō (Tokyo, 1981), esp. 58–59.

Table 1.1
Female Factory Workers in Cotton Spinning and Silk Reeling in Numbers and
Percentages of the Total Work Force

	1902	1907	1914	1919
Cotton	61,980	68,273	100,460	175,873
	79.4%	79.3%	80.6%	77.4%
Silk	120,980	148,588	209,703	278,249
	93.8%	94.9%	95.0%	93.4%

Source: Nishinarita, "Joshi rōdō no shorui gata to sono hen'yō," 11.

families. By the turn of the century these kōjo came from some of the poorest tenant-farmer villages in the entire country. The women and girls who became textile factory workers, including those from independent cultivator or prosperous farming homes, were no strangers to hard work. They knew that many generations of country women had contributed to the well-being of their families by laboring both at home and away from home. Like their mothers and grandmothers before them in pre-Meiji times, they had routinely seen female as well as male offspring of peasant families "going out to work" (dekasegi) in a place beyond commuting distance to the home village.

Women, Work, and the Peasant Family in Pre-Meiji Times

During the Edo era (1600–1867), female offspring of peasant families were sent away to labor as dekasegi workers, usually in a local village or town. This immediately reduced the number of mouths that had to be fed, and the girls might gain valuable skills and experience, eventually bringing in some remuneration. The ones who remained at home were essential workers within the peasant family economy, producing and processing food and other items for the family's subsistence, caring for the young and the incapacitated, and playing key roles in the production of marketable commodities, including silk and cotton thread.

The Confucian ideology of Japan's samurai rulers during the Edo era decreed a static, self-supporting agrarian economy as the only legitimate source of wealth. By the end of the seventeenth century, however, financial exigencies largely related to consumption patterns of the samurai class obligated rulers to permit peasant money-making and peasant-merchant collaboration in the interests of goals not attainable by Confucian-sanctioned production of food and simple necessities alone. The feudal lords encouraged cultivation of cash crops and cottage production of local handicraft specialties. Although in theory all land remained the property of the feudal lords and could not be bought or sold, within the peasant class the more fortunate were able to become de facto landlords as their poorer neighbors mortgaged their holdings to borrow funds demanded by the growing money economy and unrelenting tax burdens.[4] Well-to-do farmers and merchants increasingly employed poor peasants of both sexes—sometimes dekasegi peasants—in small, medium-sized, or large-scale enterprises such as sake brewing, bean-paste making, coal mining, and cotton or silk production. From the early eighteenth century on, there was an especially strong demand for cloth and yarn goods of cotton and silk.[5]

Although a peasant family might raise a cash crop or sell a processed or semiprocessed handicrafted product in order to pay taxes, the household economy tended to be self-sufficient.[6] The situation may have differed in the homes of a handful of relatively rich rural families, but nearly every item in daily use in families that tilled small or medium-sized plots on which they paid taxes directly, or in families that worked the land as tenants, was made by family members. And although there were regional variations regarding the division of labor along gender lines,[7] it was the female members of the family who everywhere were particularly active in the production of such items and in the processing of the family's food, clothing, and fuel supplies.

First from hemp and then from cotton plants, farm women and girls took the raw materials that required many stages of treatment before they

[4] During the Edo period there was great variation regarding the degree of penetration of the money economy, the amount of commodity production, and the number of tenants and wage laborers in literally hundreds of different rural areas under a multitude of fief administrations. Tenant farming, for instance, was most common in districts near urban centers. Ōuchi Tsutomu has estimated that at the end of the Edo period in economically advanced areas like Kinki about 31 percent of the agricultural land was tilled by tenants, in moderately developed areas about 20 percent, and in backward districts like Tōhoku about 11 percent. Ōuchi Tsutomu, *Nihon ni okeru nōmin sō no bunkai* (Dissolution of the agricultural class in Japan) (Tokyo, 1970), cited in Nakamura Takafusa, *Economic Growth in Prewar Japan* [*Senzenki Nihon keizai seichō no bunseki* (Tokyo, 1971)] trans. Robert A. Feldman (New Haven, 1983), 49.

[5] Katō Kōzaburō, "Nihon shihonshugi keisei ki" (The period of formation of Japanese capitalism), in Teruoka, *Nihon nōgyō shi*, 11–12.

[6] Household self-sufficiency was especially strong up to the end of the seventeenth century. See ibid., 9. Stephen Vlastos, *Peasant Protests and Uprisings in Tokugawa Japan* (Berkeley, Calif., 1986), 92–113, vividly describes sericulture in an Edo village that needed the income from this by-employment to pay taxes.

[7] See, for example, regional variations in jobs done by women and men processing cotton as discussed in William Hauser, *Economic Institutional Change in Tokugawa Japan: Osaka and the Kinai Cotton Trade* (Cambridge, 1974), 136–40.

became thread ready to be woven into the cloth from which the family's clothes were fashioned. Women made sandals, bags, baskets, and many other household and farming implements from straw. They were in charge of pickling vegetables, grinding grain, making salt, and all of the laborious processing of food for future use and day-to-day meal preparation—tedious and time-consuming tasks demanding skill and patience. In addition to their many labor-intensive household chores, women bore major responsibility for looking after the very young and the very old and nursing the ill or injured.[8]

At the same time, farm wives and daughters were heavily involved directly in agricultural production. They cultivated barley, beans, foxtail millet, buckwheat, and other dry-field crops, harvesting the yields when they were ready. They worked side by side with their menfolk performing similar or complementary tasks: men would turn over the soil while women planted in the areas thus prepared; men and women weeded fields together; every member of the family would turn out to bring in the rice harvest. All-important rice planting and transplanting, the religious as well as economic focus of much peasant life, had been women's special work since ancient times.[9] And threshing the rice harvest tended to be a female job too.[10]

A chapter in a warrior chronicle describing agriculture at the beginning of the Edo period portrays a farm woman who is reminiscent of the "good wife" in the Book of Proverbs:

The farmer's wife can work unceasingly. Meticulously she prepares the food, morning and night. She weaves cloth for the linen garments for spring, summer, and autumn. She grinds the barley and plants the rice fields. In autumn she threshes the rice and makes ready the tribute [rice paid as land tax]; in winter she weaves cotton robes for the New Year. She is able to take her husband's place at the plough. When the firewood refuses to burn she labors long over it because she will not serve meals that are not tasty.[11]

The picture here is of a woman who manages to do some of her husband's work, if necessary, as well as her own. Despite different customs in different areas, early seventeenth-century farm women generally performed a

[8] Nagashima Atsuko, "Kinsei josei no nōgyō rōdō ni okeru ichi" (The position of women in agricultural labor during the late feudal period), *Rekishi hyōron* (Historical review), 382 (March 1982): 55–56.

[9] Ibid., 57–60; Kanno Noriko, "Nōson josei no rōdō to seikatsu" (Labor and daily life of rural women), in *Nihon josei shi 3: kinsei* (History of Japanese women 3: Late feudal period), vol. 3 of *Nihon josei shi* (History of Japanese women), ed. Josei shi sōgō kenkyū kai (Woman's history research collective) (Tokyo, 1982), 77.

[10] Nagashima, "Kinsei josei," 57.

[11] Cited in ibid., 49.

wide variety of agricultural tasks but normally did not do the heaviest work, such as ploughing the rice fields or logging trees on the mountainsides.[12]

As time went on, however, new crops and technology brought change. By the end of the seventeenth century, cotton was rapidly replacing hemp as material for everyday clothing because it could be produced more easily and was warmer and more flexible.[13] With the spread of information about crop methodology, rice production began to be seen less as a matter of pleasing the rice god than of scientific application; and thus rice planters needed no longer to be gaily bedecked young women.[14]

Such advances did not mean that the work loads of women lessened. Because improved agricultural implements made farm work easier, it became possible for women, who continued subsistence handicraft production, housework, and child care, also to do the heaviest work that had once been performed mostly by men.[15] A passage in the 1807 *Aizu fudoki fūzoku chō* (Aizu gazetteer, compendium of customs and manners) reveals that the male author of this work was aware that women were becoming more conspicuous in all kinds of agricultural work in Aizu fief:

> In days of yore when a woman went to work it was usually to spin or weave or to do the washing. It was highly unlikely that a widow living alone could survive weeding fields and paddies in summer, cutting grass to feed the animal, planting rice and mowing it, breaking the ground with a mattock. But during the past thirty years gradually women too have been wielding mattocks and ploughing fields. In recent years they have come to do what men do. Women even go out to plough the rice paddies, and there are many among them who can surpass men when it comes to work.[16]

And if rice planting was no longer restricted to girls, this meant that women of all ages as well as men were involved in planting. There is much evidence to suggest that even after the decline of festive rituals binding village maidens and the rice deities, women were considered more skillful planters than men and were thus more likely to be involved in this work.[17]

Another factor that over time affected peasant women's work and their standing in local communities was the rapid advance of money economy

[12] Ibid., 52–53. Sometimes women were not supposed to cut trees in the mountains or to hunt because of regional taboos. But such prohibitions did not stop them from hauling the cut logs or felled deer back home to their villages. See Segawa Kiyoko, *Mura no onnatachi* (Village women) (Tokyo, 1970), 298.

[13] Hauser, *Economic Institutional Change*, 59–60.

[14] Nagashima, "Kinsei josei," 59–60.

[15] Kanno, "Nōson josei," 76–77.

[16] Cited in ibid., 92.

[17] Ibid., 77.

and commodity production clearly visible from the eighteenth century on.[18] Fief administrations of the lords demanded more and more taxes from peasants to be paid in cash rather than in rice, and hard-pressed peasants had to supplement tenancy with work as day laborers for their more wealthy neighbors or bind themselves in long-term contracts working full-time for others in attempts to earn the necessary cash.[19] They also tried to produce the salable items that were in demand in urban areas.

Farmers sold charcoal, paper, oils, lacquer, and straw handicrafts, turned local products into specialty foods, and grew such cash crops as tobacco and tea, but increasingly it was cotton and silk that were in great demand. Handicrafts, preserving and processing foods, and above all textile production had always been women's work, so females played a key role in activities that brought peasants badly needed money income.

Sometimes such production involved desperate gambles. In cotton-growing areas, huge profits could be made, but farmers could also be ruined because successful harvesting depended heavily upon the weather as well as upon fertilization.[20] Women were active in harvesting and in semi-processing cotton. In the eighteenth century when cotton-cultivating villages began to gin their cash cotton crops and in some regions took up carding, spinning, and weaving as by-employments, occupations connected with cotton kept women busier than ever.[21] As new ginning tools and looms improved peasant processing, and city cotton merchants lent villagers tools and capital and bought their semifinished or finished products, peasant women earned valuable cash for their families.[22]

Like cotton production, silk production became a common part of the work of many farm families in the eighteenth century, but, unlike cotton, silk was never produced for the farm family's consumption.[23] Silk had been named as a tax in the eighth-century Yōrō Codes, and long before the rise

[18] See such classics as Adachi Masao, *Kinsei zaigō shōnin no keiei shi* (Business history of late feudal village merchants) (Tokyo, 1955); Furushima Toshio, *Edo jidai no shōhin ryūtsū to kōtsū* (Commodity circulation and transportation during the Edo period) (Tokyo; 1951); Sydney Crawcour, "Changes in Japanese Commerce in the Tokugawa Period," in *Studies in the Institutional History of Early Modern Japan*, ed. John W. Hall and Marius B. Jansen (Princeton, 1968), 189–202.

[19] Miyashita Michiko, "*Nōson ni okeru kazoku to kon'in*" (Family and marriage in the countryside), in *Nihon josei shi 3: kinsei*, 61; Vlastos, *Peasant Protests*, 107–8.

[20] Hauser, *Economic Institutional Change* 117–20.

[21] Ibid., 136.

[22] Ibid., 136–37.

[23] What Morosawa Yōko noted in regard to the sericulture boom during the first years of Meiji applies to earlier times, too. "In late feudal times when the hemp fields were turned into cotton fields, working people's clothing became cotton. But when, with the coming of the modern period, the cotton fields were turned into mulberry fields, working people's clothing did not become silk." Morosawa Yōko, ed., *Onna no hataraki* (Women's work), vol. 3 of *Dokyumento onna no hyakunen* (Documents of a century of women) (Tokyo, 1978), 18.

of the samurai in the twelfth century it had been among the local products paid as tribute to the aristocrats who held rights to so much of Japan's arable land. Nevertheless, even during the first half of the Edo period, the most prized cloth, such as that produced by the famed Nishijin weavers of Kyoto, was woven mainly of silk thread imported from China. By the middle of the eighteenth century, acceptance of domestic thread by Nishijin and other skilled weavers was stimulating silk production in established sericulture regions and causing such activity to spread to new terrain.[24] Areas that raised silkworms for sale of cocoons or thread began to combine silkworm cultivation with weaving of cloth—all of which was women's work.[25] By the 1830s, silk thread was spun in fiefs all over Japan, and the Nishijin weavers procured raw silk from distant places as well as their established suppliers close to Kyoto.[26] In areas producing silk cloth, a thread master (*itoshi*) bought cocoons from silkworm breeders and organized peasant women to undertake reeling the thread and weaving the cloth, which he would sell in urban markets. Such wholesalers often ran fairly large-scale operations: "Even medium-sized thread masters had seventy or more families in their networks."[27]

Peasant women of course played leading roles in both cotton- and silk-textile production, as they tended to do in the production of so many of the commodities leaving rural areas for sale and consumption elsewhere. Women in poorer samurai families also spun and wove to support their families and thus became part of the thread and cloth networks of Edo Japan.[28]

Many of the peasants who went out to work for the rich in long-term service as seasonal laborers were female. The wages of wives and daughters—it was not uncommon for a husband and a wife in a poor family to be residing "in service" in different places—were often vital to family budgets.[29] According to the research of Kanno Noriko, women were generally paid less than male workers for the kind of work they did: women "in service" got about half of what their male counterparts were paid in the eighteenth century, while in the next century a female servant earned about

---

[24] Kajinishi Mitsuhaya, Tatewaki Sadayo, Furushima Toshio, Oguchi Kenzō, *Seishi rōdōsha to rekishi* (A history of silk workers) (Tokyo, 1955), 3; Katō Kōzaburō, "Nihon shihonshugi keisei ki," 11.

[25] Ibid.

[26] Kajinishi et al., *Seishi rōdōsha*, 4–7.

[27] Nakamura Takafusa, *Economic Growth*, 51.

[28] A famous illustration of women in the bottom stratum of the samurai class supporting their family through their textile skills can be found in Ariyoshi Sawako's historical novel, *The Doctor's Wife* [Hanaoka Seishū no tsuma] trans. Wakako Hironaka and Ann Siller Kostant (Tokyo, 1978).

[29] Miyashita, "Nōson kazoku to kon'in," 48, 61.

two-thirds of what a male servant earned.[30] The exception to this pattern
was rice planting, mowing, and threshing. When men and women performed the same tasks threshing rice, women received three-quarters of
what men were paid; when both sexes mowed, women made five-sixths of
what men made; when both planted rice, the sexes tended to earn equal
pay.[31]

The general picture above conceals the great variety of local custom that
existed in Japan during the Edo era. From the capital, Edo, the government of the Tokugawa overlords ruled the Tokugawa territory directly,
while the rest of the land was divided among approximately 250 lords,[32]
each ruling a fief that in many ways was really a separate "country" with its
own government, language, and traditions. Among the regions of a single
fief, customs and even language could vary greatly; in some areas geo-
graphical isolation kept villages relatively untouched by the ideology of the
samurai elite, and women's status remained high.[33] However, since the official ideology of the samurai elite was a Confucian one that "respected the
male, despised the female" (*danson johi*), and under samurai rule peasant
society itself had been forced to become heavily male oriented,[34] it is not
surprising that "women's work"—associated with housekeeping and handicrafts—was valued less than was work done by men. Although the gap
between the values placed upon "men's work" and "women's work" appears to have narrowed during the last years of the Edo era, even when
women did "men's work" they were not considered as valuable as male
workers. At the same time, the ancient religious centrality of women in
wet rice culture was remembered even after planting rituals began to decline, as the higher wages paid to female rice planters testify.

Despite regional disparity regarding sex roles and agricultural labor,
during the Edo period peasant women were respected within their own
families and communities. They may not have been as cherished as men
were, but they were valued: for the majority of peasant families survival
was impossible without women and their work. And with the respect came
self-confidence and a degree of influence in decision making within the
family and village.

[30] Kanno, "Nōson josei," 86.

[31] Ibid., 87.

[32] The precise number of lords and fiefs varied throughout the Edo period as the Tokugawa
overlords confiscated or amalgamated lands.

[33] The earlier one goes back in Japanese history, the higher is the status of women. After
the rise of the samurai class as rulers in the twelfth century, the position of females steadily
declined. In the peasant class, this decline was not as rapid or as thorough as among the
samurai elite and was marked by regional differences.

[34] The samurai rulers made and enforced laws for all segments of the population. On the
village level of administration, samurai officials of a fief dealt with males as village heads and
other functionaries.

From the eighteenth century onward, landlords and rich farmers could afford to mimic their samurai betters, accepting as brides well-bred young women upon whose labor their family did not depend; most peasant families could not do so. In a samurai or rich peasant family, a bride's primary function was production of a male heir to carry on the family line; a bride was even referred to as a "borrowed womb." In such families divorce—a unilateral privilege of the husband's family except in extraordinary circumstances—was a serious matter and was to be avoided if possible, because it usually meant disgrace for the bride and her natal family.[35] Among ordinary peasants, on the other hand, divorce was not at all uncommon: brides as well as adopted bridegrooms went back to their natal homes or off to marry someone else, little bothered by Confucian strictures against remarriage for women. If the occasion demanded, poor peasant women could even take over that bastion of male family authority, the family headship. Peasant family-registry records reveal that when male candidates for headship were thought so unsuitable as to threaten family or village well-being, headship succession and the property inheritance that accompanied it passed to a widow, a mother, a sister, or a daughter.[36] Thus, although in law laid down by samurai rulers headship was restricted to males, in practice female succession among peasants was sometimes tolerated by samurai rulers. And although female family-heads were often temporary caretakers holding the position until an absent husband, immature son, or adopted son-in-law could take over, by no means were they always such short-term intermediaries; nor did they always relinquish the headship when suitable male candidates became available.[37]

The status of Edo peasant women varied considerably. In addition to the regional differences,[38] there were important differences according to

[35] During the Edo period one opportunity for some samurai and commoner wives to unilaterally divorce their husbands was afforded by the two "divorce temples" (*enkiri-dera*), Tōkeiji in Kamakura and Mantokuji in what is now Gunma prefecture. Tōkeiji was founded as a divorce temple in 1285 by Kakusan, the widow of Hōjō Tokimune and the mother of Hōjō Sadatoki, samurai leaders of their time. Mantokuji became officially recognized as a divorce temple about 1615, after a daughter of the second Tokugawa shogun, Hidetada, took refuge in it. After a woman had spent three years—later two years—in residence at Tōkeiji or Mantokuji, she was declared free from all marital entanglements. Women came to these temples to escape pending marriage as well as to escape husbands. During the Edo period Tōkeiji and Mantokuji obtained for samurai and commoner women divorces officially granted by the commissioners of temples and shrines (*jisha bugyō*). Before the Meiji government abolished these temples' rights of divorce in 1873, the temples gave refuge to a steady stream of supplicants. In the 150 years before 1873 at least two thousand absconding wives received divorces after residence at Tōkeiji. *Nihon rekishi daijiten* (Great dictionary of Japanese history) (Tokyo, 1969), 2:113 and 7:161; *Kodansha Encyclopedia of Japan* (Tokyo, 1983), 4:115.

[36] Miyashita, "Nōson kazoku to kon'in," 42.

[37] This was especially true in farming families with small landholdings. See ibid.

[38] See Yanagita Kunio, *Japanese Manners and Customs in the Meiji Era*, trans. Charles S. Terry (Tokyo, 1957).

the stratum of the peasant class to which a woman belonged. Nevertheless, despite the fact that in all fiefs ideologies upheld the official ideals of undistilled Confucian patriarchy,[39] the vast majority of peasant women seem to have received recognition for the enormously hard work they did. Everyday experience and long-standing local beliefs often carried more weight than samurai maxims.

Japanese peasant women's participation in direct production and their skilled preparation of marketable goods were probably at least partially responsible for their relatively high status. In neighboring China (home of the Confucianism adopted by Japanese samurai of the Edo era), peasant women, who were much less likely to be involved directly in agricultural production, were held in much lower regard.[40] In pre-Liberation China (before 1949) the widespread custom of foot binding limited the amount and type of farm work women could do and thus made them less valued workers than males. As Delia Davin noted, "To be crippled physically like this in a preindustrial economy in which a peasant's income depended at least partly on strength was to be crippled economically as well."[41] The prejudice against Chinese peasant women's leaving their homes also restricted where they might work and undoubtedly helped keep their contributions to subsidiary farm occupations small.[42] Although their participation in directly productive work was unquestionably minor, that participation was perceived by their families and communities to be even less than it actually was.[43] The indispensable household work they did was not highly respected, although it was arduous and time-consuming: "Providing meals, for example, did not simply mean cooking; it could include the gathering of fuel, the drawing and fetching of water, the husking and

---

[39] In "Feminist Thought in Ancient China," *Tien Hsia Monthly* (Nanking) 1, no. 2 (September 1935): 127–50, Lin Yutang reviews what he calls the "puritanico-sadistic background of Confucianism" and the sad consequences of this for Chinese women. It should be noted that while Edo Japan's ruling class adopted Confucianism as the country's official ideology, Confucian customs of concubinage, female suicide in defense of chastity, and perpetual widowhood instead of remarriage found few enthusiasts among the samurai. Foot binding, closely tied to Confucianism in China, was never imported into Japan.

[40] Since "traditional China" endured until 1949, J. L. Buck's now classic surveys of male and female participation in Chinese agriculture during the 1920s and 1930s offer a comparative perspective. From these surveys Buck estimated that "men performed 80 per cent of all the farm labour in China, women 13 per cent and children 7 per cent." J. L. Buck, *Land Utilization in China* (Nanking, 1937), 293, and its accompanying statistical volume, cited in Delia Davin, *Woman-Work: Women and the Party in Revolutionary China* (Oxford, 1976), 117.

[41] Davin, *Woman-Work*, 10–11.

[42] Ibid., 122; Raymon Myers, *The Chinese Peasant Economy* (Cambridge, Mass., 1970), 75, 110.

[43] Davin, *Woman-Work*, 117.

grinding or polishing of grain, and the preserving of glut vegetables and fruits."[44]

Unlike her counterpart in pre-Liberation China, the peasant woman of pre-Meiji Japan was recognized by her family and her community as an important worker. While carrying an extra burden of extremely demanding household chores, she did a great deal of the same work that her menfolk did. And it was often women's skill and labor that produced the commodities which brought in vital side income. Prominent among such commodities were silk and cotton textiles. Recognition did not net Edo peasant women respect and status equal to that accorded peasant men, but they were by no means all hapless pawns as some historians have suggested.[45] Their lives were certainly difficult, but, ruling-class ideology notwithstanding, Edo peasant women were far from despised. In hard times especially— and times were generally hard for most of the peasantry—they might be victims of infanticide as soon as they entered the world; if they reached puberty they might be sold to brothels to ease the family debt; or they might go out into long years of service as bound servants at almost any time during their lives. But with the exception of the second possibility, such fates were the lot of male as well as female members of their class.[46]

In pre-Meiji times, the experience of rural women allowed many to gain confidence in labor skills that were valued by their families and communities. They were expected by their communities and families to be diligent, productive workers, and they internalized this expectation. Agricultural activities including cotton growing, sericulture, and various stages in the processing of silk and cotton thread and cloth were all part of "women's work." Leaving home to work for an employer in another village or even a town could also be women's work. When Japan's last feudal age ended and the country found itself on the fast lane to nation-statehood, girls and women of the peasantry faced a new labor demand. Parts of this demand were familiar but parts were very strange indeed.

The New Era: Change Does Not Necessarily Mean Improvement

When the Tokugawa regime bowed to enormous pressure from leading practitioners of nineteenth-century gunboat diplomacy and opened Japan

[44] Ibid., 123.

[45] See, for instance, Abe Tomio, "Kinsei nōson no josei" (Rural women in the late feudal period), *Nihon rekishi* (Japanese history) 213 (February 1966): 18–29.

[46] Infanticide, decidedly a female "affliction" in China, was practiced in Edo Japan against males as well as females. See Thomas C. Smith, *Nakahara: Family Farming and Population in a Japanese Village, 1717-1830* (Stanford, Calif., 1977), 59–85.

to foreign trade in 1859, new economic activity brought more grief to the tax-burdened peasantry. When by the terms of commercial treaties signed in 1858 and 1866, Japan was opened to almost unrestricted international trade, many handicraft industries were ruined as cheap machine-made foreign goods, like cotton thread and cloth made in India, came flooding into the hitherto-isolated island economy. The 1866 treaty in particular set tariffs—controlled by foreign signatories—so low that they offered no protection to domestic industries.[47]

Suddenly losing important sources of side income, small-scale farmers had to mortgage plots to rich peasants and merchants. By this time the lower ranks of the samurai class were full of poor warrior families who quietly manufactured handicraft commodities—often their women would spin or weave—and these folks too suffered from the foreign trade. Rich cultivators and merchants whose capital was not tied up in production and marketing of handicraft goods fared much better. When debtors lost their mortgaged land, wealthy neighbors would take them on as tenants with seasonal work obligations that went beyond farming. As fertilizer merchants, pawnbrokers, moneylenders, sake brewers, bean-paste and soy-sauce entrepreneurs, the landlord strata of the peasant class employed members of the rest of the class, who continued to struggle to produce cash income to subsidize subsistence farming.[48]

In 1868 the crumbling Tokugawa government was felled by a coalition of upstart samurai leaders. In the new era of Meiji (1868–1912) the coalition introduced a number of land-tenure and taxation reforms, but none of these were of much help to most of the peasantry. People were permitted to change their occupations; buying and selling land was legitimized. In 1873 revision of the land-tax system transformed land tribute in kind (which had always been steep but according to custom sometimes varied with the amount of harvest) due to the feudal lords into a tax to be paid in money to the new Meiji government by the registered owner of the land, regardless of the harvest's magnitude.

The revision had a dual influence upon the peasants. Peasants were not fully involved in the money economy. Under such circumstances, the payment of land taxes was changed into payment in money. This provided conditions very unfavorable for peasants who had to change their products into money. The pressure of the money economy further impoverished petty peasants and helped increase the number of peasants who lost farm land. The land tax was ordered to be paid in money. But the payment of farm rent in kind did not change. So, tenants had to buy some portion of rice for the family consumption when the rice price rose sharply during the early years of Meiji. While tenants were distressed economi-

---

[47] T. Smith, *Political Change*, 23.
[48] Nakamura Takafusa, *Economic Growth*, 51.

cally, the income for land owners increased. This resulted in the concentration of land in possession of landlords.[49]

There has been considerable controversy among Japanese economic historians over whether the growth of landlordism was heavier in late Edo times or during the early years of the Meiji era.[50] But here we are more interested in the fact that the existence of large-scale landlordism—regardless of whether it had been around for decades or was mainly a new phenomenon—pushed many peasants to struggle for additional side incomes to supplement agricultural livelihoods; so many of the fruits of their labors were devoured by landlords and the money-hungry government.

During the Meiji period those peasants who could not find a landlord to rent them land worked as day laborers, seasonally or for fixed terms, in agriculture or manufacturing. In some respects this was similar to what peasants had done during the Edo period, but now rapidly increasing numbers of men and women and boys and girls became dekasegi workers who "went out to work" to places outside of their own villages and districts. Some of the landless went to work in mines, and others moved to rural areas where silk reeling and weaving and cotton spinning and weaving had in the past provided opportunities for peasant daughters and wives to earn income. Some peasants joined the city poor, migrating to larger urban areas like Tokyo, Osaka, Kyoto, and the former castle towns of the fief lords. There they sought work as menial laborers and servants.

In addition to destitute peasants from rural areas, the poor of the cities and towns included paupers from the lowest ranks of what had once been the samurai class (*shizoku*). Some of these had quietly suffered economic distress for generations; poor samurai families in urban areas had long depended upon the handicraft production of their womenfolk to supplement meager hereditary rice stipends that samurai household heads received from their lords. The loss of feudal privilege claimed by even the poorest samurai began almost immediately after the establishment of the new government in 1868 and culminated in the complete abolition of the stipends of the shizoku in 1876.[51]

---

[49] Sumiya Mikio, *Social Impact of Industrialization in Japan* (Tokyo, 1963), 10.

[50] See, for example, Yamada Moritarō, *Nihon shihonshugi bunseki* (An analysis of Japanese capitalism) (Tokyo, 1934); Furushima Toshio, "Seiritsu jinushi no rekishiteki seikaku" (The historical characteristics of landlordism in its formative stage), *Nōgyō keizai kenkyū* (Journal of rural economics), 26, no. 3 (October 1954): 1–16; discussion of landlordism in Nakamura Takafusa, *Economic Growth*, 54–58; Katō Kōzaburō, "Nihon shihonshugi keisei ki," esp. 13–38.

[51] The Meiji government at first paid the ex-samurai pensions representing a portion of the stipends they had received from their feudal lords. In 1876 these pensions were commuted: the ex-samurai were paid off in government bonds issued with interest rates varying according

The government was extremely worried about the disastrous influence of imports upon traditional handicraft industries that had been so important to the survival of both peasant and poor samurai families. In 1874 Matsukata Masayoshi warned his colleagues in the government that the people could lose their industries completely and become abjectly poor, while Japan ended up as a producer of raw materials for the industrial West.[52] The urgency of reviving old and establishing new industries employing peasants was underlined by the two hundred agrarian uprisings during the first decade of Meiji, far more than the number of such rebellions during any decade of the Edo era.[53] Government leaders were even more concerned to extend economic aid and occupation to the poorer members of their own class, the shizoku. Some former samurai were given jobs as policemen and schoolteachers, while others were encouraged to invest their small lump-sum payments from commuted stipends in small-scale commercial or manufacturing ventures. But there were not enough jobs to provide for the poor samurai, who lacked capital as well as commercial and technical know-how. Discontent found outlets in samurai rebellions that were crushed only with all the resources of the new national army.[54]

The government's cause for anxiety increased as its own policies resulted in economic distress and dislocation during the second decade of Meiji. During the late 1870s two minor revisions in the land tax brought slight relief to some independent cultivators, but during the 1880s the famous deflationary policies of Finance Minister Matsukata Masayoshi drove large numbers of independent and tenant cultivators into extreme destitution.[55] Infanticide increased: "One social observer noted that in a Kanto prefecture most peasant families had only one boy and one girl."[56] Independent cultivators became tenants as landlords acquired land that became available through forced sales due to nonpayment of taxes and foreclosures of mort-

---

to the amounts of the former stipends. The lowest ranking ex-samurai experienced a drastic drop in income.

[52] T. Smith, *Political Change*, 30.

[53] Ibid.

[54] Hyman Kublin, "The 'Modern' Army of Early Meiji Japan," *The Far Eastern Quarterly* 9, no. 1 (November 1949): 20–40.

[55] Nakamura Masanori, *Rōdōsha to nōmin*, 56–59; Matsumoto Hiroshi, "Jinushi no shihai to nōmin" (Peasants and the rule of landlords), in *Kokken to minken no sōkoku* (The struggle between state's rights and people's rights), ed. Emura Eichi and Nakamura Masanori, vol. 6 of *Nihon minshū no rekishi* (History of the Japanese people) (Tokyo, 1974), 355–91. See also Roger W. Bowen, *Rebellion and Democracy in Meiji Japan: A Study of Commoners in the Popular Rights Movement* (Berkeley, Calif., 1980).

[56] Irokawa Daikichi, *Kindai kokka no shuppatsu* (The beginnings of the modern nation-state) (Tokyo: 1966), 320–23, cited in Mikiso Hane, *Peasants, Rebels, and Outcastes: The Underside of Modern Japan* (New York, 1982), 27.

gages. From 1884 through 1886, "roughly one-eighth of the entire arable acreage of Japan was given over to creditors in the space of but three years."[57] Desperate peasants took up arms and demanded a moratorium on debts, but they were no match for the armies of the Meiji state. Many peasants starved to death; many not quite dead crept into the cities, hoping to be able at least to beg or steal. The population of the urban ghettos swelled.[58]

Poverty and unemployment were not the only reasons the Meiji leaders were concerned about the destruction of the handicraft industries. The trade imbalance from the flood of imports was a nightmare for a government pledged to quickly build modern military might supported by industrialization and an institutional infrastructure that could put Japan on a par with the Western imperialist nations. The kind of nation building such goals involved was extremely expensive, and the costs of liquidating the old order also had to be met. The abundance of imports was rendered more problematic by the fact that shipping, insurance, and other services connected with foreign trade remained in non-Japanese hands well into the 1880s. A serious strain was placed upon Japan's specie reserves.[59] Desperately short of foreign exchange in an age when foreign loans were not easily acquired by a country like Japan, the Meiji leaders were not willing to risk the erosion of the already-restricted national autonomy that heavy foreign debts might cause.[60]

Accounting for about 35 percent of all imports during the period 1868–1872,[61] cheap cotton thread and cloth from abroad were ruining the indigenous industries. Somehow the once-flourishing network of cotton production and marketing had to be revitalized. Traditional silk production was not suffering as much, largely because of a timely pébrine blight that had temporarily disabled French and Italian sericulture. Yet silk exports had the capacity to earn valuable revenue to combat the dangerous trade

[57] Paul Mayet, "Nihon nōmin no hihei, oyobi sono kyūjisaku" (The impoverishment of Japanese peasants and policies for their relief), in *Meiji nōgyō ronshū* (Papers on Meiji agriculture), ed. Sakurai Takeo (Tokyo, 1955), 208, cited in Nakamura Takafusa, *Economic Growth*, 57. Nakamura Takafusa suggests that Mayet's estimate "is a bit exaggerated because in some cases land changed hands more than once" (ibid.). See also T. Smith, *Political Change*, 82–85.

[58] "In 1889 about 40 per cent of the slum residents of Osaka were migrants from the neighboring rural villages during the preceding four years." Sumiya, *Social Impact*, 30–31.

[59] T. Smith, *Political Change*, 25.

[60] The famous rejection in 1880 by Iwakura Tomomi of a proposal to borrow 50 million yen in London to convert outstanding paper notes reveals the Meiji government's dominant attitude toward foreign debt: "Rather than raise a foreign loan at the present time we would do better to sell Kyushu and Shikoku [the two smallest of the four major islands in the Japanese archipelago] to a foreign country." Cited in ibid., 97–98.

[61] Ibid., 27.

imbalance and provide income for the Meiji government's costly projects. Thus Japanese silk production was to be made strong enough to compete with the recovering European silk industries.[62] Strategic industry related directly to military considerations was the first priority, but the government was also determined to promote vigorous domestic production of cotton and silk.[63] Women, especially women from the countryside, were to be key figures in such production.

[62] After 1869 the silk industry in Europe was recovering. See ibid., 56.
[63] Ibid., 54–66.

2

Modern Beginnings: Reeling and Spinning

The First Modern Silk Reelers

It was certainly a stroke of luck for the Meiji government that, during the first year of Meiji, the European silkworm industry suffered a severe pébrine blight. The resulting demand for Japanese raw silk stimulated sericulture and reeling, including both the old *teguri* hand winding and the newer *zaguri* reeling.[1] The women in farm households continued to raise silkworms and to produce homespun thread, and in some regions they also wove cloth.[2] Home reelers used either teguri or zaguri tools, but the strong international demand for silk accelerated the move from the older, more cumbersome method to improved zaguri reeling, and establishments with capital and water resources made a power shift from human muscle to waterwheel.[3] Although in some households women and girls went through all the steps of raw silk production—planting mulberry trees, raising cocoons, spinning thread—many families concentrated upon raising cocoons, which they sold to wealthy neighbors who hired ten, twenty, or thirty wives or youngsters to coax the fine strands from the cocoons and reel the thread with water- or human power. Meanwhile other silkworm breeders would sell their cocoons to silk merchants; the merchants farmed them out to rural women in Gunma, Fukushima, or Nagano prefectures, who sometimes reeled on tools lent by the silk merchants. Although the old unity of silkworm cultivation and silk-thread reeling did not perish suddenly, increasingly sericulture and reeling became separated.

Desperately needing foreign exchange, the new government encouraged all efforts to meet the fortuitous demand for silk abroad. Traditional production, especially if the product was good, met with official approval; but the government was particularly eager to introduce Western-style machin-

[1] In the older of the two methods, teguri reeling, the silk was pulled from the cocoons and wound from one hand to the other. Late in the Edo period, zaguri reeling was developed. This method still involved hand reeling, but now the silk was reeled with the help of a toothed wheel called a *za. Nihon kindai shi jiten* (Dictionary of modern Japanese history) (Tokyo: Kyoto daigaku bungakubu kokushi kenkyū shitsu [National history research laboratory of Kyoto University Faculty of Arts], 1958), 221.

[2] Segawa Kiyoko, *Onna no hataraki, i-seikatsu no rekishi* (Women's work, a history of clothing customs) (Tokyo, 1962).

[3] Sumiya, *Nihon chinrōdō*, 152–53.

ery and methods that could produce thread which would please overseas buyers. Since Western-style mechanization "consisted merely in turning the reel by steam or power, rather than by hand,"[4] the prospects were neither technically nor financially daunting. And the skills of handicraft veterans would continue to be required as the cocoons still had to be prepared, the filament started on the reel, and splices made when breaks occurred—all by hand. The new government led the way by establishing model filatures to demonstrate and spread Western-style techniques and management and by encouraging the sericultural prefectures to support these establishments and set up their own local models. Government encouragement started early: sixty Italian reelers came to Tokyo to teach silk techniques in 1870, but the most ambitious plant was the large silk mill built in 1872 at Tomioka in what is now Gunma prefecture.[5]

After a careful survey of different silk-producing areas, the Tomioka site was chosen because, in the midst of a flourishing sericulture region, it was abundantly endowed with water resources. Built under the direction of the same French marine engineer who in 1865 had supervised construction of the Yokosuka ironworks for the now-defunct Tokugawa government, the Tomioka mill was designed to train groups of four hundred women in modern Western-style machine-reeled silk production.[6] With a team of eighteen French technicians, including four female reelers as instructors, training akin to study abroad awaited the privileged young women selected to be pupils there.

The problem was that eligible young women did not regard training at the mill as a privilege. Until that time, women with experience in silk reeling had usually been wives and daughters in fairly prosperous peasant families with at least middle-sized land holdings or in samurai families where women spun and wove. They had sometimes learned their skills working on the farm of a prosperous neighbor. Although they might commute to a neighbor's silk-reeling workshop daily or reside there during busy periods after cocoon harvests, neither experienced nor novice reelers were accustomed to traveling long distances in order to do their work; nor were they

---

[4] T. Smith, *Political Change*, 55.

[5] Sumiya, *Nihon chinrōdō*, 153.

[6] Wada Ei, *Teihon Tomioka nikki* (Tomioka diary, the authentic text) (Tokyo, 1976), 207–8. From about 1907 to 1912, when she was more than fifty years old, Wada Ei (Yokota Ei before her marriage) apparently wrote this famous "diary" from recollections of her youth. As Miura Toyohiko has pointed out, she tended to be nostalgic and to remember mostly the "good times." Miura Toyohiko, *Rōdō no rekishi* (A history of labor) (Tokyo, 1964), 117. See also Takase Toyoji, *Kanei Tomioka seishisho kōjo shiryō* (Historical materials regarding the factory girls of the Tomioka silk filature while under government management) (Tokyo, 1979), 106. However, since it was a very common practice for young women to keep a diary, Wada may well have kept brief diary entries during the years she worked at Tomioka and Rokkōsha and afterward used these as references for *Tomioka nikki*.

used to laboring with women and girls from distant districts with different customs and dialects. When during the first half of 1872 the government repeatedly asked young women of respectable families to travel tens to hundreds of miles—before railroads, decent roads, and other convenient means of transportation existed—in order to work with hundreds of unknown maidens from all over the archipelago, the government was asking a great deal. In the eyes of those whose lives had been lived totally within or close to the environs of their own villages, young strangers from distant prefectures were almost as foreign as the French instructors at Tomioka.[7] And mention of those French instructors struck terror into villagers' hearts.

Europeans drank red wine and cooked with lard, but the country people thought they were drinking human blood and cooking with human fat. It was widely believed that the government's eagerness to recruit young girls and send them to Tomioka was to provide the Europeans there with fresh supplies of blood and fat.[8] Despite the national government's repeated calls for young women "between the ages of fifteen and twenty-five" and its denunciations of "foolish rumors and idle talk" that spread misunderstandings about the French at Tomioka, not a single volunteer came forward.[9]

Ironically, the tone of the government's "for-the-good-of-the-nation" messages, which urged that girls be sent to Tomioka to learn trades to help meet Japan's desperate need for foreign exchange, may have compounded more fears than they allayed. The notion of sacrifice for the country's sake conjured up images of other sacrifices involving other trips for young women. Cannibalistic Europeans were the stuff of rumors, but people knew of veritable sacrifices that daughters, wives, and sisters in debt-ridden peasant families had always made for their families; when sold into prostitution, they began sorrowful journeys that took them far from their home villages.[10] Respectable families with reelers or girls who wanted to learn

[7] Indeed, one of the first Tomioka trainees, Aoyama Shina from Hyōgo prefecture, has left a description of a "European instructor" she had in 1875 who was difficult to work with because Aoyama could not comprehend a word of the foreign tongue this instructor spoke. Aoyama gave the name of this instructor in Japanese pronunciation as Endō Kō, and researchers trying to track down the identity of this "Frenchwoman" were puzzled until they discovered that a trainee from Miyashiro prefecture, who went to Tomioka even earlier than did Aoyama, bore this name. Takase, *Kanei Tomioka*, 18–22. When Aoyama called Endō a "European instructor," she may have meant that Endō was an instructor in European-style reeling. Her emphasis upon the incomprehensibility of this "foreigner's speech" underlines the linguistic differences then existing among Japanese from different parts of the country.

[8] Wada, *Tomioka nikki*, 9; Morosawa Yōko, *Shinano no onna* (Women of Shinano), 2 vols. (Tokyo, 1969), 1:208; Takase, *Kanei Tomioka*, 158.

[9] See Takase, *Kanei Tomioka*, 27–28 for government communication of May 1872 urging prefectures to recruit candidates.

[10] For accounts of prostitution during the Edo period see Yamamoto Shun'ichi, *Nihon kōshō*

reeling could not be persuaded to give up their daughters. Invitations for applicants became orders to district officials to secure quotas of trainees, but local people refused to budge.[11]

Finally the man appointed to head the new mill's management team, Otaka Atsutada, in desperation or inspiration sent to his own village in Saitama prefecture for his thirteen-year-old daughter, Yū. In Saitama, at least, this did much to puncture the frightening rumors: if the factory's highest official wanted his daughter to work at Tomioka, the place could not be so dreadful. Thirty from the vicinity of Otaka's village joined Yū for the trip to Tomioka; and other Saitama women came to the mill because of the efforts of Niratsuka Shinjirō, a rich farmer in their prefecture who struggled long and hard to manufacture the strange red bricks used to build the Tomioka structure.[12] These recruits came from villages in the northern end of Saitama prefecture, not far from Tomioka, and this may partly account for their willingness to go to the mill.

Even after Otaka's brain wave, the government had to take whom it could get. Some of the Saitama women were in their forties and fifties— one was fifty-nine and another sixty-two—considerably over the stipulated age limit of twenty-five.[13] The fifty-nine-year-old was Aoki Teru, from a rich farming family in Otaka's home village; she went to Tomioka with her seventeen-year-old granddaughter. Aoki herself had energetically sought trainees for Tomioka. Her family took a keen interest in improving its silk reeling: later both her son and daughter became prominent in silk-thread enterprises that included a filature under the prefecture and a private silk mill.[14] It is likely that the other older women were also from families interested in silk technology; some of them also became involved later in operating filatures.

With the Saitama volunteers, the mill was able to open on schedule in November 1872, but officials in other regions continued to seek recruits in vain unless they followed Otaka's example. The opening passage of the famous *Tomioka Diary* (*Tomioka nikki*) written by Wada Ei (1857–1929) describes what happened in her corner of Nagano prefecture.

> My father, one of the retainers of the old Matsushiro fief in Shinshū, was named Yokota Kazuma. About the sixth year of Meiji [1873] he was a district head in Matsushiro. Shinshū . . . was a land with a flourishing sericulture. Thus each district was instructed by the prefectural authorities to send a fixed number (actually sixteen per district) of girls between the ages of thirteen and twenty-five to

shi (History of licensed prostitution in Japan) (Tokyo, 1983), 3–64; Takahashi Keiji, *Monogatari onna ichiba* (Tales of selling women) (Tokyo, 1982), 19–27.

[11] Kajinishi et al, *Seishi rōdōsha*, 19.
[12] Ibid.; Takase, *Kanei Tomioka*, 132–40.
[13] Takase, *Kanei Tomioka*, 132–34, 135–39.
[14] Ibid., 144, 147.

the Tomioka Silk Filature. Nevertheless, because people believed they might be offered as human sacrifices, not one person agreed to go. Worried, my father did his best to persuade people, but he met with no success.

Sensational rumors had it that the girls' blood was going to be taken from them and their fat squeezed out of their bodies. One heard: "At the district head's place there is a daughter of exactly the right age. Since she is not being sent this is surely proof that the rumors are true." Thus my father decided to send me.

Among my relatives was a girl who some time ago had gone to Tokyo to learn the knitting trade and I had asked to go too. Because I was kept busy looking after four younger sisters and brothers, I had been refused permission. Disappointed then, I was highly delighted now. I stated that I wanted to go [to Tomioka] and that even if I went all by myself I wouldn't mind. . . . My grandfather said he was very pleased because even though I was just a girl it was fitting that I participate in meritorious deeds performed for the Realm.[15]

Although the very first recruits came from prosperous farming families with interests in silk production, the reaction of the grandfather of fifteen-year-old Ei reminds us that it was the former samurai who were most likely to identify with the government's call to serve the nation. It was shizoku who often let "even girls" go off to learn new skills or attend the new kinds of schools for the new order.[16] Like middle-ranking and prosperous peasants, many samurai women had long been involved in silk production. With government aid, shizoku families were attempting to establish local silk filatures during the 1870s. For successive generations women in poor but honorable samurai families had provided economic sustenance for fathers and brothers. Now such families desperately needed to find work for daughters.[17] Even previously well-off retainers had experienced drastic cuts in stipends with the Meiji era—before the abolition of the fief retainer system the Yokota house had been a 150-*koku* family, but the Yokota income had been reduced to 30 koku.[18] Thus it was not surprising that once the initial reluctance to send trainees was overcome, many of those who went to Tomioka were of ex-samurai stock.[19]

[15] Wada, *Tomioka nikki*, 9–10.

[16] Yamakawa Kikue's *Onna nidai no ki* (A record of two generations of women) begins with the journey Kikue's mother made as a young girl, leaving her ex-samurai family in the fief of Mito (to become part of Ibaraki prefecture) to go to Tokyo and search for a school that would educate her for life in the new Japan. Yamakawa Kikue, *Onna nidai no ki* (Tokyo, 1972).

[17] As we shall see, the women who worked in the first cotton-spinning mills were also from samurai families.

[18] Morosawa, *Shinano*, 1:209. The stipends of feudal retainers were officially paid in koku of rice. One koku equals 4.9629 bushels.

[19] In 1878, of the 371 trainees lodged in the Tomioka dormitory (there were also com-

Service to the nation, family economic interest, or a combination of the two brought young women to Tomioka to become part of a proud elite striving both for national goals and for regional prosperity. "Reelers Outshine Soldiers," wrote an enthusiastic Okada Atsutada with a flourish of his calligraphy brush.[20] Perhaps, after all, Tomioka training would prove to be the honor and privilege the government intended it to be.

For some at least, going to Tomioka really was like going abroad to study. Here is the memory of one of the young women in the triumphant procession from Yamaguchi prefecture in the spring of 1873.

> I was one of the thirty in the first group to go to the Tomioka filature of Jōshū in Meiji 6 [1873]. Most [of us] were samurai daughters from seventeen to thirty years of age. On April 5th we gathered in Yamaguchi, and the next day on the 6th we all went to Mitashiri harbor and left by steamboat, the *Kotohira Maru*.
>
> . . . We sailed safely to Kobe, spent one night on land, then went to Yokohama on the American mail ship, *New York Maru*. The voyage was rough and many were seasick. Because Master Inoue [Kaoru]'s nieces, the Ozawa sisters, were in our group, Master Inoue came to meet us when we docked at Yokohama. At this time Japan's first railway ran from Yokohama to Tokyo and we rode the train to Tokyo's Shimbashi station. We were put up at the Yamashiro Lodge and for several days treated to Tokyo sight-seeing by Lord Takanawa [of the Mori family, lords of Chōshū/Yamaguchi]. When we went to Tomioka in Jōshū there were about forty of us including our escorts. We rode in forty rickshaws, making two overnight stops [at Honjō and Ageo]; on the third day we arrived in Tomioka village. With forty rickshaws carrying young maidens passing one after another, all the people along the highway came out to gaze with curious eyes upon the parade.[21]

Not all of the groups traveled in such splendor. Yamaguchi, formerly a dominant fief, was the home of powerful government leaders including Inoue Kaoru. Less rich and influential prefectures were able to do much less for the recruits they sent.[22] Yet once at Tomioka all arrivals donned the new clothes made especially for the Tomioka students and began learning European machine reeling under the watchful eyes of the French technicians. The nine- to twelve-hour workday, with regular rest periods, was excellent by contemporary standards; and, unlike most working people of

---

muting trainees by that time) 40 percent were ex-samurai women. Ibid., 213; Kajinishi et al, *Seishi rōdōsha*, 20.

[20] Morosawa, *Shinano*, 1:213.

[21] Morosawa, *Onna no hataraki*, 96–97. This recollection was taken down as oral testimony from this woman in her old age.

[22] A petition to Home Minister Itō Hirobumi (a native of Yamaguchi) in 1874 requesting travel funds for girls from Miyashiro prefecture was turned down. Takase, *Kanei Tomioka*, 47.

the time, the trainees had a holiday on Sunday each week.[23] They lived in a spacious dormitory that housed from three to six individuals in each tatami-matted room. The dormitory contained a dining room where substantial fare, including beef dishes of Western cuisine, were prepared; attached to the building was a garden where trainees were to enjoy healthful exercise.[24] In case of illness, the factory had its own modern hospital under the direction of a French doctor. As encouragement and a reminder to them of their elite status, the trainees received visits from high-ranking government officials, former lords of the fiefs or their relatives, and even the empress.[25]

When students had finished their stipulated training period or were judged to be skilled, they went off to silk filatures set up in their own prefectures by the public authorities there or by private entrepreneurs.[26] After a year and three months at Tomioka the Matsushiro women, including the author of *Tomioka Diary*, were called home to work at the new Rokkōsha filature established in their native district. Like other Tomioka graduates at other regional silk mills, they found local conditions much more difficult than those at the model plant.

Teenaged Yokota Ei (later Wada Ei), as leader of the young reelers, found herself in an awkward twilight zone between frustrated reelers and dissatisfied managers. On the one hand, she was responsible for all aspects of the life-style and work performance of the girls boarding at the Rokkōsha filature; on the other, she had to persuade their male superiors to abandon zaguri winding and trust the techniques introduced by the young women. When the reelers refused to boil cocoons to high temperatures (such boiling was a common practice in zaguri reeling) because this damaged the quality of the thread, the manger-in-chief lost his temper. He brought his wife to the workshop to stoke the fires and loudly announced that boiling produced heavier thread than that drawn out by "the stuck-up Tomioka rascals." Stung by his action, the equally angry reelers indignantly compared the knotted tangles drawn by the chief's wife to their own smooth strands. They were all for quitting Rokkōsha at once. Ei calmed them down with a reminder that they could go home anytime, but if they did so, would not all their efforts at Tomioka have been in vain? She suggested a challenge: let the foreign silk traders at Yokohama choose which was the more internationally marketable thread. If they chose the thread of Ōsato Sato, the wife of Rokkōsha's head official, then the Tomioka girls would obey orders and use the zaguri method. When the Yokohoma mer-

---

[23] Ibid., 210–12.

[24] A former dormitory resident recollected that there were opportunities for lessons in reading, writing, and needlework from "an excellent teacher." Morosawa, *Onna no hataraki*, 101.

[25] Ibid., 97; Takase, *Kanei Tomioka*, 160; Wada, *Tomioka nikki*, 33–35.

[26] Takase, *Kanei Tomioka*, 75–78.

chants did not choose the heavier thread but praised the luster and unifor-
mity of the girls' product, the male management was won over to the new
method of reeling.[27]

Tomioka graduates had especially high prestige and confidence, but they
were not the only highly motivated silk workers during the 1870s. Samurai
and respectable peasant daughters who did not have opportunities to study
at the model plant volunteered to work in local filatures. When samurai
investors founded such filatures with their wives and daughters as workers,
country girls went to join them. "If we can't go to Tomioka at least we can
go to the Nijō machines and reel for the sake of the country," said the
young women of the silk areas in Nagano.[28] With government encouragement, the number of filatures increased rapidly. By 1879 there were 665
mechanical silk-reeling plants in Japan. Nagano prefecture, with 358, had
by far the largest number. Other prefectures active in mechanical reeling
were Gifu with 142 plants, Yamane with 81, Gunma with 12, Yamagata
with 11, and Fukushima with 10.[29] Until the 1880s, working conditions
in local filatures were relatively good; reelers frequently had weekly half-
holidays and freedom of movement in their nonworking hours.[30]

Although early Tomioka turned out independent, dedicated working
women, it also drew blueprints for patterns that would remain in the silk
industry long after the admired Tomioka damsel ceased to be a leader in
local silk production. Trainees came to Tomioka on contracts of from one
to three years' duration. They were not free to "go home anytime" as Ei's
colleagues at Rokkōsha seem to have been. If they made good progress in
what they had come to learn and their skills were demanded at filatures in
their home prefectures, they could be given permission to leave before the
stipulated time was up.[31] Otherwise, unless illness, family emergency, or
demonstrated incapacity to learn reeling skills caused mill authorities to
send them home early, they were bound to serve their time at the plant no
matter how homesick they might become or how oppressive they found
the regimented work.[32] One, two, or three years were not long periods of
time when compared to the time contracted by those workers of the day
who left their homes to labor as bound servants of others for many years.
However, it was the poor who went out into such service, while silk reeling
was an occupation associated with prosperous, not destitute peasants, and

[27] Wada, *Tomioka nikki*, 98–103.
[28] Morosawa, *Shinano*, 1:219. Nijō village was where Rokkōsha (founded 1874) was located.
[29] Kajinishi et al, *Seishi rōdōsha*, 27.
[30] Morosawa, *Shinano*, 1:221.
[31] Takase, *Kanei Tomioka*, 60.
[32] Ibid., 56–57, documents the plight of girls who wanted to return home because they
found the work oppressive but were unable to get permission to leave. Not every trainee had
as happy memories of Tomioka as did Wada Ei. See Miura, *Rōdō no rekishi*, 124–26.

with ex-samurai who, despite economic hardship, remained members of the social elite.[33]

In the Tomioka dormitory, girls from all over the country lived a highly regulated communal life: eating, sleeping, working, exercising, washing their clothes on Sunday. Dormitory rules divided girls into groups of twenty, placed under a room supervisor, herself chosen from among "first-class workers," trainees whose performance brought them to the attention of the management. Reporting to the administrative staff above them, room supervisors had a good deal of power over the other workers, who had to obtain permission from them for a number of actions, including leaving the plant grounds. Ordinarily girls were not allowed out of the premises except on holidays, and there was a strict curfew.[34]

By the 1880s, substantial numbers of Tomioka workers lived outside the factory walls, as whole families of distressed samurai moved to the village of Tomioka to find work for their women. In 1884 there were 129 commuting workers at the Tomioka filature and 40 nonboarding women who were labeled "day laborers."[35] As Takase Toyoji suggests, many who originally had been boarders appear to have become commuters.[36] Perhaps the splendid dormitory had become as irksome to some of its inmates as later, less grand silk-factory dormitories would be to later silk workers.

Although working hours and rest periods were considerably scheduled, not all on-the-job conditions were pleasant. Trainees were instructed sternly, and they were required to work extremely hard and quickly. They were not permitted to talk to each other at work and were penalized if they did so. At busy times they sometimes had to gulp down food while they ran their machines.[37] Despite routines stressing uniform treatment of all pupil-workers, mill managers were not above playing favorites. But when the administrative staff discriminated in favor of trainees from their own parts of the country, they faced loud protests from girls of other regions.[38]

In *Tomioka Diary* we learn that, twenty days after their own arrival at the mill, the Matsushiro girls were delighted to learn that the travelers from Yamaguchi had just reached Tomioka village. Since new recruits were put to work in the humid, steaming cocoon room, Yokota Ei and her com-

[33] In Edo times daughters of respectable farmers did sometimes "go out in service" in a samurai family's home for three years. Segawa, *Mura*, 53. But those who went for long periods of time during the Edo period were often the tragically poor, "broken farmers" (*tsubure-byakushō*) who had lost their holdings through failure to pay taxes and thus were "forced to migrate or sell themselves as indentured servants." Vlastos, *Peasant Protests*, 17.

[34] Rōdō undō shiryō iin kai (Committee for historical materials pertaining to the labor movement), ed., *Nihon rōdō undō shiryō* (Historical materials pertaining to Japan's labor movement), 5 vols. (Tokyo, 1968), 1:139–40.

[35] Takase, *Kanei Tomioka*, 152.

[36] Ibid.

[37] Kajinishi et al, *Seishi rōdōsha*, 21–30.

[38] Ibid., 24–26.

rades expected to exchange their places among the vile-smelling cocoons
for stations in front of the reeling machines. To their dismay, they were
not moved from the cocoon room, and the thirty Yamaguchi novices were
immediately assigned to learn machine reeling. Shocked and tearful, the
Matsushiro girls appealed to the mill bosses, only to be told that the unfair
preference given to the Yamaguchi group was a "mistake" made by the
foreign technicians.[39] No one believed this half-hearted, face-saving lie.
Nagano trainees were angry enough to stage a boycott of dormitory rec-
reation the next time they encountered conspicuous favoritism toward Yamaguchi natives on the part of Tomioka officials, half of whom were themselves from Yamaguchi prefecture.[40]

One sphere in which no regional or other partiality was shown was in
the rank given student-workers. Trainees were graded into categories according to their levels of demonstrated achievement: first-class worker, second-class worker, third-class worker, and unclassified worker. Ei recalls
how thrilled she was to be made a first-class worker, a goal toward which
she had been concentrating her energies. "I was seized with such joy that
the tears poured down."[41] The monetary advantage accompanying a high
rank was substantial: monthly wages were set at twenty-five yen for first-
class workers, eighteen yen for second-class, twelve yen for third, and nine
yen for unclassified workers. All workers received five-yen clothing allowances for both summer and winter; and all were charged the same seven
sen, one rin a day, then later seven sen, two rin for food.[42] Along with
binding contracts for compulsory work over a given time period, regimented dormitory life, strict discipline on the factory floor, and the problem of management favoritism, this wage classification according to skill
would remain with the silk industry decades after Tomioka's nourishing
meals, medical care, relatively short working hours with regular rest periods, and days off became a memory of the model filature days of the idyllic
1870s.

Early Machine Cotton Spinning and Spinners

Transformation to machine-spun cotton involved much more than traditional producers of cotton thread learning to spin "by steam or water

[39] Wada, *Tomioka nikki*, 22–25.
[40] Morosawa, *Shinano*, 1: 214–15; Wada, *Tomioka nikki*, 38–40. Wada Ei was chastised as
a traitor by her fellow workers from Nagano because she did not honor the boycott. Ibid.
[41] Ibid., 43.
[42] The different classifications were recognized in deductions from wages of workers who
were absent because of illness. A first-class worker who was absent had 2.9 sen deducted from
her wages, an absent second-class worker had 2.7 sen deducted, an absent third-class worker
2.5 sen. Kajinishi et al, *Seishi rōdōsha*, 21.

power, rather than by hand." Expensive to purchase and complicated to operate, spinning machinery required mastery of brand-new technologies. While international demand for Japanese cocoons and raw silk, the result of the blight in Europe, provided attractive incentives for local silk producers, domestic cotton enterprises were forced to compete with cheap, superior, foreign thread and cloth that flooded into the country under the terms of the treaties. It is not surprising that Japan's modern cotton-spinning industry began almost a decade later than machine silk reeling. Yet among the country's leaders, determination to develop cotton was just as strong as support for silk.

While those in handicrafted-cotton trades helplessly witnessed the ruin of their markets, government leaders turned their attention to the two cotton-spinning plants equipped with Western-style machinery that they had inherited from the old regime. Both had been built by the former rulers of the Satsuma fief who imported cotton-spinning machinery from England.[43] A third plant had been established in 1872 by Kajima Mampei, a Tokyo cotton merchant, with machinery ordered from England before the Meiji Restoration.[44] Despite government support of the two mills founded by Satsuma, the three could not offer much employment to dispossessed samurai or needy peasants, because the scale of their operations was small. The thread they produced was only a tiny proportion of the cotton thread sold in Japan. Until 1878 the government used one of the Satsuma plants as a teaching mill to demonstrate machine-spinning operations and encourage would-be entrepreneurs, but imitators of Kajima's perseverance were scarce.

By 1878 the Meiji government leaders had decided that the threat posed by foreign cotton imports called for more drastic measures: they resolved both to open more government mills and to subsidize private spinning ventures. The following year, the government ordered from England ten sets of spinning equipment (each consisting of 2,000 spindles) for ten private factories. Soon another three private mills had also been equipped with 2,000 spindles each, bought with government loans.[45] New government mills, opened in Ōhira in Aichi prefecture in 1881 and in Kamiseno in Hiroshima in 1882, were intended to employ former samurai as part of the government's policy of poor relief—especially for destitute samurai families—as well as to provide model factories for private investors.[46] The

[43] The first Satsuma plant was built in Iso in Kagoshima (former fief of Satsuma) in 1868; the second was established at Sakai near Osaka in 1870.

[44] T. Smith, *Political Change*, 61.

[45] Sumiya, *Nihon chinrōdō*, 177.

[46] Nagoya josei shi kenkyū kai (Nagoya women's history research association), ed., *Haha no jidai: Aichi no josei shi* (The age of our mothers: A history of aichi women) (Nagoya, 1969), 42; Kinugawa Taichi, *Honpō menshi bōseki shi* (A history of cotton spinning in Japan), 8 vols.

prefectural governments of Osaka and Hyōgo supported other plants with a 2,000-spindle capacity; additional private ventures were undertaken in Okayama, Nagoya, and Osaka.[47] The government also lent technicians to private mills after paying for their expensive training in Western technology.[48] By 1886, government efforts had helped to create the beginning of a modern spinning industry; during that year there were twenty spinning mills with a total capacity of 81,264 spindles in Japan, although most operations were small.[49]

The founders of these private mills were generally individuals of substance who had access to private fortunes as well as government funds. Itō Denshichi, for instance, the son of a rich sake brewer, established a plant in Kawashima (a village in his native Mie prefecture) with the expertise he gained at one of the former Satsuma mills and the machinery the government imported from England.[50] Others came from wealthy landlord or merchant families.[51]

Despite the optimistic expansion of machine spinning backed by public and private resources, the mill founders encountered many problems. The scale of operations was often too small to be profitable; the waterwheels that ran the machinery were not always efficient or reliable; it was difficult to find locations with convenient access to waterpower and to raw cotton; if such locations could be found, they were often far away from populated settlements where potential mill hands resided; there was limited technical expertise, and technicians were in short supply.[52]

The first demonstration mills and those built in the early 1880s employed both male and female workers. The workers were predominantly from samurai families, although peasants commuted from villages, and nonsamurai members of the urban poor were also hired.[53] The predomi-

---

(Osaka, 1937–1944), 2: 93–95; Takamura Naosuke, *Nihon bōseki-gyō shi josetsu* (An introduction to the history of Japan's cotton-spinning industry), 2 vols. (Tokyo, 1971), 1: 40.

[47] Sumiya, *Nihon chinrōdō*, 177.

[48] Takamura, *Nihon bōseki-gyō shi josetsu*, 1: 41; Ōe Shinobu, *Nihon no sangyō kakumei* (Japan's industrial revolution) (Tokyo, 1975), 41–42.

[49] Takamura, *Nihon bōseki-gyō shi josetsu*, 1: 111. Most mills had about 2,000 spindles, but Nagoya Cotton-Spinning and Tamashima Cotton-Spinning each had 4,000 and the exceptional Osaka Cotton-Spinning had 10,500 spindles. Ibid.

[50] Horie Yasuzō, "Modern Entrepreneurship in Meiji Japan," in *The State and Economic Enterprise in Japan: Essays in the Political Economy of Growth*, ed. William W. Lockwood (Princeton, 1965), 184.

[51] Sumiya, *Nihon chinrōdō*, 181; Ōe, *Nihon no sangyō kakumei*, 203–20; Horie, "Modern Entrepreneurship," 184–85.

[52] Takamura, *Nihon bōseki-gyō shi josetsu*, 1: 45; Watanabe Tōru, "Meiji zenki no rōdōryoku ichiba keisei o megute" (Establishment of the labor market during the early Meiji period), in *Meiji zenki no rōdō mondai* (Labor problems of the early Meiji period), ed. Meiji shiryō kenkyū renrakukai (Meiji historical materials research committee) (Tokyo, 1960), 125–26.

[53] Kinugawa, *Honpō menshi*, 3: 178, 269, 244; Watanabe, "Meiji zenki no rōdōryoku,"

nance of ex-samurai was not accidental, since governmental policy supported employment of impoverished samurai first, others second; in some places samurai background became a qualification for employment. In the Nagoya Cotton-Spinning Mill all the workers were samurai,[54] and in Okayama Cotton-Spinning Mill, supported by the former feudal lord of the area, "samurai wives and daughters, wearing kimonos with their family crests upon them, went in and out of the mill gate."[55] As long as the mills were established within commuting distance of settlements, there was no shortage of people willing to work in them. However, when the mills were located in mountainous terrain or other less accessible areas because of the necessity of maintaining a good water supply, managements experienced difficulties recruiting a work force.[56]

Evidence regarding working conditions in these pioneer mills is scarce, but extant reports suggest that the pay was low and the hours long. The same reports claim that morale was high among these first laborers in machine spinning. Hosoi Wakizō (1897–1925), the male cotton worker who wrote the classic study of the working lives of female cotton-mill hands, suggested that some of the magic associated with the prestigious foreign machinery rubbed off upon even the most humble of those who worked with it. Since the machines installed in the Satsuma plants were seen as something akin to marvelous new gods, daughters of the samurai families operating those machines became attendants of the gods.[57] Japanese economic historians have described employee-employer relations in these early factories as "feudalistic."[58] According to these scholars, *feudalistic* describes a situation in which workers and management were bound by a web of mutual obligations: the owners or managers would not think of discharging employees nor would workers think of leaving employment, even if it were in the economic or other interest of either to do so.[59] In such a situation, owners and workers apparently felt they shared interests

125–26; Hosoi Wakizō, *Jokō aishi* (The pitiful history of female factory workers), (1925; Tokyo, 1954), 24–25; Sanpei Kōko, "Nihon ni okeru fujin rōdō no rekishi" (History of women's labor in Japan), in *Fujin rōdō* (Women's labor), ed. Ōkōchi Kazuo and Isoda Susumu (Tokyo, 1956), 33.

[54] Kinugawa, *Honpō menshi*, 2: 481.

[55] Ibid., 3: 307.

[56] Examples are the Kuwabara mill established in 1882 in the mountains near Osaka and a mill founded in Hiroshima in 1883. Watanabe, "Meiji zenki no rōdōryoku," 125.

[57] Hosoi, *Jokō aishi*, 25.

[58] Kinugawa, *Honpō menshi*, 3: 17; Fujibayashi Keizō, "Meiji nidai ni okeru wa ga bōseki rōdōsha no idō genshō ni tsuite" (Changing phenomenon of Japanese cotton-spinning workers during the second decade of Meiji), in Meiji shiryō kenkyū renrakukai, *Meiji zenki no rōdō mondai*, 140–42. Nōshōmu-shō (Ministry of Agriculture and Commerce), ed., *Nihon menshi bōseki-gyō enkaku kiji* (Record of Japan's cotton-spinning industry) (Tokyo, 1888), cited in Sumiya, *Nihon chinrōdō*, 185.

[59] Ibid.

in a kind of master-vassal relationship in which there was no room for "the empty words" of employment contracts.[60] The atmosphere in these early plants was supposedly "family-like"—and indeed husbands and wives often worked in the same mill.[61] Such an atmosphere was possible within the small scale of operations in these establishments, which employed anywhere from forty to two hundred workers.[62]

In Itō Denshichi's Mie Cotton-Spinning plant, for instance, it was apparently unnecessary to sound the morning whistle to begin work, for the laborers immediately set about their tasks without such a warning.[63] The company took responsibility for its workers' housing: dormitory accommodation for single hands and family quarters for married ones. The work schedule was from sunup to sundown, but when the daylight hours were long, rest periods broke the monotony. Great festival days, village festival days, and a period of time from 28 December to 5 January were set aside as holidays, along with one additional day each month, although it was understood that if the mill was busy, holidays might be ignored. The dangers involved in machine spinning were acknowledged by provision of compensation to families of hands who were killed or maimed at work.[64]

When Mie opened its doors in 1882, most of its eighty workers (sixty female, twenty male) were offspring of former retainers of the Tsu fief.[65] Despite their good family backgrounds, each one had to pass an aptitude test before being accepted as a full-fledged worker. This test consisted of a twenty-day probationary period, during which the applicant was boarded in the dormitory but received no wages; or, if she paid for her own accommodation elsewhere, she received an allowance of five sen a day (seven sen for males). Depending upon demonstrated promise, after the probationary period the novice was accepted as an apprentice or an auxiliary. Apprentices, female or male, were expected to work for two years without wages before being made regular hands. However, during that two-year period they were to be provided with lodging, food, clothes, and laundry services. Little is known about the auxiliaries, but their treatment was supposedly less favorable than that accorded apprentices. When an apprentice became a regular hand, she began to be paid daily wages.

Regular hands were paid according to the wage classification they had achieved, and—since there were fifteen wage-grade classifications plus four

[60] Fujibayashi, "Meiji nidai bōseki rōdōsha," 142–43.
[61] Ibid., 141–42.
[62] Sumiya, *Nihon chinrōdō*, 183.
[63] Fujibayashi, "Meiji nidai bōseki rōdōsha," 141–42; Kinugawa, *Honpō menshi*, 2:482.
[64] Ibid., 481–87.
[65] Sanpei Kōko, *Hataraki josei no rekishi* (A history of working women) (Tokyo, 1956), 57; Sanpei Kōko, *Nihon mengyō hattatsu shi* (A history of Japan's cotton industry) (Tokyo, 1941), 377; Kinugawa, *Honpō menshi*, 2: 481.

unclassified grades—not all the grades were necessarily assigned. A worker fresh from an apprenticeship would be assigned a low classification, perhaps class eleven, at thirteen sen a day for women and twenty for men, or class twelve, at twelve sen a day for women and eighteen for men.[66] Men might be paid "a living wage," but the wages of females, while perhaps enough to feed a person in 1882, left little over for anything beyond food if the recipient of the wages was supporting herself. In all likelihood, both employer and employees saw female wages as supplementary family income that went straight to the parents or husbands of the women working in the mill.

Samurai girls went to Mie and other mills because their families needed their wages to survive, but researchers tell us they did not develop a "daily-wage mentality."[67] A girl's wage-grade classification gave her a status and income based on her skill and productivity rather than on the old hereditary principle, which was the basis of the lost rank and stipend of her family. On the other hand, her wage classification also told the world how well she was serving the cotton-spinning master who retained her directly and her whole family indirectly. Those who ran cotton-spinning mills like Mie claimed that their workers, like silk reelers, patriotically served the nation. However, the image of "family-like," patriotic mills with high worker morale began to fade after July 1883 when Osaka Cotton-Spinning Company began operations.

Osaka Cotton-Spinning Leads the Way

Scholars tend to view Osaka Cotton-Spinning as the unique creation of Shibusawa Eichi, an important figure in the Ministry of Finance before he left government service at the age of thirty-four to become one of "the most successful entrepreneurs of early Meiji."[68] Osaka Cotton-Spinning's 10,500-spindle mill, built in 1882, was certainly a central part of the entrepreneurial activity that occurred when the government began its programs of support for Western-style machine spinning. But although this company shared much with firms of "2,000- or more spindle capacity," from its in-

[66] Ibid., 481–90; Sampei, *Hataraki josei*, 57–59; Sampei, *Nihon mengyō hattatsu shi*, 377–81; Tōyō Bōseki Kabushiki Kaisha (Tōyō Cotton-Spinning Company), *Tōyō bōseki 70 nen shi* (A seventy-year history of Tōyō Cotton-Spinning) (Tokyo, 1953), 220–25. At first the mill hands were paid their wages once every six months, but this was soon changed to once every month.

[67] Fujibayashi, "Meiji nidai bōseki rōdōsha," 140–42; Sampei, *Hataraki josei*, 59.

[68] Johannes Hirschmeir, "Shibusawa Eichi: Industrial Pioneer," in Lockwood, *State and Economic Enterprise*, 216; Takahashi Kamekichi, *The Rise and Development of Japan's Modern Economy* [*Nihon kindai keizai keisei shi*], trans. John Lynch (Tokyo, 1969), 271–72; Horie, "Modern Entrepreneurship," 185–86.

ception it towered over them, with almost five times as many spindles as the next largest company. This was possible because Shibusawa was able to raise a staggering 250,000 yen in capital from "private sources"—from former feudal lords (whose income had actually come from taxpayers) and from rich merchants.[69]

#5

Shibusawa was also able to recruit and secure specialized training abroad for the company's own first-rate technicians.[70] Technological challenges were taken seriously because Shibusawa was determined to produce thread that could recapture the domestic market and eventually compete internationally.[71] The company paid close attention to its predecessors' problems: for instance, Osaka Cotton-Spinning's initial planning assumed the mill would be run by waterpower, but the difficulties water-powered plants were experiencing led to installation of steam-powered machinery.[72] Attention paid to technology and technicians quickly paid off: in 1884 Osaka Cotton-Spinning's product ranked only sixth place among the thirteen spinning companies in terms of the quantity of thread produced per spindle in a given time, but in quality Osaka Cotton-Spinning's thread topped all the others.[73]

Although Shibusawa's imaginative energy was certainly the driving force behind the firm's auspicious beginnings, as Takamura Naosuke points out, it was the large capital backing that made the successes possible.[74] Unlike Shibusawa, most of the shareholders were extremely passive, interested primarily in profitable returns on their investments. The company management under Shibusawa, ever conscious of the need for further investments to meet their goals of producing nationally and internationally competitive thread, wanted to keep its passive shareholders interested in investing in Osaka Cotton-Spinning.

#5

The way to do this was to get them a high return of profit on their investments, high enough to keep the shareholders patriotically putting their money into the domestic—and eventually international—"textile war"[75] rather than into safe remunerative investments in tenanted land and moneylending. Further application of the most modern technology available might increase production and improve product quality in the long run, but in the short and middle terms the expense of this would probably

---

[69] Takamura, *Nihon bōseki-gyō shi josetsu*, 1: 65, 66–76.

[70] The most famous of such technicians was Tanabe Takeo. The company also hired its own foreign technicians.

[71] Shibusawa's plan apparently predated the government's moves in this direction during the late 1870s. See Takamura, *Nihon bōseki-gyō shi josetsu*, 1: 64, 76.

[72] Ibid., 64–65.

[73] Ibid., 77–78.

[74] Ibid., 65.

[75] Nakamura Masanori, *Rōdōsha to nōmin*, 159.

alienate shareholders. In its quest for ever-larger profits, Osaka Cotton-Spinning looked to the work force: labor must be made to produce more at less cost. Technological change was to be initiated only if it promised short-run profits from higher labor productivity as well as longer-term improvements in quality.

Osaka was chosen as a plant site largely because it commanded access to two large populations of potential employees: the city poor of Osaka itself and farming families in villages within commuting range of Osaka.[76] Many of the former were first-generation urban dwellers who had come to the metropolitan center hungry, empty-handed, and exhausted from struggles for livelihood and land that were rife all over Japan.[77] In suburban villages were some of the poorest farming families in their districts, usually tenants who desperately needed side income to supplement precarious existences as marginal agriculturalists. Large reserve armies like these were desired by the company because cotton spinning was considered low-status work, and Osaka Cotton-Spinning managers had decided to pay male mill hands about half of what skilled urban tradesmen such as carpenters and stone-masons received at the time, and to pay female hands little more than half of what male hands would get.[78]

Osaka Cotton-Spinning's relationship with its hands definitely was not imbued with the "master-vassal" notions that apparently united employees and bosses in many of the smaller plants. Profits were seen as the key to the future envisioned by Shibusawa. On 5 July 1883, when Osaka Cotton-Spinning began partial operations, its hard-boiled approach to hiring differed sharply from practices of other companies.[79] Some mills, especially those located in remote regions, provided dormitories or boardinghouses for their workers; at Osaka Cotton-Spinning in 1883, all the hands were commuters.[80] The company did not intend to "waste" money on housing or other amenities for workers. Predictably, the wages offered were lower than those paid at most other cotton companies.

Because the first type of machinery imported from England by Osaka Cotton-Spinning was the mule-spinner,[81] requiring strong human muscles to operate it, 46 percent of the work force was male when the plant

---

[76] Takamura, *Nihon bōseki-gyō shi josetsu*, 1: 80–81. There was another reason for the choice of Osaka. Formerly the hub of the old domestic cotton industry of pre-Meiji times, the city was a place where raw cotton of good quality could be purchased. Ibid., 86.

[77] Ibid., 81, 134.

[78] Tōyō Bōseki Kabushiki Kaisha, *Tōyō bōseki 70 nen shi*, 228; Kinugawa, *Honpō menshi*, 2: 420.

[79] Takamura, *Nihon bōseki-gyō shi josetsu*, 1: 81.

[80] Ibid., 135.

[81] Also called the mule-jenny, the mule-spinner was a machine that had a moving carriage for simultaneously drawing and twisting a sliver into a thread and winding it into cops.

opened.[82] It was this 46 percent that Osaka Cotton managers focused on as they tried to make up their minds about suitable wage rates for the mill's first employees. One of those involved in these deliberations later recalled:

In December of 1882, when we came to decide upon wages for male and female workers, it was very difficult because we had no fixed standards to go by. At that time, the wages of carpenters, assistants [tetsudai], and stonemasons were usually fixed at about twenty-five sen [a day], but the cotton-spinning hands were all complete novices. Everything would have to be taught to them. The plan was to raise their wages as they acquired skill with the training they received, but it was a hard task to set beginning wages. After considerable study it was decided to pay male workers two shō of rice [then one shō cost about six sen], so the starting [daily] wage was fixed at twelve sen. Female starting wages were fixed at seven sen [a day].[83]

Interestingly, the male wage was calculated on the basis of what appears to have been per capita consumption of the basic food, while the female wage was set much lower. Since female adults could not be expected to eat drastically less than males, surely the lower wage reflects an assumption that female wages were merely supplements to family income. The male wage was eight sen less a day and the female wage six sen less a day than Mie paid workers after introductory training. Osaka Cotton-Spinning policy makers claimed they had "no fixed standards to go by," but they chose to ignore precedents set by Mie and other companies. Two shō of rice (one shō equals approximately 1.47 U.S. gallons or 1.8 liters) may have been the daily wage male agricultural day workers in the Osaka region received at this time, although elsewhere agricultural wages were certainly higher for both males and females.[84] Evidently Osaka Cotton-Spinning's management felt that cotton-thread workers, recruited from the swelling slum districts within Osaka and in nearby villages, should be at the bottom of the employment ladder. In the middle of the Matsukata deflationary distress, with wages generally going down and a nationwide tendency toward general impoverishment in full swing, the company could easily hope to attract employees.[85]

[82] Takamura, Nihon bōseki-gyō shi josetsu, 1: 82.

[83] Kinugawa, Honpō menshi, 2: 420.

[84] Tōyō Bōseki Kabushiki Kaisha, Tōyō bōseki 70 nen shi, 226, claims that two shō of rice was the daily wage of male agricultural workers at the time. However, national statistics do not support this. In 1882 the national average agricultural daily wage for male workers was 22.1 sen and for female workers 14.2 sen. Sumiya, Nihon chinrōdō, 135. For measurement of income in terms of annual low-grade rice requirements, see Masayoshi Chūbachi and Koji Taira, "Poverty in Modern Japan: Perceptions and Realities," in Patrick, Japanese Industrialization, 363–89.

[85] Sumiya, Nihon chinrōdō, 94–99, shows such a trend using a case study of impoverishment in Yamanashi prefecture as an illustration. See ibid., 135, for data on the decline in wages during the decade following introduction of Matsukata's financial policies.

Osaka Cotton's managers planned for the future: they established twelve wage-grade classifications and subclassifications according to skill and experience for both male and female workers. Wages for workers in each classification were calculated on the basis of a set daily-wage rate. The starting daily wage for a man in the lowest grade was ten sen. When the mill began operations in 1883, 77 percent of the male workers were classified as grade-eleven workers, entitled to twelve sen a day; 40 percent of the female workers were classified at the very bottom in grade twelve earning seven sen a day, but by the end of the year the latter had become more than 59 percent of the work force.[86] In that year the highest-paid male workers (11 out of 128) were in grade five (twenty-four sen) and the highest-paid female workers (11 out of 144) were in grade seven (seventeen sen).[87] A three-sen-a-day difference between the wage rate for men and that for women existed at all levels in the classification system.[88] Cotton machinery, especially mule-spinners, stood too high to permit children to do many of the related jobs, but for those under fifteen years of age who were employed as "male apprentice workers" or as "female apprentice workers," there were separate wage classifications: grade six to grade one for boys, yielding from four to nine sen a day, and from three to one for girls, yielding from four to six sen a day.[89] Osaka was not the first company to institute a wage-grade classification system; as we have seen, Mie Cotton-Spinning Company, founded in 1882, had one. But Osaka Cotton-Spinning developed its wage grades, often with subgrades, in an extremely thoroughgoing fashion, making this system the central pillar of its employer-employee relations.

When the Osaka Cotton-Spinning mill opened its doors, it offered lower wages than most other mills; the average wages of its female workers ranked tenth lowest among the thirteen cotton-spinning firms in operation in 1884.[90] Still, Osaka Cotton's workers had to be paid something, and it would be some years before training could produce any highly skilled workers. If the shareholders were to be persuaded to keep their money in the company, hands must be made to produce more.

Again, the best answer seemed to be an innovation observed elsewhere: night-shift operations, which Kuwabara Cotton-Spinning had begun about two months before Osaka Cotton's mill opened.[91] Even before Kuwabara began nighttime work, cotton-spinning companies had tried to increase the productivity of their expensive machinery by running it longer

[86] Takamura, *Nihon bōseki-gyō shi josetsu*, 1:85.
[87] Ibid., 138–39.
[88] Ibid.
[89] Ibid.
[90] Ibid., 79.
[91] Sumiya, *Nihon chinrōdō*, 189.

44

hours. In Kajima Mampei's pioneer mill, from about 1879, two shifts of workers were employed in order to keep the machines running at least twelve hours.[92] By 1883, Kuwabara Cotton ran machinery for twenty-two consecutive hours a day, with night crews working under dangerous oil lamps.[93]

Advantages to be gained from maximum exploitation of plant machinery were immediately obvious to the profit-hungry management of Osaka Cotton-Spinning. On 26 August 1883, less than two months after the company had begun operations, Osaka Cotton began its first twelve-hour night shift. This initiative was quickly copied by other companies: by the end of the following year, five firms in addition to Kuwabara and Osaka had night shifts, and thus almost half of the cotton-spinning works in the country were running through the night as well as during the day.[94]

For the hands working under kerosene lamps and unfamiliar with fire-prevention methods, this meant tragedy almost nightly.[95] Fire danger had haunted the mills even before all-night operations were introduced.[96] Operations the size of Osaka Cotton-Spinning, which utilized 650 lamps, risked enormous damage. Indeed there was a serious fire on the third night of that company's night-shift operations,[97] and frequently twenty or thirty small fires occurred during a single night. The danger was so great that a proposal to give up the night shift was seriously considered by the company.[98] Always a leader, Osaka Cotton decreased fire hazards when it installed electric lighting in 1884, and eventually other firms followed suit.[99] Still, Osaka Cotton-Spinning's great fire of 1892—years after electrification—destroyed buildings and machinery, razed thirty-four private residences beyond the mill grounds, and killed ninety-five (mostly female) workers and seriously maimed twenty-two others.[100] For profit, the company was willing to risk workers' lives and perhaps even take chances with its expensive machinery.

Despite electrification, the night shift continued to be unpopular with Osaka Cotton's workers, who were paid slightly higher wages for night

[92] Kajima Cotton-Spinning Company's machinery did not run all night long. Kinugawa, *Honpō menshi*, 6:344.

[93] Ibid., 2:233.

[94] Sumiya, *Nihon chinrōdō*, 189. Shimotsuke Cotton-Spinning's factory in Tochigi had run night shifts from the time it was opened in 1885. See Kinugawa, *Honpō menshi*, 2:267.

[95] Kinugawa, *Honpō menshi*, 2:393–94; Sumiya, *Nihon chinrōdō*, 189.

[96] The night-shift innovator, Kuwabara Cotton-Spinning, experienced that danger for years because its mill was not electrified until 1896. Kinugawa, *Honpō menshi*, 3:28.

[97] Takamura, *Nihon bōseki-gyō shi josetsu*, 1: 102.

[98] Kinugawa, *Honpō menshi*, 2: 392–93.

[99] Sumiya, *Nihon chinrōdō*, 190.

[100] Kinugawa, *Honpō menshi*, 2: 426.

work in acknowledgment of their distaste for it.[101] Sunday, officially a day off for Osaka Cotton hands, became the day the shifts changed. This meant that those getting off work Sunday morning, after serving for a week on the night shift, had two choices: they could either try to struggle through the day without sleep and sleep Sunday night in preparation for the twelve hours' strenuous labor required of them on Monday's day shift; or they could try to sleep through to Monday morning. Not surprisingly, given workers' feelings about it, the rate of production on the night shift was 15 to 20 percent below that of the day shift.[102]

Twenty-four-hour operations did, however, boost production enormously, and profits rose accordingly—Osaka Cotton's profit rate in 1884 was 31.6 percent.[103] Like the wage-grade system, which did not originate with Osaka Cotton-Spinning but was adopted and shaped by that firm until it became not only its own hallmark but a characteristic of cotton-spinning enterprises everywhere, the night shift, which began as an experiment in a smaller company, became another essential element in Osaka Cotton-Spinning's success. The rest of the industry would emulate these systems.

Initial hesitation overcome, traditional reelers of silk and young women who sought to learn reeling skills, as well as to earn money for their families, took up the Meiji government's challenge. Many but not all of those who went to learn machine reeling in order to be able to "perform meritorious deeds for the realm" were from proud samurai or established peasant families. Whether from ex-samurai, substantial peasant, or poorer peasant backgrounds, the girls and women who went to Tomioka and other filatures came from homes where "women's work" was recognized and respected, even if it was not always accorded high status. During the 1870s, the prestige of female silk workers was elevated: they were regarded as teachers of modern techniques as well as laborers. Their working situations, while not easy, usually allowed them to perform their tasks with dignity and to enjoy regular periods of rest and enough food to nourish their active and often growing bodies. As we shall see in the following chapter, these tolerable conditions changed drasticaly during the 1880s.

With greater technological and financial hurdles to overcome, early machine spinning of cotton developed more slowly. This industry too found many, perhaps most, of its first workers among the members of the former samurai class. Samurai daughters and samurai sons—in the beginning there were many male hands—were usually from impoverished families,

---

[101] Takamura, *Nihon bōseki-gyō shi josetsu*, 1: 103–4.
[102] Ibid., 103.
[103] Ibid.

who nevertheless had cherished ruling-class pedigrees for generations. In such families, female status was officially low, but as the returns from female work were often essential for survival, mothers, wives, and daughters—or at least their earnings—were grudgingly valued. Morale was high in the "feudalistic" atmosphere of the early cotton mills. Mie mill's shrill whistle woke up workers, their families, and neighbors when it blew each morning: workers did not own clocks, and the whistle's blasts told them when it was time to get up and when it was time to get ready to leave for work. Yet in those early days, the workers were at their places in the mill and already working before the blast marking the beginning of the day's operations. However, after Osaka Cotton-Spinning established large-scale operations near reserve armies of urban and suburban poor and scheduled day and night shifts, taking a "profit first" attitude toward its mill hands, the scene was set for a less happy world for cotton workers. We shall examine this world in later chapters.

3

Silk: Poor but Independent Reelers

A New Type of Reeler in a Harsher Setting

During the 1880s and 1890s the proud, confident reeler from an ex-samurai or well-to-do commoner family was replaced by a silk worker with a different background, the daughter of marginally independent cultivators or tenant farmers. This individual would commute daily from her home in the vicinity of a village or town housing a number of silk mills, or—and over time this became the dominant pattern—she would leave her family to go out to work in a mill in another part of her prefecture and eventually in another prefecture. In the beginning especially, such women and girls often went to the mills with some cocoon and reeling experience because they came from sericultural districts. Increasingly, however, as they came from poorer and poorer families with little or no sericultural side jobs, they learned their skills at the mills.[1]

During the optimistic 1870s, Tomioka and the prefectural filatures offered demonstration models and technical assistance to private silk manufacturers setting up or expanding their own operations. During the next decade, small-scale investors suffered as government aid to private enterprises became one of the many budget casualties under the drastic retrenchment and deflation policies of Finance Minister Matsukata Masayoshi, beginning in 1881. Silk works that survived had to face a number of problems, chief among which was Italian and French competition in world markets. The apparatus that sixty Italian reelers brought to Tokyo in 1870 and the French machinery introduced at Tomioka in 1872 had been similar to the equipment French and Italian silk reelers used in the 1860s and 1870s.[2] But during the next two decades reeling apparatus was vastly improved in Europe, and this trend continued in France and Italy up through the second decade of the twentieth century.[3] Japanese reeling, on the other hand, did not manage to keep pace with European improvements in labor technique and machinery: it was not until the 1920s that indigenous inventions dramatically upgraded reeling technology in Japan.[4] The poor

[1] According to Sumiya, *Nihon chinrōdō*, 165, hiring from among the daughters of poor families began with the sharp increase in the number of filatures that dated from 1876.

[2] Ishii Kanji, *Nihon sanshi-gyō shi bunseki* (An analytical history of the Japanese silk-reeling industry) (Tokyo, 1972), 245.

[3] Ibid.

[4] Ibid., 245–47. Ishii concluded that although in the Suwa district of Nagano prefecture

quality of silk cocoons raised in Japan was also an obstacle to production of the superior silk thread demanded abroad.[5]

In order to overcome competitive disadvantages in world markets, Japanese silk manufacturers enthusiastically turned to low wages. This is clear, although precisely how low wages actually were for silk workers in Japan during the late Meiji period has long been a hotly debated issue.[6] Certainly they were lower than wages paid to contemporary European silk workers, and they were probably lower than those paid to silk workers in mills in Shanghai, China. Ishii Kanji convincingly argues that, in early twentieth-century Japan, silk workers were paid roughly one-half of what their counterparts in France and Italy were paid and from 70 to 100 percent of what Shanghai silk workers received.[7]

The low wage costs of Japanese silk manufacturing were attained and maintained through long working hours, few rest periods, and provision of worker accommodation close to the factory floor so that almost every waking hour could be a working hour. Low wage costs to employers were also facilitated by delayed payments or nonpayments of portions of wages earned and by a complicated system of wage-grade classification, which rewarded a very small number of extraordinarily productive workers with relatively high wages and penalized the vast majority of the work force with very low wages.[8] These developments will be examined in detail in chapter 4. Here attention is drawn to the link between employers' successful reduction of real wages during the 1880s and the appearance of a new type of silk worker during that decade. The low wages, which enabled Japanese thread exports to hold their own against competitors in Europe, in-

---

technological improvements pioneered by such big firms as Katakura Gumi put Suwa's productivity ahead of that of the nation, at the turn of the century in Japan as a whole the productivity of a silk-mill worker was approximately one-half of the productivity of the same kind of worker in Italy and France. See also Kiyokawa Yukihiro, "Enterpreneurship and Innovation in Japan: An Implication of the Experience of Technological Development in the Textile Industries," *The Developing Economies* 22, no. 2 (June 1984): 211–36.

[5] See Ishii, *Nihon sanshi-gyō*, 373–77, for a discussion of the low quality of Japanese cocoons in comparison with those in France and Italy.

[6] For the basic contentions in this controversy see Yamada *Nihon shihonshugi bunseki*, and Sakisaka Itsurō, *Nihon shihonshugi no shomondai* (Problems of Japanese capitalism) (Tokyo, 1937).

[7] According to Ishii's calculations, if the 1903 daily wage of a Shanghai reeler is represented by 100, an Italian reeler's daily wage for that year is 140, a French reeler's 180, and a Japanese reeler's 70–100. Comparing hourly wages paid French, Italian, and Japanese silk workers in 1910, Ishii concluded that in that year a French reeler's average hourly wage was 61 sen (1 franc, 60 centimes), an Italian's was 46 sen (1 lira, 20 centesimi), while that of a reeler in the Koguchi Company in Suwa was 24 sen. Ishii, *Nihon sanshi-gyō*, 247.

[8] Nishinarita Yutaka, "Nihongata chinrōdō no seiritsu" (Formation of the Japanese pattern of wage labor), in *Kindai Nihon keizai o manabu* (Studying the modern Japanese economy) ed. Ishii Kanji, Uno Fukuju, Nakamura Masanori, Egusa Tadaatsu, 2 vols. (Tokyo, 1977), 1: 114–15.

delibly colored the working lives of those newcomers from poor peasant families who entered the silk mills after the 1870s; there they found an atmosphere considerably different from that familiar to the proud patriotic reelers of the previous decade.[9]

Longer working hours for factory workers in many industries became a general trend during the hard times of the 1880s. While government-run enterprises with eight- or nine-hour days lengthened working hours as budgets were squeezed and management problems arose, a longer work day became even more conspicuous in private businesses.[10] Indeed, when, as part of the Matsukata restraint policies, government enterprises were sold to individuals and private companies from 1884 on, the working day was often extended: this was the case with both the Kawasaki Shipbuilding Works and the Tomioka Silk Mill.[11] Longer and longer hours became especially noticeable in privately owned silk filatures.

Longer hours in silk reeling at first followed seasonal patterns: employers would squeeze what extra work time they could out of the dim morning light and the evening sun's vanishing rays. "The employees at silk manufacturing factories worked from sun rise to sun set originally. But by the middle of the 1880's, they were working from dawn to twilight every day."[12] Even longer working hours became possible with the introduction of artificial light, which provided silk-plant owners a way to get more out of their hands without increasing wages. Osaka Cotton-Spinning Company began night-shift operations under dangerous gas lamps in August 1883, introducing electric light the following year. Other cotton-spinning firms quickly followed suit, and soon gas and electric lighting had spread to the silk-thread industry.[13]

The extension of working time became possible as darkness at night—the most important "natural restriction"—was removed by the adoption of such modern lighting facilities as electric or gas lamps. The management sometimes neglected even the physiological requirements of girl workers in order to exploit their labor to the maximum. Their humanity was ignored and they were something like parts of machines. Their factory dormitories functioned as storerooms of machines furnishing labor.[14]

[9] One can argue that the difference in working atmosphere for silk workers in the two eras was largely a difference in degree, not in kind. Nevertheless, the perception by others and by the workers themselves of the silk factory girl was different before and after the early 1880s.

[10] Factories operated by the navy moved from an eight-hour to a nine-hour day in 1883, although eight-hour shifts were maintained during the winter. The navy's factories changed to a ten-hour day in 1886. The government printing bureau switched from nine daily hours to nine and a half hours a day in 1879. Sumiya, *Social Impact*, 43.

[11] Ōe, *Nihon no sangyō kakumei*, 174–76.

[12] Sumiya, *Social Impact*, 43.

[13] Sumiya, *Nihon chinrōdō*, 190.

[14] Sumiya, *Social Impact*, 43.

Although longer hours and harsher working conditions became widespread during the 1880s, this general trend by no means affected all silk workers uniformly. There were regional variations in the length of the workday as well as in wages and treatment accorded workers.[15] Some individual factories stuck to earlier practices regardless of changing norms within their regions.[16] Even in the greatest of the silk prefectures, pacesetting Nagano, where deterioration of the silk workers' lot was earliest and most thorough, there were a few managers like Ōsato Chūichirō of the Rokkōsha Mill who reportedly said, "Other silk companies sometimes run nighttime operations, but this is the result of the abominable, slipshod manufacturing [practices] they have accepted."[17]

The "slipshod manufacturing" Ōsato disapproved of often survived and expanded, while silk filatures with more humane working conditions went under during the early 1880s. Increasingly, the surviving plants hired young women from poor rather than respectable rural families. These young women became available as the Matsukata economic policies drove large numbers of independent cultivators and tenant cultivators to destitution: ruined peasants migrated to villages, towns, and cities with industry, while the swelling ranks of the starving who remained in the countryside eagerly sent children away to earn wages that might help to keep members of their families alive.[18] Workers from such families expected less than had their predecessors, but they too were not without pride and independence of spirit—as any employer who pushed them too hard might discover.

Resistance in Kōfu and Tomioka

Employers in the city of Kōfu, the center of Yamanashi prefecture's silk-reeling heartland, discovered this in 1886.[19] Turning out almost a quarter

[15] Ishii, *Nihon sanshi-gyō*, 254–57. In 1900 Nagano, Fukushima, and Gifu silk filatures paid wages once a year, while mills in the Kansai area and prefectures elsewhere aimed at monthly payment of wages. Wages varied in different prefectures from about fourteen to nineteen sen a day. Opportunities for female workers to rise to minor supervisory positions existed in some regions, but in Nagano, the greatest silk-producing prefecture, only men were employed as supervisors. See ibid.

[16] Ibid., 256.

[17] Quoted in ibid., 257.

[18] From 1881 when the Matsukata deflation began, for six years the prices of silkworms and rice repeatedly fell sharply. Yet farmers still had to pay taxes, and tenants had to pay rent to landlords who passed their tax burdens on to their tenants. See Nakamura Masanori, *Rō-dōsha to nōmin*, 56–59; Matsumoto, "Jinushi"; T. Smith, *Political Change*, 78–80.

[19] Most of the commercial development in Yamanashi during early Meiji was related to production and sale of cocoons and production of silk thread and cloth. In the old days, rural families in Yamanashi both raised silkworms and reeled thread, which they sold for valuable supplementary income. However, by the second decade of Meiji parts of the prefecture were

of the prefecture's raw silk by 1883, Kōfu mills were larger and employed more people than mills elsewhere in Yamanashi; they also ran for more days in the year.[20] Receiving generous aid and encouragement from the prefectural administration during the 1870s, Kōfu filatures were also among the earliest in the country to switch from traditional zaguri reeling methods to mechanical reeling.[21] The women who worked in the Kōfu mills came either from the urban poor (former samurai families or landless peasants who had migrated from the countryside) or from farming families in villages within walking distance of the city.[22] Commuters from neighboring villages were definitely in the majority.[23] "Carrying their lunches, they came to town every day to work for a fixed rate of so many sen."[24]

Despite the keen need of many families for side incomes, by 1880 the rapid expansion of mechanical reeling in Kōfu had outstripped the pool of available workers. Labor shortages began to worry mill managers. Those who did not treat their reelers well soon lost them to another establishment: since the young women were paid their wages each working day, it was not difficult for them to switch employers. "It was not the custom in the prefecture to provide factory dormitories for female workers, and thus all commuted to work. One day a worker would go to one silk mill to work; the next day she would enter another silk mill. A mill that was not good to her had no right to censure her; if she was censured, the next day she would just go elsewhere."[25] In 1881 a prefectural report on silk establishments noted that in Kōfu mills hands "are happy working for a firm that does not have a lot of rules. If Firm A has strict rules that they [mill hands] find hateful, on the morrow they will quit that firm and go to work for Firm B [with few rules]."[26] Filature owners might wring their hands and mutter darkly about local "customs of self-indulgence," but the young women did the best they could for themselves and their families each day as they sold their skills in the Kōfu labor market.

In 1885 a Kōfu company that practiced favoritism, being more generous with its pretty and single female employees than it was with its plain or

---

beginning to split into areas that specialized in cocoons and others that produced silk thread. By 1883, the district (*gun*) of Nishi Yamanashi (West Yamanashi), the largest producer of raw silk in the prefecture, boasted thirty-eight thread mills—thirty-seven of which were located in the city of Kōfu. Yoneda Sayoko, "Meiji 19 no Kōfu seishi jokō sōgi ni tsuite: Nihon ni okeru saisho no sutoraiki" (The Kōfu silk-factory girls' dispute of 1886: Japan's first industrial strike), *Rekishi hyōron* 105 (May 1959): 71.

[20] Ibid., 71–73.
[21] Ibid., 73–74.
[22] Ibid., 78.
[23] Kajinishi et al, *Seishi rōdōsha*, 37.
[24] *Seishi shijun kai kiji* (Report of the Association for Inquiry into Silk Reeling), 22, quoted in Yoneda, "Meiji 19 no Kōfu sutoraiki," 77.
[25] *Seishi shijun kai kiji*, 72, quoted in ibid.
[26] Ibid.

married ones, found itself facing a plant full of united, angry strikers. Their action was effective because the only strikebreakers the company managed to bring in were much less skilled than the original workers.[27] The strikers did not hesitate to take action despite the fact that, largely as a result of the Matsukata deflationary policies, 1885 was a year of serious economic depression. The following year, also a time of economic hardship, working women in Kōfu would cause an even bigger disturbance.

Early in 1886 Yamanashi silk manufacturers and merchants formed an employers' alliance under the general auspices of the newly established national Silk-Reeling Industrial Alliance (Seishi Sangyō Kumiai).[28] Although organizationally the Yamanashi silk employers' alliance conformed to the national body's constitution and bylaws, the regulations of the Yamanashi alliance contained a number of items regarding control of female mill hands that were not in the Silk-Reeling Alliance's regulations.[29] Yamanashi regulations, which declared that the employers' alliance would unilaterally set wage rates each year, included the stipulation that workers be allowed to work at only one mill during the year, denying them the right to change employers. The regulations also contained the provision that an employer was to be permitted to discharge a worker at his convenience, but a worker who left an employer at her convenience was not to be hired elsewhere until a period of six months—or one year if the worker's resignation inconvenienced her former employer—had elapsed. In the regulations was an arrangement for 2 percent or more of a worker's wages to be deducted by her employer and held back as forced savings, while regular payment of wages was to be monthly instead of daily. The most shocking of all the provisions in the regulations involved a system of "fines and rewards": heavy fines were to be levied for a long list of minor infractions of factory discipline. Fines one could incur in a month could reduce one's wages to zero, while the highest reward one could attain in a month equaled three days' pay.[30]

[27] The management tried desperately to train their scabs, but the newcomers were not skilled enough to do the work. The favoritism involved advance-loans on future wages: to the fair of face and the unmarried went loans of five yen while the others were extended loans of only one yen. See *Yamanashi rōdō undō shi* (A history of the Yamanashi labor movement) (1952), as reproduced in Akamatsu Ryoko, ed., *Rōdō* (Labor), 377–78, vol. 3 of *Nihon fujin mondai shiryō shūsei* (Collected documentary materials concerning Japanese women), hereafter *NFMSS*, 10 vols, (Tokyo, 1977–1980).

[28] The aim of the national organization, established in 1885, was government support for the silk industry, which was suffering in the economic depression that had begun in 1881. Nationally, the Silk-Reeling Industrial Alliance worked on regulation of export of raw silk; regionally, it encouraged the silk-producing areas to set up their own industrial alliances. Cocoon breeders and cocoon merchants also formed an alliance in Yamanashi in 1886. Yoneda, "Meiji 19 no Kōfu sutoraiki," 79.

[29] Ibid.

[30] Ibid.; *Yamanashi rōdō undō shi*, reproduced in *NFMSS*, 3: 380–82.

The national alliance may have been designed to regulate the raw-silk industry as a whole, but in Yamanashi employers were more interested in curtailing the bargaining power and independence of their workers. The plan was to use the new regulations to get more work out of Yamanashi silk workers for lower wages in order to keep Yamanashi silk exports competitive in international markets, despite the advantages of superior raw materials and technology held by silk producers in France and Italy.

The agreement and regulations of the Yamanashi alliance went into effect in mid-May 1886; by early June silk workers in Kōfu responded with the first of a series of strikes. The mill owned by Amamiya Kihyōei, where the first strike occurred, was a fairly large plant: the number of workers it employed is not precisely known, but newspaper accounts mentioned 114 and 196 workers, and any mill with more than 100 employees was large by Kōfu standards.[31] The work stoppage was undertaken to protest longer working hours, lowered wages, and arbitrary fines introduced with the Yamanashi employers' agreement.

During the months of May and June, working hours at the Amamiya mill, extended to match the summer daylight hours, had always been long. Factory operations began at 4:30 A.M. and continued until 12:30 when workers took their midday meal. At 1:30 it was back to the machines, and everyone worked until 7:30 P.M. This meant a long day away from home even for women who lived in town, but those who commuted from nearby villages added an hour to the end of each working day. During the 1880s, Kōfu and its environs were unsafe after dark: bands of thugs loitered about, ever ready to fight, rape, or relieve the unwary of their earnings.[32] There was always the possibility that the women might be kidnapped and sold into prostitution.[33] The risks faced sound very much like those Emily Honig describes in her account of the dangers encountered by Shanghai textile workers in pre-1949 China:

> Local toughs—many of whom belonged to Shanghai's powerful gang organizations—gathered at the mill gates, then flirted with and even pursued women walking home from work. On payday they seized women's wages, and on ordinary days they collected some cash by engaging in an activity called "stripping the sheep"—robbing a woman of her clothes, which they then sold. . . . All women workers had family members or friends who had been raped, beaten, or kidnapped by neighborhood hoodlums.[34]

[31] Ibid., 382; Kajinishi et al, *Seishi rōdōsha*, 36.
[32] *Yamanashi rōdō undō shi* in *NFMSS*, 3: 382.
[33] Ibid.
[34] Emily Honig, "Burning Incense, Pledging Sisterhood: Communities of Women Workers in the Shanghai Cotton Mills, 1919–1949," *Signs* 10, no. 4 (Summer 1985): 703.

Like Shanghai textile workers, Kōfu mill women tried to travel to and from work in groups of three or more.[35] If a woman who was ready to set off for work in Kōfu at 3:30 A.M. did not have company, she would wait until dawn rather than risk attack or intimidation in the dark. Then, hurry as she might, she was sure to arrive at the mill after operations were supposed to have been begun. Women did not like to be late, but their guiding principle was "Better late than molested." With the new regulations, tardiness, regardless of its cause, brought a reeler a stiff fine. Even women who came on time were docked twenty minutes in wages if they brought children to work with them—which married women frequently did. The new regulations introduced speedups and longer work periods: reelers were not permitted to go to the toilet or even to pause for a drink of water, and the hour-long break at noon was cut in half. Fines were freely imposed. Wages were cut from thirty-two or thirty-three sen a day to twenty-two or twenty-three.[36]

On 12 June more than a hundred Amamiya hands left their machines, streamed out the plant doors, and headed for a temple in the town to discuss and plan action against the capricious unfairness of their employer. They agreed to send a delegation to parley with the mill management, which eventually agreed to some of their demands: reelers who could not arrive before operations began in the morning were no longer punished, and the mill returned to the fourteen-hour day that was standard for June. Before the women agreed to go back to work on 16 June, the management also promised to think of "other ways to improve conditions."[37] This may not appear to be a great victory, especially as it is not entirely clear precisely how this promise was kept, but Yoneda Sayoko, a scholar who has carefully examined the documentary evidence regarding this strike, has concluded that in the end the women, not the company, were the winners.[38]

The Amamiya strike was followed by four other walkouts in June, July, and August, which involved about 275 workers.[39] These protests were also against the unilateral imposition of the new regulations. The results were mixed: there were some victories and some disappointments for the women who walked out of their factories, found meeting places large enough to accommodate them, elected representatives to negotiate with employers, and encouraged each other to maintain solidarity in their ranks. Employers both sought help from third-party mediators and negotiated directly with angry women who, in at least one of the strikes, were willing

[35] Ibid., 704.
[36] *NFMSS*, 3: 383.
[37] Ibid.
[38] Yoneda, "Meiji 19 no Kōfu sutoraiki," 81.
[39] *NFMSS*, 3: 382.

to take evidence that their employer had violated their contracts to a court of law.[40]

The underlying theme of the protests was "unfair treatment": summarily imposed fines, more difficult working conditions, longer hours, lower wages, favoritism. Yet much more damaging to the silk workers' situation were the regulations halting easy movement from one employer to another, along with those defining the new arrangements for monthly rather than daily payment of wages and the withholding of forced savings. These government-backed innovations were soon to put an end to the freedom of the Kōfu mill hand to sell her labor daily in the town's labor market. But in 1886, even Kōfu silk workers who were happy with their mills (and there continued to be a few outstanding mill operators with contented employees)[41] were still employed under short seasonal contracts, usually during spring, summer, or autumn. Not yet bound to an employer in continuous factory work during a season that lasted almost a year, and in great demand as mechanized silk reeling expanded, a skilled reeler was confident that she could find somewhere to work no matter how the strike ended. Thus the danger of the prohibitions against worker-initiated change of employer and the unpopular monthly wage payment apparently did not seem as pressing as the need to resist work-floor restrictions, arbitrary fines, lower wages, and longer hours.

Kōfu employers, on the other hand, had definitely agreed not only to stop raiding each others' work forces but also to stop hiring workers who had recently been employed elsewhere. They were also determined to enforce the new wage schemes that would make it very difficult for future strikes to succeed. The employers' success was evident six years later in a Kōfu strike in which 150 silk workers took action against a company that had lowered basic pay from fifteen to thirteen sen a day. The company sent a popular theatrical performer to inform the strikers that a return to the fifteen-sen rate was possible, but the strikers demanded immediate payment of the daily two sen they had already been docked. In order to safeguard their solidarity, the women pledged themselves liable for financial forfeits if they broke ranks. But the mill management locked them out and halted production. Without resources and with other employers refusing to hire them, the hands could not hold out; on the fourth day of the lockout the women sadly sent five delegates to negotiate a mass return without conditions.[42]

Nothing in the Kōfu employers' or silk workers' actions suggests the much-vaunted feudal relationship that supposedly dominated employer-

[40] Ibid., 383.
[41] Ibid., 384, mentions one such employer the women were happy to work for.
[42] Kajinishi et al, *Seishi rōdōsha*, 44.

employee connections in industrializing Japan. "The employee relation was seen as one between status unequals, similar to the relations between lord and vassal, master and servant, parent and child, calling for benevolence on one side and loyalty and obedience on the other":[43] so writes the historian Thomas C. Smith. Yet the descriptions of Kōfu silk workers before the 1886 regulations do not suggest that the women perceived their employers in such terms. Neither during nor after the strikes of that year is there any hint of this kind of relationship. As a worker ceased to be an independent seller of her labor power, she did not necessarily look to her employer for benevolence to accompany the new dependence. Ōmori Matsu, a Kōfu silk worker who wrote to a local newspaper about her employers in 1888, did not find them benevolent: "Silk thread manufacturers, using contracts as a shield, treat us abominably. They think we are like slaves, like dirt. We think the silk-thread bosses are vipers, are our bitter enemies."[44] And employers, for their part, do appear to have readily changed the rules of employment in the interest of profit maximization.

A strike in 1898 at that proud showpiece, the Tomioka Silk Mill, is instructive. In 1893 the government sold Tomioka to a private concern, the Mitsui firm, which by that time was already well on its way to becoming one of Japan's most powerful *zaibatsu* (a financial combine composed of a number of interlocking companies). The sale was not a happy one for the women working at Tomioka, who were no longer trainee-workers sent by prefectural administrations all over Japan but were now mainly daughters of the poor farm villages in the economically disadvantaged northeast.[45]

In the dormitory dining room, meal portions became smaller and contained coarser food than before. The New Year's holiday was reduced from fifteen to seven days, and workers were no longer paid wages during the holiday. Payday was moved from the tenth to the fifteenth of each month, and wages held back as forced savings no longer seemed to be accruing their former level of interest. Sunday was no longer a regular day off. Revised scheduling of work hours clashed with the need for rest periods and meals. By early 1898, Tomioka reelers decided they could no longer tolerate the general deterioration that had been occurring steadily since the sale.[46]

[43] Thomas C. Smith, "The Right to Benevolence: Dignity and Japanese Workers, 1890–1920," *Comparative Studies in Society and History* 26, no. 4 (October 1984): 589. Unsurprisingly Smith's examples of employee–employer relationships are not drawn from the textile industries.

[44] *Kyōyōkō shinbun* (Kyōyōkō newspaper), 26 to 29 August, carried Ōmori's contribution, cited in Kajinishi et al, *Seishi rōdōsha*, 42. Another silk worker wrote against this in another newspaper in September, but her sycophantic description of employers reads suspiciously as if her prose had been dictated by them. See ibid.

[45] Ibid., 26.

[46] Articles in the *Tokyo Asahi shinbun* (Tokyo morning sun newspaper) published 14 and 16 February 1898, reproduced in Rōdō undō shiryō iin kai, *Nihon rōdō undō shiryō*, 2: 55.

On 9 February 1898, the 281 women who operated the "new machines" at Tomioka got permission from the gateman to go to the factory office. The office staff responded with cold laughter to their questions about the decline in conditions. One of the women was promptly fired and thirty-five others were told they could not leave factory premises. The mill's commuting workers reacted immediately with a strike. After talking about a work slowdown, dormitory workers joined them. The following day commuters and boarders alike went to a theater in the town of Tomioka to discuss and debate. When a second visit to the management produced no satisfactory results, the women assembled in another theater and drew up their grievances and demands:[47]

1. When ownership was transferred from government to Mitsui, nothing had been said to the workers about Mitsui's getting a loan of five days' wages from each worker. Yet Mitsui was now claiming that this arrangement had been made. The workers asked to examine plant ledgers in order to verify this claim.

2. When Tomioka was under government management, 10 percent of the workers' wages had gone into savings; but the workers had received the interest accumulated on those savings, and that interest had been clearly marked in each worker's savings account book. Under Mitsui, workers received their savings, but they no longer had savings account books and the savings were coming to them with little or no interest. The workers demanded that rates of interest be fixed and complete records of that interest be entered in savings account books.

3. The workers demanded that all wages owing be paid on the tenth day of the month as before.

4. The workers demanded Sundays off as before.

5. The workers demanded that the hours of work be as before, pointing out that it was especially important to have a free period for a morning meal.

6. The workers demanded that wages be paid during the long holiday as had been done previously.

7. The workers demanded that the management apologize to two workers who had been particularly insulted.

8. The workers demanded that management lift the ban which prohibited the thirty-five "gated" workers from leaving plant premises.

All of the 462 operators of the "old machines" and all of the 281 operators of the "new machines" signed the list of demands and elected representatives to speak for them. With work in the plant at a standstill, individuals from the town tried to mediate, but their efforts were rebuffed by the company. In the end, even some of the silk workers' fathers came down and joined the striking throng in front of the mill.[48] The strike lasted a full

[47] These grievances and demands were printed in *Tokyo Asahi shinbun*, 16 February 1898, in an article reproduced in Rōdō undō shiryō iin kai, *Nihon rōdō undō shiryō*, 2: 55–56.
[48] Ibid.

week, but Mitsui was a powerful concern and not surprisingly the end involved compromises on the strikers' part.[49]

Silk workers who went to work in new and old mills during the 1880s were usually from poor—sometimes desperately poor—homes. In generally declining working conditions that affected those who labored in other trades and occupations too, machine-reeling women and girls labored longer hours for lower wages and found their freedom of movement from factory to factory increasingly restricted. Their families appreciated what they earned, but the social prestige of these daughters of the poor did not match that accorded the highly respected pupil-workers and teacher-workers at filatures during the optimistic 1870s, when so many of the reelers had been samurai women. Yet the newcomers had as much pride as their high-caste predecessors. Employers who expected them to make do with less and less in hard times or who heaped indignities upon them could find themselves facing militant ranks of united, angry strikers.

Employers took the rebels' solidarity and will to fight back seriously. As we shall see in the next chapter, silk manufacturers soon took steps to develop long-range strategies aimed at averting the kind of strikes that had erupted at Kōfu, Tomioka, and other plants in the country. These strategies led to changes that increasingly tightened the silk manufacturers' grip on the women and girls who reeled in their mills.

[49] Ibid., 2: 56.

4

Silk: Tightening the Screws

THE long-range responses of silk-mill owners to worker autonomy and defiance, as demonstrated in the strikes discussed in the last chapter, were fivefold. The owners began to exploit the advantages to be gained by seeking employees in areas distant from their factories among young women who would not have local friends or relatives to provide support during a strike. They began to build dormitories to house such recruits, who could be locked in after working hours. As competition among mills for skilled reelers intensified toward the end of the century, silk manufacturers followed the example of their counterparts in Yamanashi and formed alliances and signed agreements designed to prevent workers from changing employers. They fashioned a wage-payment system that made the cost of leaving an employer enormously high. And they worked their hands so long and hard in such dreadful conditions that mere survival absorbed most of the workers' energies.

Recruiting in the Hinterland

Beginning in the 1890s, recruitment from districts farther and farther away from the mills became common.[1] This practice was closely linked to the acute shortage of silk workers created as the industry expanded and as cotton spinning also drew the daughters of the poor, but employers also showed a preference for women without supportive local connections. In Nagano's booming silk center, Suwa, this trend is very clear. By 1900 about 60 percent of the silk workers of Suwa came from outside the Suwa district, and about 10 percent of Suwa's silk workers were from other prefectures, primarily neighboring Yamanashi and Gifu.[2] A decade later about 72 percent were nonnatives of Suwa district and about 23 percent were from prefectures other than Nagano.[3] As the research findings of Ishii Kanji and Nakamura Masanori demonstrate, Suwa employers generally recruited workers from prefectures and districts with tenancy rates higher than the national average and from areas where agricultural productivity

[1] Sumiya, *Social Impact*, 81–84.
[2] Ishii, *Nihon sanshi-gyō*, 262.
[3] Ibid., 264.

was low.[4] Thus the women who came to the mills not only traveled greater and greater distances from their villages; they also came from poorer and poorer villages and families.[5]

Each year employers sent both their own employees—often overseers who supervised women in the factories—and independent labor recruiters to distant villages to sign up new workers and make sure old ones returned. Whether or not a full-time company employee, a recruiter was usually male and a native of the area in which he sought recruits. To poor peasant girls and their families he would promise the sky: tasty food in abundance, spacious dormitory rooms, health care, unlimited cultural and educational opportunities, and, most important of all, excellent wages. Recruiters' tales dazzled the desperately poor. Over and over again the shock of discovering the difference between the recruiter's glowing descriptions and the realities of mill life resounds in the songs women sang to keep themselves awake at their machines:

> I didn't know
> I would end up in such a company;
> I was fooled by a recruiter.[6]

A line from a worker's song entitled "Song of the Living Corpse" sums up the mill hand's experience with the recruiter: "I was deceived by a fox without a tail."[7]

Recruits and their families were often completely unaware when a girl agreed to go to a mill that all the recruiting agents' expenses—such as their lodging, transportation, meals, entertainment, traveling clothes and gear, little presents that farm families were so grateful for, as well as fees charged to companies for signing women up—would actually be borne by the girl herself. A sum, called "preparation money," ostensibly to finance a girl's preparation for the journey but actually to be used immediately by her needy family, was often handed over to the recruit's father. Such sums and all transportation costs were routinely deducted, along with the interest on them, from future wages.

Heavier debts were incurred when recruiters advanced fathers "earnest

[4] Ibid., 265–66; Nakamura Masanori, *Rōdōsha to nōmin*, 91–92; Kajinishi et al, *Seishi rōdōsha*, 30–31.

[5] Nakamura Masanori found that in Yamanashi in 1910, 81 percent of female silk workers were from peasant families holding 3 *tan* (1 tan = 0.245 acres) or less of land. In 1910, 92 percent of Yamanashi's female silk workers were from families holding 7 tan or less land. Nakamura Masanori, *Rōdōsha to nōmin*, 91. See also Nakamura Masanori, "Seishi-gyō no tenkai to jinushi sei" (Advance of silk reeling and the landlord system), *Shakai keizai shigaku* (Social and economic history) 32, nos. 5–6 (1967): 46–71.

[6] *Jokō kouta* (Factory girls' ballads), quoted in Nagoya josei shi kenkyū ka, *Haha no jidai*, 59.

[7] Hosoi, *Jokō aishi*, 409.

Table 4.1

Female Silk Workers (Machine Reelers) in Major Silk-Reeling Prefectures in 1900 and 1912

	Machine Reelers of Silk[a]	
	1900	*1911*
Nagano	32,813	56,289
(Suwa district in Nagano)[b]	(11,180)	(23,445)
Gifu	9,886	13,187
Yamanashi	7,721	14,099
Aichi	6,062	18,286
Shizuoka	5,835	6,260
Yamagata	3,400	5,831
Gunma	3,019	6,588
Saitama	1,386	10,344
Fukushima	1,637	4,141
Others	46,102	56,830
Total	117,861	191,855

Source: Nōshōmu-shō, nōmu-kyoku, *Dai san, roku, kyū jizenkoku seishi kōjō chōsa* (Third, sixth, ninth surveys of silk factories), 1902, 1913, as organized in Nakamura Masanori and Molteni, "Seishi gijutsu," 48.

[a] Does not include zaguri reelers.

[b] These separate figures for Suwa district are not included in the totals.

money"—out-and-out loans against their daughters' future wages. Fathers, not the girls themselves, sealed the contracts, although young women were usually consulted and, upon hearing the recruiter's "sweet words," were usually eager to go. After all, the prospects at home were often dreary.[8] Advance-loans became increasingly common from the 1890s.[9]

[8] See Hane, *Peasants*, 180–81.

[9] In Hirano, a major silk village in the Suwa district, around 1890 approximately two-thirds of the silk factory workers were paid advance-loans of about one yen each at the time their annual contracts were sealed. Those who received loans generally came from homes outside of the Suwa district. By 1900 virtually all Hirano silk workers were coming to the mills after advance-loans of between one and five yen had been paid to their fathers or guardians. In 1903, when the silk producers' league of Suwa set advance-loans at five yen, some companies advanced additional sums calling them by other names. Ishii, *Nihon sanshi-gyō*, 169–70.

Advance-loans, paid as "earnest money" when contracts were sealed, played a critical role in the family economies of poor tenant farmers. For instance, in the regions in which silk companies of Hirano, an important silk village in Suwa, sought recruits, a tenant family's average expenditure of cash was fifty-nine yen in 1899. Such a family could expect to receive up to five yen as a cash advance when a daughter, sister, or wife was recruited for a Hirano mill. Since recruitment was done during the agriculturally slack months of January and February, a five-yen advance-loan was even more welcome than it might have been at other times. To pay back both these loans and the interest on them, a girl might work all year for nothing. If the loan was repaid before the year's end, families who could not wait until their daughters returned at the end of the year might request another advance, and, at the end of her term, the girl would come home empty-handed. She might even owe the company money that she would have to start paying off the following year.[10]

Table 4.2 illustrates how borrowing money against a worker's wages reduced the wage packets that the girls and women took home at the end of the year. In 1909, the families of the workers in this Suwa mill tended to borrow heavily. Consequently, many year-end payments were not large, and fourteen of the thirty-seven workers in the mill left for home at the end of 1909 with less than one yen in cash. Ten of these went off without a single rin. Nine of these ten owed the company substantial sums: their families had mortgaged the girls' futures long before the recruiters made their annual rounds in the new year.

Those who left the mills for home at the year's end knew that their parents were eagerly waiting for their earnings to pay pressing debts. Let us look for a moment at the *Kosaku nisshi* (Diary of tenant affairs) kept by the Nezu family of landlords in Yamanashi prefecture:

28 December [1911]: It rained and was very cold. On this day I demanded the rents in Kuwado. At Oki Nobuhei's place he was out and I pressed his wife hard to pay off everything. She said that when her husband returned she would give him the message, and they would try to pay off at least some of it within the year. Sekimatsu Tarō was also out and I gave a severe warning to his wife. Furuya Teizō was also out and I got nowhere. I left a stern warning with his family and told them to pay off some of it within the year. Motegi Heijirō was out. *I warned his wife who said, "On the 30th we will receive wages from the silk factory where our daughter works and as soon as we get them we will pay you some."* Tanaka Mohachi was out. I left a warning with his wife. *Nagasawa Yokichi, Kawai Sadatoshi, and*

[10] Nakamura Masanori, *Rōdōsha to nōmin*, 92; Ishii, *Nihon sanshi-gyō*, 326–28; Nōshōmu-shō, shōkō-kyoku (Ministry of Agriculture and Commerce, Commerce and Industry Department), ed., *Shokkō jijō* (Factory workers' conditions), originally published in 1903, to be found in *Seikatsu koten sōsho* (Classics of everyday life series), 8 vols. (Tokyo, 1971), 4: 141.

Okuta Chōhei of Kamimanriki all said that as soon as they received their daughters' wages they would pay immediately or, at the latest, by 10 January. They beseeched me to wait until then. Mayakawa Shusaku and Kanai Isaku both said that, whether in cash or in unhulled rice, they would pay off everything by early January, or in any case, by mid-January. Yamashita Sajurō is also supposed to pay something during the year. Even if he is delayed he should pay something, no matter how small, by mid-January.[11] [Italics mine]

Family need was an effective way of binding a recruit to a factory where she had to work hard to pay off her family's debts. Contracts sealed at the time advances were received legally mortgaged a reeler's working future and made her father liable for heavy financial penalty should she be unable or unwilling to pay off the mortgage. If a girl did run away, the company was legally entitled to punish her and her family as it saw fit. Here are two contracts that were included in the Ministry of Agriculture and Commerce's report of 1903 on factory workers' conditions (*Shokkō jijō*).[12]

Contract for Employment of Female Silk Worker

1. Amount _____ , being the earnest money for the employment of
   __(name)__ , silk worker (born _____ year _____ month)

We confirm that in return for contracting the above person employed as a female operative at your filature in the _____ year of Meiji, we have received the said earnest money in full. Moreover, she shall commence work from the coming spring in _____ month, _____ day, or the coming summer in _____ month, _____ day without further notice and shall work without lapse until the cessation of plant operations. And no matter what unforeseen circumstances may arise, during this term we will not have her work for any other silk manufacturer. *If there should be any infringement of this contract whatsoever, as reparations we will pay without question a sum equal to twenty times (20x) the said earnest money.* In witness whereof we set our seals to this contract, accepting joint responsibility. [Italics mine]

_____ Prefecture _____ District _____ Hamlet _____ Number.
Meiji __3?__ Year, _____ month, _____ day.
Name. _____
_____ Prefecture _____ District _____ Hamlet _____ Number.
                                                    Name. _____

[11] Quoted in Matsumoto, "Jinushi," 366.
[12] Nōshōmu-shō, *Shokkō jijō*, 144–45.

Table 4.2
Advances on Wages and Year-End Pay in a Silk Mill in the Suwa District of
Nagano in 1909 (in yen. sen. rin)

Female Worker's Name	Home Village or Town	Money Lent against Wages	Money Taken Home at Year-End
Hayashi, Seki	Takane village	22.97.	3.44.
Nakai, Shisu	Takane village	17.41.5	31.47.5
Uesaki, Kiyo	Takayama town	30.05.	−13.35.
Yamamoto, Shizu	—	14.10.	−7.60.
Yamaguchi, Ei	Furukawakami town	12.94.	42.56.
Kama, Jitsu	Kokufu village	19.97.	30.47.
Hashimoto, Raku	Kuguno	11.97.	34.94.
Kama, Kise	Kokufu village	9.05.5	20.16.5
Ema, Tō	Takayama town	41.53.	48.59.
Ema, Ei	Takayama town	31.40.	46.15.
Ueda, Moto	Takane village	22.07.5	19.08.35
Morishita, Koma	Takane village	23.86.	47.43.
Ema, Yū	Takayama town	27.75.	38.55.
Mise, Fusa	Miya	24.87.	−4.49.
Yamakoshi, ?	Ōnada village	18.83.	5.97.
Kubota, Sue	—	5.88.	0.09.
Inamoto, Naka	—	10.35.	0.60.
Nishizawa, Chiyo	—	15.20.	00.00.
Uchimoto, Sue	Miya	5.18.	34.15.
Mizoguchi, Tono	Miya	16.78.	−9.43.
Motonaka, Shizu	Ōnada village	5.12.	1.04.
Yamashita, Kita	Takayama town	30.07.	59.37.
Kiriushi, Toya	Kuguno	17.29.	57.11.
Kiriushi, Haru	Kuguno	12.09.	36.00.
Yoshida, Tama	Takayama town	19.31.	14.61.
Hashido, Hana	Ōyaka village	10.96.	31.89.
Takeda, Naka	—	62.82.	−3.02.
Takeda, Shina	—	5.00.	−2.69.
Aramoto, Yasu	Takayama town	21.25.	−8.45.
Takiguchi, Kiyo	Takayama town	21.16.	0.97.

Table 4.2 (*cont.*)

Female Worker's Name	Home Village or Town	Money Lent against Wages	Money Taken Home at Year-End
Tajima, Kiyō	Takayama town	30.87.	2.40.
Hashido, Shō	Ōyaka village	8.36.5	26.92.5
Tanaka, Fude	Yamaguchi	45.32.	− 26.98.
Ikedo, Nara	Takayama town	30.05.	13.80.
Sora, Toku	Takayama town	31.03.	− 14.33.
Otake (Kotake?), Chika	Ōnada village	22.82.	0.79.
Tsudake, Etsu	Nada	19.19.	6.82.

Source: Yamamoto Shigemi, *Aa nomugi tōge*, 197.

[a] The above information was taken from the mill workers' account books. Perhaps the account books which did not indicate a home town or village belonged to local girls and women who lived near the mill.

Silk Reeler's Contract

Female worker's registration address:

_____ Prefecture _____ District _____ Number.

Female worker's present address:

_____ Prefecture _____ District _____ Number.

Female worker's name: _____

Female worker's place and date of birth and age: _____

Status and name of female worker's guardian: _____

Contract Articles:

Duration of silk-reeling labor contract:

From Meiji _____ year, _____ month, _____ day

To Meiji _____ year, _____ month, _____ day

Working a full _____ year(s) service

If, due to illness, more than one month's work is lost, a doctor's examination shall be done and the results submitted at appropriate times. Moreover, the number of days lost shall be made up by continuing work after the full term of the contract.

If the operative withdraws from the company in order to get married, when the registration is transferred, the head of the ward or village shall receive a certificate of notification. In return for the favor of employment according to the above contract, your company's regulations shall be faithfully observed, and during the

term of the contract she shall apply herself to her work with diligence. If she should go to another company before her full term is up or *if she should withdraw from your company for insufficient cause, no matter how you handle this I can have no complaint.*
In witness whereof I set my seal to this covenant. [Italics mine]

Meiji _____ year _____ month.
Guarantor _____

These contracts are extremely one-sided. Undoubtedly illiterate fathers did not always understand everything they were agreeing to when they set their seals on these documents. But one-sided contracts were nothing new in the lives of poor tenant families. The following contract, dating from the 1890s, bound tenants of the Otaki landlord family in Yamagata prefecture.

To Otaki Saburoemon:
[Description and Designation of the land . . . Rent . . . Surcharge. . . .]
I hereby certify that, from this year and for such time as the relationship between us shall last, I have undertaken tenancy of the above land. I undertake to deliver, by 31 December each year, at such place as you shall direct, the above rent and surcharge in selected rice, carefully and conscientiously baled.
I beg that in years of bad harvest through natural causes you will, on inspection of the crop, make such reduction in rent as seems to you fit. In the case, however, of a fall in yields resulting from my own bad management and affecting myself alone, I undertake to ask for no reduction in rent. I shall, of course, make no attempt to sell the right of tenancy, nor be indolent in cultivation of the land, nor engage in any other unjust conduct. In the event that I should break contract, irrespective of whether I am resident in the village or not, the guarantor will pay full compensation. In such circumstance, or, indeed, at any other time, I undertake to raise no single word of complaint should you, as your convenience makes necessary, decide to terminate my tenancy.
In sign whereof and for future reference.
Tenant . . . .
Guarantor . . . . [13]

[13] R. P. Dore, *Land Reform in Japan* (London, 1959), 33. In a footnote on the same page Dore explains the "surcharge": "The surcharge (*kuchimai*) dates from the Tokugawa [Edo] period and is found generally throughout the country. Bales which were transported to the central markets inevitably suffered some wastage from theft and leakages. In order that they should contain the standard amount of rice when they arrived, they had to start with a little more than the standard. It was one of the facts offered as evidence of the Otakis' benevolence that they demanded a surcharge of only 2 per cent. compared with the 4 per cent. of many landlords."

For many poor farming families, the silk reeler's contract was merely a variation on the unequal relationships they had previously been forced to enter.

Imprisoned in Dormitories

With recruits coming from distant places, company dormitories became common features of silk establishments. Dormitories kept workers from going elsewhere to work or running home, but they also enabled managers to extract longer hours from workers who no longer had to be allotted time to commute home and prepare meals there. Under strict discipline, dormitory inmates could be controlled so thoroughly that nearly all their energies were spent on thread production. Sumiya Mikio's blunt assessment is accurate: "The dormitory system was originally developed to the convenience of employees from distant places, but it now functioned virtually as detention houses."[14] Solidly constructed and equipped with heavy metal screens, dormitories were surrounded by eight-foot fences or connected to the adjacent plant by a bridge high above ground. Sometimes fences were crowned with broken glass, sharpened bamboo spears, barbed wire, and other forbidding objects to discourage runaways. Management claimed that workers were locked in after working hours "to protect their morals."[15] However, that claim rings hollow. The women and girls endured sexual abuse at the hands of male managers and supervisors as well as male workers.[16]

Dormitory sleeping quarters were drafty, Japanese-style tatami-matted rooms crammed full of workers. Even in winter there was no heat, and in the bitter cold the inmates huddled together under thin bedding. At best a resident might have one tatami mat of about six feet by three feet as her living space, but ten individuals were often squeezed into an eight-mat room. There was no place for an ailing worker to convalesce unless she was at death's door, in which case she would be isolated in a shed awaiting a member of her family to come and take her or her corpse away. Toilet and washing facilities were limited, and access to them was permitted only at stipulated times.[17] Lice were an ever-present annoyance. Dormitory in-

[14] Sumiya, *Social Impact*, 86.

[15] Nōshōmu-shō, *Shokkō jijō*, 303.

[16] Sexual abuse is discussed later in this chapter, but strong evidence of it appears in many sources, including *Shokkō jijō*. Sakura Takuji, a male employee in silk mills during the 1920s, offered a chilling eyewitness account of sexual harassment in the silk mills and dormitories continuing far beyond the Meiji period. See his *Jokō gyakutai shi* (A history of the ill-treatment of female silk-factory workers) (1927; Nagano City, 1981), esp. 163–68.

[17] Sakura, *Jokō gyakutai shi*, 76.

mates were closely supervised in their rooms by veteran female workers in supervisory or semisupervisory positions.[18] In case of fire their nightly imprisonment could and often did mean death.[19] Although everyone was urged to be careful, the danger from fire remained high. Wooden structures full of inflammable materials, some silk mills used kerosene lamps well into the twentieth century.

Many small mills did not have bathing facilities, so workers might be given permission to leave the premises to go to the public bath. They were encouraged to visit the public bath in groups rather than to go alone; any worker suspected of being a potential runaway might be refused permission or be allowed to go only if supervisory personnel went along.[20]

Dormitory meals consisted of small portions of coarse food. Food was, of course, also scarce and coarse in the rural homes the women came from, as Mikiso Hane has correctly pointed out.[21] But the skimpy bowls of grain and a few pickles, or thin soup with occasional minute portions of bean curd or dried fish, did not provide enough nourishment for young people putting in up to seventeen strenuous hours plus machine-maintenance time.[22] In many mills there was very little protein, the side dish consisting of a few vegetables or thin soup. Native rice mixed with barley or with rice imported from Korea, Taiwan, or China may have been as nutritious as Japanese rice alone, but its taste did not please those who, perforce, ate it greedily. Continual hunger drove dormitory residents to spend any pocket money they had—and they usually received a little from the company once or twice a year, notably at New Year's and the midsummer Obon holiday— on sweets and other edibles. As an elderly sweet seller reported to officials from the Ministry of Agriculture and Commerce in 1902, silk workers bought sweet potatoes, fish products, and other treats from him when they could because the meals they received at the dormitory were not enough to fill their stomachs.[23]

Dormitory life offered none of the flower arranging or music lessons or classes in basic letters and arithmetic that boarders at the grand Tomioka mill had enjoyed. A few mills made halfhearted attempts to schedule classes in writing or sewing after working hours, but as the authors of *Shokkō jijō*

[18] Even in Nagano where only men were employed as factory-floor supervisors or overseers (*kenban*), senior female workers would act as supervisors in the dormitory.

[19] Nōshōmu-shō, *Shokkō jijō*, 154.

[20] See Yamamoto Shigemi, *Zoku aa nomugi tōge* (Ah! The Nomugi Pass: The sequel) (Tokyo, 1982), esp. 195–201.

[21] Hane, *Peasants*, 181.

[22] Sakura, *Jokō gyakutai shi*, 134–40; Nakamura Masanori, *Rōdōsha to nōmin*, 82; Nōshōmu-shō, *Shokkō jijō*, Furoku 2 (Appendix 2), 560.

[23] Nōshōmu-shō, *Shokkō jijō*, Furoku 2 (Appendix 2), 608; Nakamura Masanori's elderly informant also remembered a need to buy sweets to fill stomachs. Nakamura Masanori, *Rōdōsha to nōmin*, 82.

noted in 1903, this sort of program usually fared badly because the operatives were too exhausted by their long hours of work to learn anything.[24] The prefectural authorities in Nagano tried to encourage companies to take up the cause of schooling for young children, but with little success. Worried about the increasing number of young girls in the prefecture not attending school as the silk industry expanded, school officials in Nagano supported a government proposal of 1898 to limit the work hours of children aged fourteen or younger. Vehemently opposed by silk manufacturers in Nagano, this proposal did not come to fruition.[25]

An attempt was made to set up "special education" classes in local elementary schools in areas where silk workers were recruited. The hope was that when the girls returned to their homes at the end of December they would go to school at least until they departed for the filatures in February or March. But a month or two of instruction each year did not seem to impart much literacy, and there was great difficulty in getting the mill girls to attend these classes. In silk-mill villages in Suwa, female attendance at elementary school was extremely low. Mill owners and managers did not give much support to special classes during the short period the mills were closed, unless they could use a display of apparent support in an advertisement to girls living in other areas—girls they were attempting to lure to their mills.[26] As a conference of educators in Suwa noted in 1901, almost no silk factories in the area organized educational courses in their dormitories.[27]

During the next decade the situation did not improve noticeably. In 1907 compulsory elementary education was extended from four to six years of schooling, but neither the special education classes for returned silk workers nor instruction within the mills made any progress. Talk of abolition of child labor within the mills continued to meet with strong opposition from mill owners, who pointed out how dependent upon the wages of their offspring were the families of the children who worked in the mills. Recommendations like the one that educators in Shimo Ina district in 1911 put to more than thirty district mill owners, that they employ only those who had finished compulsory elementary education, were not welcomed by silk employers.[28]

The girls and women endured wretchedly uncomfortable sleeping quar-

---

[24] Nōshōmu-shō, *Shokkō jijō*, 156.

[25] Kōzu Zenzaburō, *Kyōiku aishi* (The pitiful history of education) (Nagano City, 1978), 377.

[26] Ibid., 383.

[27] Ibid.

[28] Ibid., 416. Only in 1916 when the Factory Law of 1911 went into effect did employers in Nagano and elsewhere have to begin providing elementary education for school-aged children.

ters, limited food, rigid routines, little spare time, close and often severe supervision, few educational opportunities or other amenities, and almost no entertainments other than the midsummer Obon festival. There was little joy in the dormitories:

> More than a bird in a cage,
> More than a prison,
> Dormitory life is hateful.[29]

Thus sang the female silk workers.

For some silk workers there was a fate even worse than life in the company dormitory. Girls who toiled in small-scale zaguri operations were boarded in their employers' homes in even less pleasant circumstances.[30] Each of the zaguri factories, especially numerous in Fukushima and Gunma prefectures,[31] usually employed fewer than ten young girls. Although they lived with the factory owner's family, they were certainly not treated like family members. In the winter, each girl would take her turn rising in the morning at about 3:30 to prepare breakfast for the group. About 4:00 or 5:00 A.M., the others would get up and eat a skimpy meal of three parts rice to seven parts barley and a little bean-paste soup. All day they would work, turning their reeling apparatus by foot pedal and hand. During the day the owner's wife watched them closely: the best worker would be placed farthest away from the wife, while the novice would be right under her critical gaze. After the sun went down, lamps were lit and the girls continued at their assigned places far into the night. Yokoyama Gen'nosuke observed zaguri reelers in Maebashi, the center of Gunma's zaguri production, working until midnight. The evening meal was exactly like the one served in the morning. Although they boarded with the family, Yokoyama described their sleeping quarters as "pig pens." And every minute that was not spent in the workplace, the youngsters were on call to wait on the master and his family. They were not allowed to leave the premises unless carefully supervised, probably because employers feared they would run away.

Even Yokoyama Gen'nosuke, who thought he had been hardened by the poverty and hardship he had seen all over the country and most recently by his experiences in weaving districts, was shocked in 1898 by the conditions of the Maebashi zaguri reelers. In exchange for the right to work these children—eleven- and twelve-year-olds were common, most were

---

[29] Yamamoto Shigemi, *Aa nomugi tōge*, 388. See Nōshōmu-shō, *Shokkō jijō*, 154–55, on dormitory conditions.

[30] Ibid., 157–59; Yokoyama, *Nihon no kasō shakai*, 149–50; Ishii, *Nihon sanshi-gyō*, 320–33.

[31] In Gunma about one-third of the prefecture's silk was manufactured in zaguri factories. Ishii, *Nihon sanshi-gyō*, 326. See also Yokoyama, *Nihon no kasō shakai*, 148.

about fifteen years old, and few were over twenty—for five to seven years, zaguri bosses paid advance-loans (of from fifteen to thirty yen at the turn of the century) to each girl's father or guardian. And the boss agreed to feed and clothe each girl during the period she was under contract. If she became ill, he was obligated to look after her for a period of up to three weeks. But there was no agreement binding him to feed or clothe his workers adequately. Food was generally poor and not very abundant; clothes were seldom new. The best worker might get some decent clothes occasionally, but the least productive operatives would be given only rags to wear. The girls might get a few sen for spending money twice a year, but mostly their lives were pure drudgery. There was no schooling for zaguri reelers, and some of them did not even know their surnames. Unsurprisingly, morale was low. According to *Shokkō jijō*, "There were those [zaguri workers] planning suicide."[32] The same study sadly noted that those who did return home after their contracts had been completed were often found unfit for agricultural work and were therefore sent out again to another zaguri silk establishment.[33]

Did conditions have to be so miserable? Was it possible to run a mill and offer humane treatment to the girls and women who lived and worked there? Yes, said education administrators of Nagano prefecture in 1909, pointing to a model silk factory in Shimo Ina district, which had been in operation for more than thirty years.[34]

This company, the Yoshizawa Silk Mill, founded in 1875 with fifty reeling machines, made relatively low profits. However, since its policy of worker-owner cooperation made it an attractive place to work, the owner, Yoshizawa Koheiji, and his wife, Yoshizawa Saku, did not have to spend money on recruitment. Highly respected in their district, the couple had good contacts with both silkworm brokers and farmers engaged in sericulture. Thus they were also able to purchase silkworms of good quality at cheap prices.

Proclaiming a "familial ideology," the owner and his wife took pains to ensure the well-being of their workers and to encourage good employer-employee relationships. They argued that, in a small enterprise at least, health, education, and kindness were partners with profit. The Yoshizawa familial ideology was self-consciously paternalistic: employees were instructed to call the Yoshizawa couple "father" and "mother" and to develop siblinglike relationships with their co-workers.

Yoshizawa Saku was in charge of the health needs of the girls who

---

[32] Nōshōmu-shō, *Shokkō jijō*, 159.

[33] Ibid. For a comparison, including other Meiji Japanese factory workers toiling in difficult laboring conditions, see Yokoyama, *Nihon no kasō shakai*, and Yokoyama Gen'nosuke, *Naichi zakkyo go no Nihon* (Japan since the opening of the country) (1899; Tokyo, 1954).

[34] Kōzu, *Kyōiko aishi*, 416–23.

Table 4.3
Apportionment of Female Silk Workers' Wages Paid by the Kasahara Company of Nagano in 1891 and 1909 (in yen. sen)

	Preparation Money[a]	Advance- Loans[a]	Sums Paid While Working[a]	Year-End Payment[a]	Obon Pocket Money	Other Pocket Money	Held-back Wages[b]	Total Wages Paid by Company
1891								
Total payments for 44 workers	27.50	0.0	132.50	432.55	5.50	110.96	80.89	789.90
Average Payments per worker	1.45	0.0	6.02	12.02	0.78	3.70	1.84	
% of total wages paid	3.5	0.0	16.9	54.8	0.6	14.0	10.2	100
1909								
Total payments for 102 workers	319.0	255.80	628.12	2,571.00	56.50	312.23	304.22	4,466.87
Average payments per worker	3.54	12.29	11.02	25.21	2.97	3.06	2.98	
% of total wages paid	7.2	5.8	14.1	57.8	1.3	7.0	6.8	100

Source: Nakamura Masanori, *Rōdōsha to nōmin*, 99.
[a] paid directly to father.
[b] kept by the company until the following year.

worked in the filature. Because she strongly believed in wholesome physical exercise, she installed a playground with swings. After the evening meal, she and her husband led the girls outside for exercise there. What a strange sight it must have been for the people of the area to see factory girls enjoying themselves on playground equipment built especially for them. Saku made sure the reelers were fed enough nourishing food. Clothes were washed often and bedding was also cleaned frequently. Each employee received a space of two tatami mats to sleep on. Saku also made sure that air was circulating within the factory. And her concern for cleanliness made the Yoshizawa mill one of the first to introduce aprons to help keep factory clothes clean. A doctor was hired to examine the girls regularly, and the company was justifiably proud of the illness-free records of its operatives.

Saku's other major responsibility was education, and, perhaps because she came from a family of teachers, she took this very seriously too. During working hours she taught reeling techniques to the girls and women. The mill opened a night school where every evening basic reading and writing were taught for thirty minutes to an hour. Saku was probably the main teacher of these lessons, although for a time they were given by a village schoolteacher who stayed at the Yoshizawa home. After the youngsters had struggled with their letters, Saku rewarded them with another hour of instruction in sewing, a skill many were more eager to learn. Language and sewing instruction were available, but "moral education" was compulsory: all workers had to attend the formal morality lessons taught several times a week by a primary-school teacher and his wife.[35]

The hours at the Yoshizawa mill must have been shorter than at many mills, since the workers were allowed to exercise in the early evening and given time to study later on. One may well believe that any vacancies in the work force were soon filled. Yoshizawa Saku was eventually honored by the prefectural government for her accomplishments in factory health and education, and by 1909 Nagano educators had publicly recognized achievements of the night school. Yet even after the Yoshizawa Silk Mill became famous as a positive model, there is no evidence that other silk companies made serious efforts to emulate it.

Registration: Becoming Employers' Property

Throughout the 1890s, as expanding silk operations contended with a shortage of skilled laborers, during the rare occasions when female workers were permitted outside the mill walls they were in danger of being lured away or kidnapped by agents of another factory. Well-dressed men would

[35] Ibid., 423.

meet the trains bringing girls to a silk district and carry them off, by force if necessary, to a mill other than the one they had been hired for or sell them into prostitution. Sometimes kidnappers would not take their booty directly to a rival mill but would hide the girls in a farmer's house for a while. When they thought the coast was clear, they would smuggle them into the mill. In time, companies made sure female hands were accompanied by a male employee whenever they left factory grounds—to insure that the women were not captured, as well as to prevent their running away.[36] Violent raiding of each other's workers was such a grave problem by the turn of the century that silk manufacturers banded together to halt it; in the process they took away the little leverage female silk workers had gained as a result of the labor shortage.

As they often did, Nagano mill owners took the lead. In 1898 some of them united in a plan to keep workers from changing employers. The idea was to entice young women to stay put by offering such amenities as sewing classes and calligraphy lessons after work.[37] This effort became a model for the famous Suwa Silk-Manufacturers' League (Suwa Seishi Dōmei) founded two years later; but the league, emphasizing compulsion rather than enticement, was closer in spirit to the Yamanashi alliance of 1886 discussed in chapter 3.

The articles of the league's agreement, which first went into effect in 1901 for silk plants in three Suwa villages, were aimed at stopping employers from stealing each others' reelers. By 1903 the Suwa Silk-Manufacturers' League had devised a system of registering silk workers that effectively prevented them from working for any company except the one they were registered with currently. Each league member, when recruiting each year, had the exclusive "right" to reengage his former employees, who remained registered with him after the year's work was finished. Other members of the league could not offer employment to these individuals until the company that "owned" them notified the league's central headquarters that it was releasing them. Any company attempting to hire a rival's "property" risked a heavy fine. Thus, even after a reeler had fulfilled her year's contract and paid back her family's debt to the company, she was not permitted to choose a different employer. Back in the 1880s only about 30 percent of a mill's reelers had returned to the same mill for a second consecutive year. About the time the league began registering workers, more female silk workers were returning to the same mill after the year's work had ended, but many still changed employers (see table 4.4).[38] With reg-

[36] Nakamura Masanori, *Rōdōsha to nōmin*, 101–2.

[37] Kajinishi et al, *Seishi rōdōsha*, 58.

[38] Ishii, *Nihon sanshi-gyō*, 270–71, 276, 284; Iwamoto Yoshiteru, "Suwa seishi dōmei no seiritsu ki ni okeru katsudō" (Activity during the period of establishment of the Suwa Silk

Table 4.4
Turnover among Female Workers in Silk-Reeling Mills in 1901 (number and percent)

Length of Time Worked	205 Mills in Nagano Prefecture		29 Mills in Other Prefectures
	Suzaka and Matsushiro Districts	Suwa District	
Less than 6 months	478 (11.5)	837 (10.0)	340 (11.7)
6 months–1 year	651 (15.6)	2,221 (26.5)	342 (11.8)
1–2 years	687 (16.5)	1,752 (21.0)	484 (16.6)
2–3 years	787 (18.9)	1,480 (17.7)	478 (16.4)
3–5 years	791 (19.0)	1,287 (15.4)	763 (26.2)
More than 5 years	771 (18.5)	787 (9.4)	502 (17.3)
Total	4,165 (100)	8,364 (100)	2,909 (100)

Sources: Nōshōmu-shō, Shokkō jijō, 145–46; Ōishi, Nihon sangyō kakumei kenkyū, 172.

istration, a woman had to go back to the same mill. In theory she could stay home for a year and then go to work for a different employer, but most workers' families were too poor to exercise this option. The league also set amounts for advance-loans handed over when contracts were sealed: they could be up to five yen.[39] Rapidly the league became a national organization of silk manufacturers, which by 1922 (four years before registration was finally abolished) was operating in one metropolitan district (fu), twenty-six prefectures, and the colony of Korea, registering 76,812 female workers.[40]

Working for Wages

Probably the most important of the contrivances to keep reelers quietly on the job was the complicated wage-payment system adopted by silk manufacturers. It kept silk workers at their machines for long hours at low pay,

Manufacturers' League), in Nihon kindai ka no kenkyū (Studies in Japanese modernization), ed. Takahashi Kōhachirō 2 vols. (Tokyo, 1972), 1: 350.

[39] Ibid.

[40] Ishii, Nihon sanshi-gyō, 277–84; Nakamura Masanori, Rōdōsha to nōmin, 101–5; Kajinishi et al, Seishi rōdōsha, 56–67; Sakura, Jokō gyakutai shi, 28–41; Iwamoto Yoshiteru, "Suwa seishi dōmei," 349–70.

fashioning thread of good quality from poor raw materials. With its many wage classifications, few rewards, and many punishments, this system enabled Japanese silk firms to rise above the primitive technology and low-grade raw materials that hampered them as they competed with better-equipped Italian and French manufacturers. Nagano, which managed better than other Japanese silk areas to keep up with European competitors, unsurprisingly pioneered acceptance of the wage-classification system.[41]

As we have seen, in Yamanashi it was not until 1886 that silk producers switched from daily to monthly payment of wages to keep their hands from leaving plants at will. Despite this change in the timing of wage payments, wages continued to be fixed as before: at this time in Yamanashi, as in Fukushima and Gunma, silk mills paid wages according to wage-grade classifications for workers at different skill levels, but the wage rates were fixed—a certain average denier (fineness) and quantity of thread corresponded to one of a number of wage grades netting that grade's wage rate.[42] This resembled the fixed wages according to workers' skill originally established at Tomioka, which in wages as in most other matters took French custom as its model.[43]

In Nagano's Suwa district, however, a different system was evident as early as the late 1870s, and by the turn of the century this was rapidly spreading through the country.[44] According to this system, which scholars have termed a "relative wage-classification system," wages in each classification were not set amounts but fluctuated according to the average and highest productivity of workers within a given mill and according to the few rewards and multitude of fines that went with the system. Until the 1930s (when a key technological breakthrough was achieved) quality and quantity of thread heavily depended upon the skill of the reelers' fingers.[45] Until then it was this "relative wage-classification system" that raised production and profits—at the expense of the women and girls who worked in the thread factories.

The relative wage classifications were decided on the basis of ratings ascertained according to the quantity, weight, denier, and luster of thread reeled by an individual worker. Everyone's production according to these four categories was measured daily, and average production (quantitatively and qualitatively) in the mill was established. From this average, management fixed wage classifications moving both upward and downward. The highest classification was awarded the plant's top producer as measured by the four categories. This was usually labeled first class. The next highest

41 Ishii, *Nihon sanshi-gyō*, 247. See also Nishinarita, "Nihongata chinrōdō no seiritsu."
42 Ishii, *Nihon sanshi-gyō*, 299–300, 342–48.
43 Ibid., 343.
44 Ibid., 300.
45 Nakamura Masanori, *Rōdōsha to nōmin*, 96.

producers would be designated second class, third class, and so on, sometimes for as many as fifty classifications.[46] Every day each woman's work
was closely inspected and marked strictly. Not only would her wage classification be changed according to her daily output, but she might also
have fines deducted from her wages for a variety of infractions of petty
factory rules, as well as for not making improvements in the grade of the
thread she reeled. This was in spite of the fact that thread quality was to a
considerable extent dependent upon the quality of the cocoons the reelers
worked with—poor cocoons could not produce excellent thread, no matter
how skilled the reeler's hands: "No matter how much of a genius the female worker unraveling thread may be, if the larvae are not thick, cluster
by cluster, and the fiber is not long . . . it is not humanly possible to make
the reeled thread uniform."[47]

Fines and poor cocoon quality could actually reduce wages to zero or
less: a worker could end up owing the company money for her room and
board or be obligated to work year after year to pay off advance-loans made
to her family. Workers in ill health, who could not keep up with stronger
workmates, often became desperate as supervisors passed among the lines
of reeling women, hitting them with sticks and urging them to reel faster
and better. Because, under such pressure, factory averages went up, a
woman would of course have to produce more just to maintain the wages
she had been getting, and slower workers were paid even less than previously: classifications were always *relative* to average and highest production
rates. Each and every hand was urged to become a top producer, a "hundred-yen factory girl" (*hyaku en kōjo*) who received a bonus at year end. But
since becoming a hundred-yen factory girl meant doing better than almost
everyone else, this was an impossible dream for most of the factory force.

As the entries in the account books of the workers of the Yamanoue
Kairyō Company suggest (see table 4.6), some skilled, diligent workers did
become ill but carried on their work nevertheless. Some girls may have
been able to spend some of their earnings on items for trousseaus, but most
of their pay went straight to their families.[48] Preparation money and the
year-end wage packet went as a matter of course to the girl's father. The
case of Nakamura Shiyaso in 1893 stands out as an exception in the ac-
count-book records: her uncle, mother, and father all came to collect portions of her wages during the working year.

Ishihara Osamu, the medical doctor who became familiar with condi-

[46] Ibid.

[47] Sakura, *Jokō gyakutai shi*, 85.

[48] Even held-back earnings, when or if they were eventually paid by the company, went
straight to the worker's father or guardian. Often a recruiter would take these held-back earnings to a girl's home in the spring and hand them over to her family only after her guardian
had sealed another contract binding her to work during the coming year. Ibid., 46.

Table 4.5
Daily Wages in 205 Nagano Silk-Reeling Mills by Region in 1901

Daily Wages	Suzaka		Matsushiro		Upper Suwa		Lower Suwa		Total Workers	% of Total Workers	% of Female Workers
	Male	Female	Male	Female	Male	Female	Male	Female			
10 sen or less	67	827	2	85	8	165	38	649	1,841	13.52	13.79
11–15 sen	41	1,112	22	279	21	405	166	1,169	3,215	23.60	23.68
16–20 sen	34	874	23	231	47	522	112	1,775	3,618	26.56	27.17
21–30 sen	42	442	19	175	68	733	125	1,692	3,296	24.20	24.30
31–40 sen	24	30	12	94	41	326	73	657	1,257	9.24	8.84
41–50 sen	3	4	3	10	20	61	41	155	297	2.18	1.84
51–60 sen	1	2	2	0	8	5	16	30	64	0.47	0.30
61–80 sen	0	0	0	0	1	0	10	10	21	0.15	0.08
81 sen–1 yen	0	0	0	0	0	0	7	0	7	0.05	0.00
More than 1 yen	0	0	0	0	0	0	4	0	4	0.03	0.00
Total	212	3,291	83	874	214	2,217	592	6,137	13,620	100.00	100.00

Source: Nōshōmu-shō, Shokkō jijō, 148–49.

Table 4.6
Payments of Earnings Recorded in the Account Books of Female Silk Workers
Employed by the Yamanoue Kairyō Company of Suwa District in Nagano in
1893, 1895, and 1900

Worker's Name	Type of Payment	Amount (yen. sen. rin)	Date
1893 (In 1893 the price of a postcard was 5 rin; an egg, 1 sen; a glass of milk, 3 sen, 5 rin; cold cream, 4 sen.)			
Sakai, Naka[a]	Preparation money	1.00.0	21 Mar.
	Payment when returning home	0.50.0	1 May
Sazawa, Fude[a]	Preparation money	1.00.0	1 Feb.
	Payment when returning	1.00.0	1 May
Nakamura, Shiyaso[b]	Payment	0.08.3	1 May
	Payment to Dr. Shibukawa	0.24.0	undated
	Preparation money	1.00.0	"
	Payment to father	1.00.0	"
	Payment on returning home	0.50.0	"
	? (meaning of entry unclear)	0.50.0	"
	Payment to mother	1.30.0	"
	Payment to uncle	1.00.0	"
	Payment to uncle	1.00.0	
	Payment to company store	0.50.0	"
	Payment when returning home	0.70.0	"
	Shopping	1.00.0	"
	Payment to uncle	4.00.0	"

Source: Yamamoto Shigemi, *Aa nomugi tōge*, 184–90.

[a] Returned home after spring season of silkworms; did not return to work during the summer season.

[b] This worker's home was probably close to the mill, as seemingly her father, mother, and uncle all came to the company to collect portions of her wages.

Table 4.6 (*cont.*)

Worker's Name	Type of Payment	Amount (yen. sen. rin)	Date
Nakamura, Shiyaso[b] (*cont.*)	Payment when returning home	1.00.0	"
	Payment to father	1.00.0	"
	Shopping	3.00.0	"
Arai, Iku[c]	Medicine from store	0.11.0	10 Apr.
	Payment to Dr. Shibukawa	0.24.0	10 Apr.
Odagiri, Kei[d]	Preparation money	1.00.0	undated
	Payment when returning home	0.30.0	"
Makino, Isa	Preparation money	1.05.0	21 Feb.
	Payment when returning home	0.50.0	1 May
	"One-way" payment[e]	0.20.0	1 Sept.

1895 (in 1895 the price of rice was 3 sen for 1 shō; a newspaper reporter's monthly salary was 12 yen.)

Worker's Name	Type of Payment	Amount (yen. sen. rin)	Date
Ayuzawa, Aki	Payment to Dr. Shibukawa	0.16.0	Oct.
	Payment to Dr. Shibukawa	0.10.0	Nov.
	Store-bought medicine for worms	0.10.0	3 Sept.
	Medicine for TB cough	0.10.0	28 Oct.
Takei, Moto	Money remaining after payment for silkworms[f]	0.50.0	25 Aug.
	In total[f]	Balance[f]	undated

[c] Since she received no year-end payment, this ill worker was probably sent home to recover or die.

[d] Because her year-end pay was so low, one might surmise that Odagiri joined the company late in the working year. Perhaps she was a novice.

[e] Meaning unclear. Perhaps this sum was to pay her travel expenses home, since she quit in midyear.

[f] Meaning unclear.

Table 4.6 (*cont.*)

Worker's Name	Type of Payment	Amount (yen. sen. rin)	Date
Yamada, Owa[g]	Preparation money	1.00.0	2 Apr.
	Payment to Dr. Shibukawa	0.75.0	30 Aug.
	Payment to Dr. Shibukawa	0.52.0	1 Sept.
	Payment	10.00.0	29 Dec.
Odagiri, Fu[h]	Preparation money	1.00.0	25 Jan.
	Payment to Dr. Shibukawa	0.08.0	28 Aug.
	Payment to Dr. Shibukawa	0.38.0	Dec.
	Payment to doctor	1.30.0	undated
	Medicine for September	3.08.0	"
Yamaoka, Tomo[i]	Preparation money	5.00.0	undated
	—	3.00.0	14 July
	—	1.00.0	14 Aug.
	Money to buy lumber	2.38.0	undated
	Money to buy lumber	13.10.0	"
Koushi, Hisa[j]	Shopping	0.30.0	14 Nov.
	Shopping	0.30.0	17 Dec.
	Payment to worker	5.00.0	undated

[g] This worker was ill, but, judging by the year-end payment, still a good worker.

[h] Odagiri appears to have been seriously ill. Since there is no record of a year-end payment, she may have died.

[i] There is no clue why Yamoka Tomo's preparation money is 5 yen when 1 yen appears to have been the amount normally provided. The lumber may have been for her family's house-building endeavors.

[j] Koushi seems to have joined the company late in the working year. If so, 5 yen at year end was very good pay.

Table 4.6 (*cont.*)

Worker's Name	Type of Payment	Amount (yen. sen. rin)	Date
1900 (In 1900 the price of a postcard was 1 sen, 5 rin; an umbrella, 1 yen, 50 sen; 1 shō of rice, 12 sen, 3 rin.)			
Hanaoka, Asano	Preparation money	3.00.0	undated
	Paid from wages earned	0.30.0[k]	28 Dec.
Morozumi, Makie[l]	Paid from wages earned	55.00.0	30 Dec.
Shinoda, Machi[m]	Preparation money	3.00.0	undated
	Money to buy rice	10.00.0	14 July
	Owed to dye works	2.50.0	28 Aug.
	Doctor's fee	1.00.0	4 Sept.
	Doctor's fee	1.00.0	29 Nov.
	Paid from wages earned	20.00.0	undated
Saito, Suge	Preparation money	3.00.0	13 Oct.
	Shopping[n]	5.00.0	14 Nov.
	Paid from wages earned	25.00.0	30 Dec.

[k] The 30 sen is probably an error. This probably should have read "30 yen," because 30 sen is much lower than typical low year-end payments in 1900. Because this 28 December payment was made from wages earned, one can assume that the company was holding back the rest of the wages earned during the year. However, there is no indication regarding how much was held back.

[l] This worker received no preparation money, so she took home a larger wage packet at the end of the year. As her year-end payment was from wages earned, the company was probably keeping back some of her earnings to be paid only after she returned the following year. Since she received no small allowances paid by the company, she may have been receiving pocket money from home.

[m] Even though she was ill. Shinoda Machi managed to earn more than a total of 37 yen, 50 sen. The amount of her held-back wages is unknown. She took home 20 yen at the end of the year, despite medical and other expenses. Perhaps the substantial expenditure to the dye works was for cloth being prepared for her marriage trousseau. She was a skilled worker.

[n] The expenditure for shopping was paid to a large merchandising firm. Thus the items bought may have been goods acquired by a young woman preparing for marriage or they may have been good desired by her family.

tions in the textile mills near the end of the Meiji period, when he conducted an extensive survey of workers' health and sanitation conditions in
these factories for the government, accurately described the companies'
strategy in sending portions of the workers' pay to their fathers.

> Money is sent to a girl's home and a letter written to her father or guardian
> stating that "your daughter is healthy and really working well and thus we are
> able to send you this monetary token. . . ." Because the father doesn't know
> much about the [factory] conditions he takes [the company's letter] at face value.
> He tells his daughter, "We're very grateful that we received the money you
> earned. It's a good factory so do your best and work hard. . . ." When the girls
> themselves tell their fathers about the hardships of the work, the fathers just
> think their daughters hate the work because they are self-indulgent.[49]

The hundred-yen factory girls appear to have been comparatively rare.
Studying the archives of the village office of Kokufu in Gifu prefecture,
Yamamoto Shigemi found that of 458 females who left the village to work
elsewhere in silk factories during 1900, only one made a high enough wage
to be called a hundred-yen worker. This one worker earned the high wage
of 150 yen for the year. Most of the others earned from ten to thirty yen,
with some earning as little as two to five yen during 1900. The annual
average wage among these workers from Kokufu was twenty-eight yen,
fifteen sen.[50]

Despite the difficulty of becoming a top earner, supervisors urged all
hands to compete with each other and bitterly humiliated those with the
lowest production, regardless of the reasons for their lesser achievements.
Sometimes a plant's workers were divided into competing teams, and the
winners won small prizes like sweet potatoes—which, while warmly welcomed by the ravenous reelers, were petty when compared to the heavy
fines and overtime work without pay routinely imposed. And the losers
could be made to pay for the winners' prizes. The overseer of the winning
team might be awarded a one-yen bonus the day his team won. But that
bonus would be taken from the wages of the workers and overseer who
performed least well. Such an arrangement was designed to make the fined
overseer push his team into producing more.[51]

Girls and women from one region were often kept working together as
a unit under an overseer who was also from the workers' part of the country. Thus companies were able to use regional solidarity to encourage frenzied competition. Playing upon the girls' attachment to home and local

[49] Ishihara Osamu, *Jokō to kekkaku* (Female factory workers and tuberculosis), originally
published in 1913, to be found in *Seikatsu koten sōsho* (Tokyo, 1970), 5: 185.
[50] Yamamoto Shigemi, *Aa nomugi tōge*, 198, 405–9.
[51] Ibid., 83–84.

prejudices against strangers from other villages, overseers were able to foster keen rivalry among the teams of workers.[52]

As silk workers frantically tried to draw heavier, finer, and glossier thread in greater quantities from stubborn cocoons, the songs they sang suggest they were not without bitter awareness of their exploitation.

> To kill a factory girl
> You don't need a knife;
> You just strangle her
> With the weight and denier of the thread.[53]

> How are you doing, reeler of thread?
> Are you drawing the weight out?
> You either get the weight or you get the sack.

> How are doing, sister?
> Are you drawing the weight out?
> It's either the weight or tears for you.

> How are you doing, young miss?
> Are you drawing the weight out?
> It's either the weight or a tongue lashing.[54]

And the singers knew that the lashing might just as readily be delivered with a sturdy bamboo stick.

The ones most likely to be thrashed were workers who, no matter how hard they tried, never managed to acquire the skills needed to be a good reeler. Sakamoto Kō, a silk-mill veteran by the end of the Meiji period, remembered such workers.

> Once I took on the training of five new workers at the same time. At the end of a year, two out of the five had become good factory girls but the other three just didn't get the knack of it. When I think back over the long years I spent as a silk worker, I can say that out of ten, two or three workers were really good. Then there were three or four more who managed because they were enthusiastic and made great efforts. But as for the remaining two or three, no matter how many times you taught them, or got angry at them, or beat them, these people just didn't have it in them to be reelers. It was hopeless to get angry at them.[55]

[52] Nakamura Masanori and Corrado Molteni, "Seishi gijutsu no hatten to joshi rōdō" (The development of silk-reeling technology and female labor), in *Gijutsu kakushin to joshi rōdō* (Technological innovation and female labor), ed. Nakamura Masanori (Tokyo, 1985), 63; Takizawa Hideki, *Nihon shihonshugi to sanshi-gyō* (Japanese capitalism and the silk-reeling industry) (Tokyo, 1978), 395–408.

[53] Nakamura Masanori, *Rōdōsha to nōmin*, 98.

[54] Yamamoto Shigemi, *Aa nomugi tōge*, 386.

[55] Ibid., 124.

In her mellow later years, Sakamoto might say that "it was hopeless to get angry at them." But while she was teaching such people, she probably did feel and vent such anger. Unfortunates who just could not "get the knack of it" were yelled at, fined, humiliated, and hit by all of their superiors. Worse, when the year ended, they would have little or no earnings to take back to their waiting parents. If the father of such a girl had received a large advance-loan at the time her contract was sealed, her inability to develop earning skills might land her family in serious trouble. With ratings on all workers posted each day or every other day and all praise and prestige going to the most productive operatives, the working lives of the unskilled must have been very miserable indeed. The saddest aspect of their failure to learn skills is surely the blame that they heaped upon their own heads, as they internalized the low repute in which they were held by employers and by fellow workers who were proud of their own acquired skills.

Enduring or Escaping

Working conditions were as harsh as the wage system. Workers were expected to rush to their machines at 4:30 or 5:10 A.M.; rest periods during the day were short and few. At most they might consist of fifteen-minute breaks in the morning and evening with thirty minutes for food at noon, but breaks could be ten- and fifteen-minute intervals instead. When the mill was busy, operators remained at their machines until ten in the evening. Speedups and suspension of breaks forced workers to stuff food into their mouths as they manipulated machines, cocoons, and threads. Not surprisingly, utter exhaustion at the end of thirteen to seventeen hours of work left the women and girls in a semistupor. An elderly woman recalled her experience in a Suwa filature during the 1890s: "In the lamplit factory we worked from morning darkness to about ten o'clock at night. By the time we had finished work we could hardly stand on our feet. After our nighttime soup we occasionally received a sweet potato. Then we had to wash and to fix our hair. When we were through, it was about eleven o'clock."[56]

With operatives dead on their feet it was easy for accidents to occur and for exhaustion to become illness. In 1975 an old woman who began as a silk worker at the age of nine in 1895 described the greatly swollen feet, serious influenza, and pneumonia she remembered.[57] Hands that were constantly plunged into boiling water were raw with burns. Influenza and pneumonia were contracted or worsened as workers raced from freezing dormitories to steaming factories. Workplaces were tightly sealed from

[56] Ibid., 176.
[57] Nakamura Masanori, *Rōdōsha to nōmin*, 83.

drafts, and the humidity was kept high to reduce the chances of thread breakage. This was unbearable enough in winter, but coupled with the stifling heat of summer it took a perilous toll on overworked, undernourished bodies; stomach disorders and heavy colds were commonplace. The fine floss in the air caused breathing problems. Workers were completely covered in silk dust, and the pores of the skin on their faces became blocked. Long hours under poor lighting ruined eyesight and reduced resistance to eye diseases. Ishihara Osamu observed that the growth of many silk workers was stunted: they were smaller than average for their ages.[58]

By 1900, beriberi and tuberculosis were killing and disabling at much higher rates among silk and other textile workers than among the population at large.[59] Tuberculosis hit the young especially hard, and most of the silk workers were young: according to a government survey in 1898, of 13,620 silk workers in 205 mills, 1 percent were under ten years of age, 16 percent were under fourteen, and 47 percent were between fourteen and twenty. The rest were mainly in their early twenties.[60] Since employers never sent ailing workers home unless they were dying, everyone dreaded the prospect of being sent home sick. Her comrades knew that the woman waiting patiently to be fetched home by a relative would die on the way to her village or soon after her arrival there. "If you were going home, it was the end," remembered one retired silk worker.[61]

Another, Sakanoue Jitsu, vividly recalled for Yamamoto Shigemi the sad autumn of 1907 when a number of seriously ill silk workers left Hirano village mills for their homes on the other side of the Nomugi Pass.

Right after I went to work in the Yamaichi silk plant in Shinshū, my younger sister Aki came to work in the same factory. Maybe she worked for about two years. Then she got peritonitis and was in bed at the factory. At that time, there were about thirty sick people. Those who clearly had lung disease were quickly sent home. The song "Takeo and Namiko" was a hit tune then so everybody was afraid of TB and wouldn't go near [sick people]. It wasn't long before my sister Aki was also sent home and she died shortly afterward. She was thirteen. She had come determined to become a hundred-yen factory girl and make our mother happy. I will never forget her pallid face and sad eyes when she left the factory. I saw her off as far as the gate but no words came out of my mouth. Surely this sick person cannot cross the Nomugi Pass and walk more than thirty miles! That's what was in my mind. But they wouldn't let her stay at the factory.

[58] Ishihara, *Jōkō to kekkaku*, 179.
[59] See chap. 9.
[60] Nōshōmu-shō, *Shokkō jijō*, 163; Sakura, *Jokō gyakutai shi*, 143–45.
[61] Nakamura Masanori, *Rōdōsha to nōmin*, 83.

There was no money to send her to the hospital. There was nothing else but for her to go home.[62]

Table 4.7
Ages of Silk Workers in 1901 (number and percent)

	205 Mills in Nagano			29 Mills in Other Prefectures		
	Males	Females	Total	Males	Females	Total
Under 11	3	150	153	0	0	0
	(0.3)	(1.2)	(1.1)			
11–14	54	2,135	2,189	2	305	307
	(4.9)	(17.1)	(16.1)	(1.0)	(10.5)	(9.9)
15–20	274	5,999	6,273	19	1,607	1,626
	(24.9)	(47.9)	46.1	(9.5)	(55.2)	(52.3)
Over 20	770	4,235	5,005	179	997	1,176
	(69.9)	(33.8)	(36.7)	(89.5)	(34.3)	(37.8)
Total	1,101	12,519	13,620	200	2,909	3,109
	(100)	(100)	(100)	(100)	(100)	(100)

Source: Nōshōmu-shō, *Shokkō jijō*, 132–33.

Stricken workers returned to their villages to infect relatives and neighbors with the communicable diseases they were carrying. In this way the hazards of mill life were added to the hardships of those who stayed behind in the countryside.

Working conditions were harsh at home in the villages, too. In mountain hamlets where folk lived by gathering acorns and horse chestnuts in the forest and growing the millet and other coarse grains they did not find tasty, people "worked so hard that even four meals a day could not fill their stomachs."[63] Where raising silkworms was an important by-employment, superhuman efforts were required to make sure the demanding larvae reached maturity: day and night the insatiable insects had to be fed and kept dry and warm.

Silkworms sleep only four times, each time for about twenty-four hours, before spinning cocoons, and if not sleeping they will eat voraciously day and night. As the larva grows from a newly hatched "ant" to full size, it consumes 30,000 times

[62] Yamamoto Shigemi, *Aa nomugi tōge*, 149. Presumably Takeo and Namiko are the names of the lovers in the song about love and TB.
[63] Segawa, *Onna*, 66.

its body weight in mulberry leaves, which must be picked, chopped, and distributed fresh at every feeding. Moreover, it is very particular about what it will eat, choosing only the tenderest portions of the leaf. Experiments have shown that silkworms consume at most 12 percent and as little as 6 percent of the prepared leaves.[64]

All hands in a family or even a village might be involved in this work when the demand was greatest, but it was the womanfolk who directed and provided most of the exhausting labor for this cottage industry that, since before the Meiji Restoration, had been enabling peasant families to continue living on their precarious land holdings.[65] And it was women's work to grow the mulberry plants needed to feed the silkworms.

Women worked in the fields as they had done in earlier times. In rice paddies they planted, transplanted, weeded, and hoed: bent over and aching, their bodies felt the sharp rays of the sun and the pelting rains while leeches clung to their legs. To prepare the ground for drier crops like millet, barley, and barnyard grass, they would dig large boulders out of the inhospitable earth. They cut down trees in the mountains, hauled the logs back, and along with the men in their families carried heavy loads of firewood, produce, and other burdens on their backs. In addition, the farm woman's special domain included endless household chores of food preparation for immediate and future use, making and repairing the family's clothing, and weaving cloth for the family and perhaps some to sell. When seasonal work used up energy faster, they had to find even more food and cook it more often: not only the silkworms but all who looked after them had to be fed. In poor families this was a far from easy task. In the peasant household, women worked late into the night, even when they knew they needed hours of sleep to be able to carry on. As the refrain of a mountain song put it:

Go to bed quickly
Tomorrow we have to go out to work![66]

Seasonal efforts and everyday demands certainly took a toll of undernourished bodies in the countryside. Certainly, as one old grandmother remembered, farm women "worked so hard that we couldn't squat over the toilet because our legs were so sore."[67] Yet sometimes farm women

---

[64] Vlastos, *Peasant Protests*, 97.

[65] Segawa, *Onna*, 70, points out that after the first decade of Meiji, hand reeling, which in pre-Restoration times had been an integral part of so many families' sericultural activities, declined rapidly.

[66] Segawa, *Mura*, 11. This collection of recollections tells us much about the life and work of Meiji farm women. See also Segawa, *Onna*, esp. 61–103, and Nagoya josei shi kenkyū kai, *Haha no jidai*, 12–38.

[67] Segawa, *Mura*, 126.

were able to work at a less frenzied pace, for instance, when the silkworm season was over. Routines were varied as countryfolk performed a variety of tasks, at least some of which were done in the fresh air.[68] The women in the silk mills were fed regularly, but their working environment was less healthful than that of their sisters and cousins at home in the villages.[69]

Bodies of mill women and girls were assailed not only by disease and illness. As administrators of fines and punishments on the work floor, male employees had "considerable arbitrary power over the young opera-tives. . . . The young operatives, single and vulnerable, were open targets for personal whims and sexual abuse by these low-ranking supervisors, and provocations led to constant tension between textile hands and their over-seers."[70] Owners and managers were often as abusive as their male subor-dinates, and unlike ordinary workers these men usually had keys to the women's dormitory rooms.[71] When rape and intimidation resulted in pregnancy, the male employee or employer had little to fear: he would pay the unfortunate woman a small sum, and that would be the end of the matter for him.[72] Verses that reelers sang warned against sexual harass-ment, mentioned it as an ordinary fact of life, and expressed bitter resent-ment at their humiliating powerlessness. The following stanzas appear in a number of different songs.

Don't fall in love with male workers.
You'll end up discarded like tea dregs.

At parting one is like a fan,
Discarded when a breeze is no longer needed.

Meet him often and the factory gets upset.
Don't meet him and the master gets upset.

This company is like a brothel;
We are whores who live by selling our faces.

[68] Laura Strumingher makes this point in comparing the working conditions of silk work-ers who went to reel in the filatures established in the city of Lyons from 1830 to 1840 with the working conditions of rural women who reeled silk in addition to performing their other agricultural jobs. See Laura Strumingher, "Les canutes de Lyon (1835–1848)," *Mouvement Sociale* 105 (October–December 1978): 60–61.

[69] This is not to say that the country environment was always healthful. Farm women worked in the fields in all kinds of weather, and they met with accidents while hauling logs back from the mountains or out fishing.

[70] Gary Allinson, *Japanese Urbanism: Industry and Politics in Kariya, 1872–1972* (Berkeley, Calif., 1975), 50. See also Kajinishi et al, *Seishi rōdōsha*, 89.

[71] Sakura, *Jokō gyakutai shi*, 163.

[72] See ibid., 163–68, for some sordid details.

In Suwa geisha get thirty-five sen.
Common prostitutes get fifteen sen.
Silk reelers get one potato.[73]

Despite all the bonds welding them to the miserable conditions in the mills, many silk workers did run away—jumping over fences or failing to come back from rare holidays outside the factory gates. As the folk wisdom of the silk-producing districts put it: "The day may come when the cock ceases to crow but never the day when factory girls stop running away."[74] Without food or financial resources, the trip back home was extremely difficult, and once there a girl faced anxious parents who had long ago spent the advances on their daughter's wages. Runaways often ended up in prostitution or as aimless wanderers easily located and returned by police or the male employees sent after them. Sometimes they were not so easily returned, as a former male worker recalled:

> It's a strange story because ironically we young boys felt like running away too, but we had to go chasing after fleeing female workers. Once I chased factory girls from Hida who were avoiding the main road, going around to the back roads. I had no option but to go ahead to the station and hang about there all night. Carrying their wooden clogs in a bundle and wearing straw sandals, the factory girls crossed the pass during the night. In the morning when they arrived tired at Shiojiri station I caught them. They were Fumi (eighteen) and Ise (eighteen), factory girls who were natives of Hida near Nomugi Pass. The two of them cried and begged me to let them go. I was just a simple nineteen-year-old then so I asked them to please come back to the factory to save my face, but they said they wouldn't return even if it meant their death. I told them if they ran away I would be fired but it was no use. I said I'd let them go if they would be sure to come back in two or three days and I left. But they never came back. Later I heard that the company seized their families' entire summer harvest of cocoons.[75]

Those who were brought back to their employers were punished cruelly.[76] Suicide was another avenue of escape to which girls were driven: "In the silk plants of the Suwa region, despairing girls often committed suicide by jumping onto the giant waterwheels in the Tenryū River."[77] Probably many more wanted to run away than actually did. The distance to their homes and the metal screens and thick wooden bars of the dormitories presented formidable barriers. After the alliance agreements went

[73] Yamamoto Shigemi, *Aa nomugi tōge*, 393–95. The payments mentioned in the last verse are presumably all for sexual favors.
[74] Ibid., 97.
[75] Ibid., 98–99.
[76] See for example ibid., 94–95.
[77] Hane, *Peasants*, 188. See also Yamamoto Shigemi, *Aa nomugi tōge*, 197–98, and Nakamura Masanori, *Rōdōsha to nōmin*, 98.

into effect, reelers could not easily get silk work elsewhere if they ran away. They were held by the wage system, which encouraged them to strain their health to become hundred-yen factory girls, held back wages to be paid only after a worker returned to the mill for another year, and got them and their families into debt through advance-loans. By the early twentieth century, the turnover rates—including the escape rates—in the mills had dropped drastically.[78] This drop does not indicate, however, that employee satisfaction had risen. The inexperienced continued to be lured by "sweet words," but such innocents had to be sought in districts further and further away from the mills. As factory conditions became known in the more accessible villages, families refused to give up their daughters. As Ishihara Osamu reported:

> There are many who run away home because they cannot endure the severe illness caused by their work. The factories have tried various policies to deal with these women but no matter what public pronouncements the companies put out, the conditions in the factories become known in the countryside. Meanwhile, those who went to the factories come home with tuberculosis and die. Thus even families that are ground down by rural poverty stop sending their daughters out to be mill hands. They absolutely refuse [to send their daughters]. Because of this, I am told, companies go to new districts where recruiting has not occurred before and—hiding the facts—open up these districts as recruiting grounds. After three years in a new place [recruiters] have to give up this territory too and go elsewhere to recruit mill girls. In Japan there are fewer and fewer untapped districts left.[79]

The recruiter's tasks thus became more inconvenient and costly, but for many years after the Meiji era had ended he was able to find poor families who would send their womenfolk to the mills.

Both veteran reelers, driven by need or ambition, and innocent novices, who had arrived full of hope, would continue to sing together:

Factory work is prison work
All it lacks is iron chains.[80]

[78] The silk manufacturers' registration of workers played an important role in this reduction in the turnover rate.
[79] Ishihara, *Jokō to kekkaku*, 185.
[80] Yamamoto Shigemi, *Aa nomugi tōge*, 388.

5

Silk: Working for the Nation?

RECOGNIZING that a work force composed of individuals who felt they were treated as convicts promoted neither productivity nor profit, silk manufacturers made special efforts to raise the morale of their female employees. They taught the women company songs, arranged for them to hear uplifting lectures on moral themes, and had simply written ethics texts distributed to those few who could read. Employers stressed the importance of silk reeling for both the modernizing nation of Japan and the poverty-stricken families back home in the countryside. Loyalty to the company was offered as a means to both national and family prosperity. Silk factory women, for their part, noticed contradictions between the high esteem their bosses displayed for the fruits of their labor and the low regard those same bosses accorded them individually and collectively. As we shall see in this chapter, the mill hands did not always respond to patriotic or company exhortations as their employers would have liked.

"Girls to the Factory"

From the time they were recruited, young women were told that national, company, and personal interests were identical. We see an example of this in Yamamoto Shigemi's vivid portrait of the women and girls who each February struggled through the icy snows and winds of the Nomugi Pass between Gifu and Nagano prefectures on their way to the silk-factory district of Suwa.[1] As they were led by company representatives in single file through the frozen pass, the strains of a hearty song came from the front of the line.

> We don't cross the Nomugi Pass for nothing;
> We do it for ourselves and for our parents.
> Boys to the army,
> Girls to the factory.
> Reeling thread is for the country too.[2]

[1] This is memorably portrayed in the 1979 film *Aa nomugi tōge* (based on the book of the same title), directed by Yamamoto Satsuo. The sequel to this film, a movie based on *Zoku aa nomugi tōge*, was made in 1983.

[2] Yamamoto Shigemi, *Aa nomugi tōge*, 16.

Once the girls reached the silk factory, the company continued to provide uplifting tunes with lyrics to inspire patriotic effort.

> Raw silk,
> Reel, reel the thread.
> Thread is the treasure of the empire!
> More than a hundred million yen worth of exports,
> What can be better than silk thread?

> Factory girls,
> We are soldiers of peace.
> The service of women is a credit
> To the empire and to yourselves.
> There are trials and hardships, yes,
> But what do they matter?[3]

Such songs present toil in the silk mills as the source of blessings for the individual worker, her family, the nation.

> Put all your strength into your work.
> It's for yourself,
> It's for your family,
> It's for the country of Japan.[4]

As soon as the young women arrived, they were lectured by their employers on the importance of what they would be doing: their work, which would benefit themselves and their families, was precious patriotic labor that would enable Japan to take its rightful place among the nations of the world. Such lectures would be repeated periodically; by the end of the Meiji period their messages had been printed in textbooks designed for young female textile workers. These books were short (usually under a hundred pages) and written in simple language—phonetic *furigana* script provided to gloss all Chinese ideographs made them even easier to read.[5] These texts served as references for employers' instant lectures; they were also intended for the minority of mill hands who could read a little, although even by the end of the Meiji era barest literacy was far from being

---

[3] Seishi orimono shinposha (Silk-Reeling and Woven Goods Press), ed., *Shūshin kunwa kōjo no kagami* (Moral discourses: A mirror for factory girls) (Tokyo, 1912), 82–83. These are the first two of fourteen stanzas. To paraphrase Pete Seeger, each one of them is drearier than the last.

[4] Takenobu Toshihiko, ed., *Jokō tokuhon* (Factory girls' reader) (Tokyo, 1911), 5.

[5] Written Japanese of the period employed the two indigenous, phonetic scripts, *hiragana* and *katakana*, along with a large number of ideographs from the Chinese language. Since only the well educated could read many of the Chinese ideographs, *kana* readings (furigana) were sometimes placed beside each ideograph.

the norm.[6] These books, which linked duty owed to parents with duty owed to nation and urged self-sacrifice in the interests of both, give us a detailed picture of employers' messages to the young girls and women in the silk-thread industry.[7]

The first lesson in *Factory Girls' Reader*, published in 1911, is as follows:

Working for the Sake of the Country

Everyone, if you all work to the utmost of your abilities from morning to night, there can be no loyalty to the country greater than this. If you do not work thus and stay idly at home, the country of Japan will become poorer and poorer. Therefore, work with all your might for the country's sake, enabling Japan to become the greatest country in the world.

Every one of you, no matter what your age, you would not want to become a burden to your father and mother who have to toil unceasingly. Now that you have gone out into this great world, work well every day and you will bring great peace of mind and happiness to your parents, your elder brothers, your elder sisters.

For everyone to do her factory work to the utmost of her abilities is, as I have said, loyalty for the sake of the country, filial piety for the sake of the family. You must do your work unselfishly. In the old alphabet song, does it not say, "One can't buy the kind of progress the young can make"? For your own sake, for your family's sake, for your country's sake, devote yourself heart and soul to your work.[8]

The first chapter in the 1912 text, *Moral Discourses: A Mirror for Factory Girls*, has even more emphasis on patriotism. It describes Japan as the land of the gods, "the country of the rising sun" (*hi no de no kuni*), a small island nation that defeated gigantic China and Russia, invincible in war with its special spirit and hundreds of thousands of loyal troops. With factory girls' brothers in the army, the army is victorious and the country is strong. Yet even a strong country needs money, so its soldiers' sisters go to the mills to serve there as combatants. They fight "the peace war," producing silk

[6] Yokoyama, *Nihon no kasō shakai*, 179–80; Yamamoto Shigemi, *Aa nomugi tōge*, 411; Uga Kiyoshi, ed., *Bōseki shokkō jijō chōsa gaiyō sho* (Summary report of the survey of conditions among cotton-spinning workers), not for sale (Osaka, 1898), 125–27. See also Hanai Makoto, "Seishi jokō to gakkō kyōiku" (Silk manufactory girls and school education), *Nihon shi kenkyū* (Journal of Japanese history) 19 (July 1978): 25–47, for Aichi prefecture's female factory workers' education levels: as late as 1920, 5,412 or 7.43 percent of the female factory workers in Aichi had received no formal education at all, while another 23,484 or 32.31 percent of the prefecture's female factory workers had received some elementary schooling but had not completed elementary school.

[7] *Shūshin kunwa kōjo no kagami, Jokō tokuhon*, and the other two textbooks quoted from in this chapter appear to have been published especially for textile employers' purposes.

[8] Takenobu, *Jokō tokuhon*, 1–3.

thread, cotton thread, and woven silk to enable Japan to accumulate money through exporting to foreign countries. This noble work also allows the girls to demonstrate the filial piety they owe their parents as they send their wages back home. At the same time, they evince loyalty to the emperor. Awake or asleep, they should never forget loyalty and filial piety; to do so would inevitably bring punishment from heaven.[9]

Published in 1910, *Factory Girls' Lessons* begins with a chapter yet more riddled with national chauvinism. After a jingoist version of Japan's past military glories, the author claims that the Russo-Japanese War of 1904–1905 left the country with a debt amounting to six yen, fifteen sen, nine rin per person. Because of this debt, the need to produce money-making silk is urgent.[10] *Factory Girls' Lessons* reminds its readers that even the first family of the realm acknowledges the importance of the raw silk industry: from the time of the visit of the empress dowager and empress to the government's pioneer mill at Tomioka in 1879, illustrious members of the imperial family have visited mills and taken a personal interest in silk production.[11] These textbooks and others like them went on to urge unswerving obedience to factory rules and superiors, punctuality and conscientiousness at work, moderation in eating, drinking, and speech, patience, forbearance, honesty, frugality. Care was taken to enmesh such virtues within the main theme of patriotic endeavor for the empire and filial recompense to the family: "Many soldiers died in the Sino-Japanese War and much money was spent in order that Japan could become a first-class country. So let's work hard, make good thread, sell it abroad, and take those high foreign noses down a peg."[12]

Conduct toward the factory owners, often referred to as "your second parents," was also prescribed. The second chapter in *Moral Discourses* told the factory girl that her master (the employer) worried about her as if she were his own child. According to this text, he treasured her even more than he did his own child. As in other readers for silk hands, the girl was told to obey the master and all his management subordinates. If the master only thought of profit and not of her welfare, the chapter explained, then the company would surely fail. "So pay off the debt of gratitude you owe him by working as hard as possible."[13] Chapter 3 of *Factory Girls' Reader* spelled out the company's role in loco parentis even more clearly:

> In your home it is father, mother, elder brother, elder sister who are your elders. In the company it is first and foremost the company president, then office offi-

[9] Seishi orimono shinposha, *Kagami*, 1–6.
[10] Katō Tomotada, *Kōjo kun* (Factory girls' lessons) (n.p., 1910), 1–8.
[11] Ibid., 14–15.
[12] Ibid., 47.
[13] Seishi orimono shinposha, *Kagami*, 9. In this volume, see Lesson 2, "Your Employer Is Your Second Parent," 7–9.

cials, engineers, supervisors, section heads who are your elders, and there are many of them. Make sure you do everything these elders tell you to do. And it is not enough just to do what they bid; you must show respect toward them at all times. At home if you did not obey your parents or were rude to your elder brother and elder sister, what would the neighbors think? They would certainly decide that you were an unfilial daughter. If you acted like that you would not be cherished by your parents, your elder brother, or the neighbors. Similarly, if you do not obey your elders in the firm and are rude to them . . . the loss will be yours alone.[14]

Company profits, workers' material benefits, and service to the country were carefully woven together in *Factory Girls' Lessons*: "If you produce good thread, the factory's profits will increase. Your wages will increase and you will be wrapped in honor—for the country, for your parents, for your employer, for yourself."[15]

The intention of employers' songs, lectures, and textbooks is crystal clear: the highest worker productivity must be attained and maintained. Yet at the same time, as we saw in the previous chapter, factory owners were busy devising other, more practical means of extracting as much work as was possible from their hands. Thus, the reality that greeted the young women who arrived in Suwa and other silk-producing districts contrasted sharply with those glowing depictions of factory life that delineated stellar roles in factory, family, and state assigned by employers and government to the female textile workers of Meiji Japan.

Company Songs Were Not Workers' Songs

Silk production had flourished during the first decade of Meiji: the blight in Europe was a boon to Japanese exporters at the time of the Restoration, and a short while later Tomioka and other government filatures were enthusiastically spreading new reeling technology. Some of the prestige of important government initiatives rubbed off on the women and girls learning machine reeling. Regarded as teachers as well as workers, they enjoyed the exciting optimism and relative material prosperity of the period. It is no wonder that calls for patriotism met with ready responses—especially from those with samurai backgrounds.

Those who became machine reelers during the next three decades were not so fortunate. When the Meiji period ended in 1912, the country's silk mills were full of anxious, harassed, half-starved daughters of rural Japan's poorest families—no one would mistake them for the proud samurai and

[14] Takenobu, *Jokō tokuhon*, 7–8.
[15] Katō Tomotada, *Kōjo kun*, 27–28.

prosperous farming lasses who patriotically reeled at Tomioka and elsewhere during the 1870s or for Kōfu's spirited strikers of the 1880s. They
did not mistake themselves for their more fortunate forerunners. They
knew where they stood in the social pyramid:

If a woman working in an office is a willow,
A poetess is a violet,
And a female teacher is an orchid,
Then a factory woman is a vegetable gourd.[16]

Yet it was the fingertip skill of these poor daughters rather than superior
raw materials or efficient machine technology that enabled the silk industry
to hold its own against foreign competitors in world markets. The women
themselves—even when resigned to their humble status—realized this and
resented the lack of respect accorded them:

Don't sneer at us
Calling us "Factory girls, factory girls"!
Factory girls are
Treasure chests for the company.[17]

Management's major contribution to productivity was to invent ways to
keep every possible ounce of worker energy and every possible moment of
worker time devoted directly to producing silk. The measures they took to
do so were brilliantly successful, but they did not endear employers or the
nationalist cause they espoused to the women and children in the mills.

Despite the rhetoric to which they were subjected, by late Meiji many
daughters of the poor knew exactly why they were in the silk factories.
Employers and distinguished visitors might talk about reeling for the empire and working for the sake of the country, but the country had not done
much for the young women in the factories. Samurai women had traveled
in style from Yamaguchi to Tomioka, but ill-clad girls from mountain villages in the Hida region in Gifu trekked eighty-five miles through treach-
erous mountain terrain, their bleeding feet staining the snow red.[18] Aoki
Teru and her granddaughter took Tomioka reeling skills back to a family
that prospered in the silk industry which also helped to fill the state's cof-
fers. But Hida families and their daughters received only low wages for
which they themselves often paid in humiliation, health, and even lives.
The patriotic songs that were taught in the mills were not the songs of
youngsters from Hida and other areas. Nor do the young women appear
to have been taken in by employers who referred to themselves as "your

[16] Yamamoto Shigemi, *Aa nomugi tōge*, 395.
[17] Ibid., 396.
[18] Ibid., 19–22.

second parents." Often the owner who lectured his hands about his parental concern for their welfare and the transferred filial duties they owed him
was also the boss who was responsible for exhausting, underfeeding, fining, beating, confining, and perhaps even sexually attacking them. Silk
workers obeyed their male superiors because they had to, not because, in
the words of a distinguished scholar, "the conditions under which they
lived and worked reinforced in their minds traditional patterns of feudal
servitude."[19] Many of the reelers' own songs—as opposed to company an-
thems—make their feelings about employers, supervisors, and work conditions quite clear.

My Factory

At other companies there are Buddhas and gods.
At mine only demons and serpents.

When I hear the manager talking,
His words say only "money, money, and time."

The demon overseer, the devil accountant,
The good-for-nothing chrysalis.

If you look through the factory's regulations,
You see that not one in a thousand lies unused.

We must follow the regulations;
We must look at the foreman's nasty face.[20]

The Prison Lament

Factory work is prison work,
All it lacks are iron chains.

More than a caged bird, more than a prison,
Dormitory life is hateful.

Like a horse or a cow,
The reeler is fenced in.

Like the money in my employment contract,
I remain sealed away.

If a male worker makes eyes at you,
You end up losing your shirt.

[19] Ōkōchi Kazuo, *Labor in Modern Japan* (Tokyo, 1958), 2.
[20] Yamamoto Shigemi, *Aa nomugi tōge*, 391.

How I wish the dormitory would be washed away,
The factory burn down,
And the gatekeeper die of cholera!

At six in the morning I wear a devil's face,
At six in the evening, a smiling face.

I want wings to escape from here,
To fly as far as those distant shores.

Neither silk-reeling maids nor slops
Are promoted or kept for long.[21]

There were, of course, those who did not struggle against their fates or even complain very much about their working lives, but such workers did not show much enthusiasm for service to the nation or company either. They were busy surviving. When they had time for reflection it was their families, not the nation or the company, that they thought about. Here is the story that a twelve-year-old silk hand in the city of Maebashi told a government investigator in October 1902.[22] The explanatory statements in parentheses were provided by the investigator who wrote down what she told him.

I came to this city in May of last year. I didn't come because I wanted to. I was only doing what my mother told me to do. Someone who was a recruiter or a letter carrier brought me here. With others I was brought here to————in this city where I did nothing for ten days. Then it was decided that I would work at the firm I had been brought to. I wasn't told what the wages, pocket money, or anything would be like. But I did hear that the contracted term would be five and a half years.

In this place there are twenty-five or twenty-six female hands. They have all worked for a long time and many of them do more than the work of one operative. There are those earning wages who are about twenty-five years old who have been working for five or six years straight. I don't have a person called a supervisor (*kantoku*) over me, but I work under a twenty-year-old girl called a "lookout" (*banshū*) and she acts as our supervisor.

During this season we get up at four in the morning and work for two hours before breakfast. When the meal is ready, all the factory women eat it together and then go right back to work. At first I cleaned the floor but after a while I began to be sent over to where thread is drawn out. Then, little by little, I began doing something like work. Up until then, I had believed that the cruelest hardship was what I did when it was my turn to be on duty (*tōban*). (What she referred to as "on duty" involved getting up at three o'clock in the morning, one

[21] Ibid., 388–89.
[22] Recorded in Nōshōmu-shō, *Shokkō jijō*, Appendix 2, 600–601.

hour earlier than the other female operatives did, in order to light the fire, to heat the water, to get things ready for work, and then to wake the sleeping workers.) After everybody gets up you wash your own face and then go with everybody to the workplace and start to work. In the summertime you are just a little sleepy but in winter even getting up is a great effort because, with fatigue from work in the daytime and the cold, it is hard to leave your bed. Squirming away under the covers, you know you'll be late for work if you are slow so you get up all right. But I find this the hardest thing.

This firm begins operations a little early [in comparison with other firms] in the morning but we stop working at night after the lamps have been lit. Since the boss does not let you go to bed as soon as you want to, even when you have nothing to do you have to stay up until about 9:00 P.M. Some girls sew after they finish work but most just gossip and fool around. There are two holidays: a half day off (of course they work in the mornings) at New Year's and Obon midsummer festival. There are no fixed rest periods. We go to work immediately after we finish eating so there are virtually no rest periods at all.

As for meals, in the morning the meal is half rice and half coarse grains with a side dish of bean-paste soup (or eggplant pickles). At noon we get pickled radish or occasionally cooked beans. In the evening there is soup and pickled radish. It's the same throughout the year except on a holiday when we are given salted fish. There is no limit to the number of bowls of rice one is allowed.

Because last year when I became sick I was given bought medicine and looked after, I got well quickly. It wasn't a serious illness so I didn't need a doctor.

At Obon and New Year's we are given clothing. The striped cotton clothes I am wearing now I received this year at Obon. Ordinarily we don't get any pocket money, but at Obon we got fifteen sen and at New Year's twelve sen.

The little girls usually get their hair done by the older girls, but in exchange you've got to listen obediently to whatever the older girls tell you. I can't talk back to them. If you do talk back to them they will soon call you all kinds of bad names, treat you dreadfully, and make you do almost impossible jobs.

Constantly I think of my mother at home in my native place. When you are treated badly your great longing to see your mother grows even stronger. But nowadays no matter how much I want to see her, during my five-and-a-half-year term I can't see her. I have to be resigned to this.

The government investigator who listened to this child reported that while the girl spoke her eyes were filled with tears. He noted that for a young girl she appeared surprisingly resigned.

Resigned or defiant, reelers were working for their parents and their siblings back home. As Ariga Kono—an elderly woman interviewed by Nakamura Masanori in 1975—explained, "For poor people, going out to work (dekasegi) was the thing to do. One was happy if one thought one was able to help one's family."[23] And help their families they did. They

---

[23] Nakamura Masanori, *Rōdōsha to nōmin*, 84.

knew how important this aid was: many of them stayed at their machines because they knew their earnings, forwarded to parents or brought home at the year's end, were literally keeping the folks back home alive.

Adding verse after verse to old tunes as they struggled to maintain the rhythm of their tasks and their own spirits and stamina, girls composed bittersweet songs that expressed pride, affection, and longing not for the country or the company but for their homes and parents.

Homesick

On rainy days and at night,
I think of home.

The factory closes and I return to the dormitory,
To think of home where frogs croak at night.

Is it the misty valley or just the steam from the silk?
Is it the temple bell on a sunny day or just the noon bell?

Looking out at the growing darkness,
I recall the evening bell at Takayama Temple.

When my term expires I'll cross the Nomugi Pass
And they'll say, "Our daughter is home!"

When the double yellow rose blooms,
I am beckoned home via Nomugi.

Autumn is lonely, overwhelmed by turning leaves.
In the moonlight I long for Hida.

As I go toward my home,
I look back at the hateful chimneys.[24]

My Two Parents

When I left home my parents
Told me always to behave myself.

On days when the rain falls,
On nights when the wind blows,
I remember my parents.

Listen folks, because I want
To be filial to my parents
I crossed Miyama and came
All this way to suffer in Shinshū.

[24] Yamamoto Shigemi, *Aa nomugi tōge*, 389–90.

How bitter, how bitter I think, but
When I remember my parents it's not bitter.

I want to go and cross the mountain,
If I go my little sister will be there,
And my parents too.

Let the year's end come quickly,
I want to tell my parents
About this cruel factory.

We don't cross the Nomugi Pass for nothing,
We do it for ourselves and for our parents.

When the season of painful reeling is over
The world will be bright again,
And maybe I'll be able to get married.

Because I am poor, at age twelve
I was sold to this factory.
When my parents told me, "Now it is time to go"
My very heart wept tears of blood.

Let the year end, let the year end,
I want to fly to my parents' side.

Mother! I hate the season in the silk plant;
It's from 4:00 P.M. to 4:00 A.M. . . .

I wish I could give my parents rice wine to drink,
And see their happy tears fall into the cup.

In this troubled world
I am just a silk-reeling lass,
But this lass wants to see
The parents who gave her birth.

Their letter says they are waiting for the year's end.
Are they waiting more for the money than for me?[25]

[25] Ibid., 390–91.

6

Cotton: The Reserve Army

The Initial Reserve Army

The Osaka Cotton-Spinning Company's dramatic breakthrough in 1883 provided a model for other entrepreneurs attempting to organize large-scale machine-spinning operations. As small and large plants proliferated, the capacity of Japan's machine spinning grew steadily: by the end of the 1880s there were thirty-four cotton-spinning firms, including ten that owned more than eighteen thousand spindles apiece. These ten, boasting 74 percent of the industry's spindle capacity, clearly dominated their smaller competitors.[1] Large enterprises located their mills in urban areas, Osaka and its environs being by far the most popular choice. Like Osaka Cotton-Spinning, companies like Dōjima, Tenma, Kanekin, Settsu, Izumikawa, and others chose Osaka or adjacent locations mainly because of the number of poor people living in the city and surrounding countryside.[2]

Throughout the 1880s, refugees from famine in the countryside poured into Osaka in search of work and food.[3] As a local newspaper noted in 1889, the connection between the swelling ranks of poor migrants and the opening of large spinning mills was a close one.[4] Slums within the city were bulging with poor people, but villages and towns not far from the city limits were also full of desperate folk.[5] In 1885, Osaka officials were

[1] Takamura, *Nihon bōseki-gyō shi josetsu*, 1:111.

[2] As the former center of the old cotton trade, Osaka was a logical choice for other reasons, too. Merchants who invested in machine spinning often had been merchants involved in the pre-Restoration cotton trade. For example, Okahashi Jisuke, the first president of Tenma, had been a cotton-thread merchant. Kitazaki Toshiji, "Bokkō ki ni okeru waga kuni bōseki-gyō to rōdō mondai: Meiji 22 nen no Tenma bōseki ni okeru sutoraiki o chūshin ni" (The sudden rise of the Japanese cotton-spinning industry and labor problems: The Tenma Cotton-Spinning Company strike of 1889), *Rekishi hyōron* 113 (January 1960): 61. The Osaka region was close to domestic sources of raw cotton; this remained important until 1896 when the tax on imported raw cotton was abolished. But the main reason for choice of Osaka, as contemporaries and scholars agree, was its proximity to a large pool of cheap labor.

[3] Between early 1881 and late 1889 Osaka's population increased 42 percent. Of the newcomers to the city, 47 percent came from prefectures other than Osaka prefecture (fu). Takamura, *Nihon bōseki-gyō shi josetsu*, 1:135.

[4] *Osaka mainichi shinbun* (Osaka daily newspaper), 31 January 1889, cited in ibid., 1:134.

[5] See Suzuki Umejirō's 1888 report on the great Osaka slum of Nago-machi in *Jiji shinpō* (News of the day), reproduced as "Ōsaka nago-machi hinmin kutsu shisatsu ki" (Observa-

confronted with the results of a local study entitled "Nōkōshō suitai ni kan suru hōtōsho" (Answers regarding the decline of agriculture, industry, and commerce), which drew attention to the heavy burdens of local farmers under the new tax system. Such burdens, the study found, left many poor cultivators without enough food to survive between harvests.[6] According to a Ministry of Agriculture and Commerce survey four years later in Sumiyoshi district, the home of many girls and women working in Osaka's spinning mills, 60 to 70 percent of the inhabitants were members of farming families—often tenant cultivators—who were struggling in conditions of extreme poverty.[7] Some of the abysmally poor folk in Sumiyoshi and other districts near Osaka may have moved there from neighborhoods within Osaka proper: in 1888 the Osaka police energetically began to implement an ambitious city sanitation plan that "cleaned up" poor people's ghettos by driving their inhabitants out to towns and villages beyond the city limits.[8]

Before the tottering Tokugawa government signed the commercial treaties that let in cheap foreign thread, the Osaka region had been the busy center of a flourishing cotton trade. Although raw cotton and cloth transactions had dominated the market, there had been a trade in thread too. Cotton thread, spun on hand tools by skilled craftfolk in towns or by the women of farm households, was drastically undercut by the cheap foreign threads that came with the treaties, but some hand spinners in the Osaka region did manage to continue their craft during the early years of the Meiji era. Then, about 1887, they were invaded on another front: the machine-spun thread of the modern mills built in Osaka could be produced more cheaply than the traditional products of hand spinners in suburban districts like Nishinari and in Higashinari city workshops. As the price of raw cotton rose steeply while machine-spun thread remained relatively inexpensive, hand spinners were paid less and less by the merchants who bought their finished wares or, as part of the "putting out" network, engaged them to turn raw cotton into thread. The government's agricultural survey of 1889 reported that "previously they [hand spinners] received eight sen for one hundred *me* [1 me or 1 *monme* = 0.1325 ounces] of

---

tions of the Nago-machi Ghetto of Osaka), in *Meiji shoki no toshi kasō shakai* (Early Meiji society's urban lower classes), ed. Nishida Taketoshi, vol. 2 of *Seikatsu koten sōsho* (Tokyo, 1970), 123–52.

    [6] See "Nōkōshō suitai ni kan suru hōtōsho" (Answers regarding the decline of agriculture, industry, and commerce), reproduced in Ōsaka shi-yakusho (Osaka City Hall), ed., *Meiji Taishō Ōsaka shi shi* (A history of Osaka City during the Meiji and Taisho eras), 8 vols. (Osaka, 1932), 7:819.

    [7] *Nōji chōsa: Osaka no bu* (Agricultural survey: Section on Osaka), pt. 3, cited in Kitazaki, "Meiji 22 Tenma sutoraiki," 63.

    [8] Chūbachi and Taira, "Poverty in Modern Japan," 403–4.

thread. Now they do not get even a third of this."[9] Hand spinning, as even a limited source of side income for cash-hungry villagers and city dwellers, began to disappear rapidly.

Connected with neither the traditions of ancient skilled crafts nor the joys and sorrows of tilling the land, cotton-factory work was something new. It was generally considered to be extremely low status labor, and wages were not high enough in the cotton mills to raise that status. Wages listed in table 6.1 are rough estimations. However, they do allow us to compare women's wages in cotton spinning with earnings in other working-class occupations halfway through the third decade of Meiji when the cost of rice was from 9 to 9.6 sen per shō (1.477 U.S. gallons).[10]

Male mill hands were paid much less than artisans in traditional crafts, made about one sen a day less than day laborers, and earned a little more than agricultural wage-workers. The latter two occupations, which were inclined to be seasonal, may have offered less steady employment than cotton spinning. The wages of female operatives in cotton were approximately half those of male operatives. Women could make as much or more money as agricultural laborers, but again agricultural wage-work may not have been as steady. Silk reeling appears to have been considerably more remu-

Table 6.1
Average Daily Wages Earned in 1892 (in sen)

Occupation	Sex	Average Daily Wages
Cotton spinning	female	8.9
Cotton spinning	male	17.4
Silk reeling	female	13.4
Weaving	female	8.0
Agriculture	female	9.4
Agriculture	male	15.5
Carpentry	male	26.7
Metal working	male	25.1
Day laboring	male	18.3

Sources: Kitazaki, "Meiji 22 Tenma sutoraiki," 67; Ishii, Nihon sanshi-gyō, 303; Ōe, Nihon no sangyō kakumei, 225; Sumiya, Nihon chinrōdō, 135; Sanpei, "Nihon fujin rōdō," 42.

[9] Nōji chōsa, pt. 3, 60, cited in Kitazaki, "Meiji 22 Tenma sutoraiki," 62.
[10] Sumiya, Nihon chinrōdō, 135; Sanpei, "Nihon ni okeru fujin rōdō no rekishi," 42.

nerative than other female occupations; but, as we saw in chapter 4, silk workers tended to work longer than the twelve-hour shifts in the cotton mills, and thus the hourly wage of silk workers may not have been greater. Weaving, a trade with probably the longest hours of all, paid less than cotton spinning.

With so many people in adjacent regions and in the city proper needing income, cotton-company owners and managers of Osaka were correct in assuming that prejudices and traditional preferences would not keep workers away from their mills. In the past, peasant families had sent young family members to work for more prosperous neighbors on the land or in sideline businesses producing finished or semifinished products for market.[11] Now they sent sons to munitions plants and brick works and daughters to match factories and cotton-spinning mills in the city.[12]

The earliest mechanized cotton operations had employed approximately as many males as females. But after 1886 mule-spinners were rapidly replaced by another import, ring-spinners, which produced thread more efficiently, demanded much less training time for operatives, and required less physical strength to manipulate. As a result, ring-spinners could easily be run by "weaker-muscled females."[13] By 1889 there were more ring- than mule-spinners in Japan, and female spinning hands outnumbered males two to one. A decade later 77 percent of the machine-cotton work force was female.[14] This development must have pleased profit-hungry managers because in nearly all occupations females were paid much less than males of corresponding levels of skill. From about 1887, the ranks of the girls and women who trooped daily from urban neighborhoods or suburban villages to the spinning companies included hand spinners whose occupations had been ruined. Experienced but now unemployed spinners were

[11] On sideline businesses during the Edo period, see Nakamura Takafusa, *Economic Growth*, 51.
[12] *Nōji chōsa: Ōsaka no bu*, cited in Nakamura Masanori, *Rōdōsha to nōmin*, 159.
[13] Murakami Hatsu, "Sangyō kakumei to josei rōdō" (The Industrial Revolution and female labor), in *Nihon josei shi 4: kindai* (History of Japanese women 4: Modern period), vol. 4 of *Nihon no josei shi*, 87. The mule-spinner was invented in 1779 and was first imported by the cotton-spinning mill in Kagoshima. Invented in 1830, the ring-spinner was displayed to the industrializing world at the Paris Exhibition of 1877. Osaka Cotton-Spinning tried ring-spinners first on an experimental basis, purchasing 4,000 spindles from Platt Brothers. The ring overtook the mule quickly: in 1885 out of a total of 79,264 spindles in Japanese cotton-spinning plants 71,125 were mules and only 5,892 were rings; by 1889 there were 113,768 mules and 151,248 rings in Japan. Kajinishi Mitsuhaya, *Nihon kindai mengyō no seiritsu* (Formation of Japan's modern cotton industry) (Tokyo, 1950), 100–108. The ring's production was 40 percent higher than that of the mule. Murakami Hatsu, "Sangyō kakumei to josei rōdō," 87.
[14] Takamura, *Nihon bōseki-gyō shi josetsu*, 1:136–37. Nōshōmu-shō, *Shokkō jijō*, 43–44; Rōdō undō shiryō iin kai, *Nihon rōdō undō shiryō*, 1:119–20.

apparently keen to earn wages even if they were low.[15] Others were equally eager for an opportunity to be able to make even small contributions to their family incomes.

With such a large reserve labor-army, companies viewed workers much as they regarded another resource in the Osaka region, raw cotton. Bonds between master and hand in the early mills supposedly had been close, but then the early mills had been connected with the government's policy of relief first to members of its own class, the ex-samurai, and second to "deserving" but impoverished commoners.[16] The large firms of the late 1880s were private ventures getting less and less aid from an increasingly cost-conscious government. Like Osaka Cotton-Spinning, these firms were in business for profits and not to provide welfare for the unemployed. If, however, extending a little incidental poor relief would facilitate production, companies were happy to get involved: when earthquakes, floods, or other natural disasters in various parts of the country swelled the ranks of the Osaka region's population, cotton entrepreneurs sometimes helped disaster victims make the move.

In 1889 the human tragedy caused by a flood in the Tanabe region of Wakayama prefecture gave the Dōjima Cotton-Spinning Company a golden opportunity to recruit sorely needed female operatives among the victims who had lost parents and other relatives and needed to support themselves. Dōjima reached potential recruits through prefectural officials who passed along to village headmen the company's request for young women between the ages of thirteen and twenty. Dōjima was able to collect about 180 hands in this way.[17] Two years later Settsu Cotton-Spinning Company also found aid to the destitute to be profitable. "Shortly after Settsu Cotton-Spinning began operations, the Nobi earthquake occurred. With the object of carrying out relief for the distressed, the company recruited female hands in Gifu prefecture. . . . The female hands who came because of the earthquake contributed a great deal to the operation of Settsu's Number Two Factory."[18]

---

[15] Nōji chōsa, pt. 3, cited in Kitazaki, "Meiji 22 Tenma sutoraiki," 63.

[16] Fujibayashi Keizō suggested that even before the proliferation of large cotton-spinning companies in the late 1880s, not all managers were as benevolent and not all workers were as loyal as portrayed in Kinugawa Taichi's classic Honpō menshi bōseki shi. See Fujibayashi, "Meiji nidai bōseki rōdōsha," esp. 166–68.

[17] Ōsaka asahi shinbun, 6 October 1889, cited in Kitazaki, "Meiji 22 Tenma sutoraiki," 64.

[18] Kinugawa, Honpō menshi, 4:286. Unfortunately we do not know what conditions were like in the Number Two Factory in 1891, but Ushiyama Saijirō found conditions in Settsu's Number One Factory to be among the worst he had seen in the many mills he visited in 1897. See Ushiyama Saijirō's articles published in Jiji shinpō in 1897, reproduced as "Kōjō junshi ki" (Records of an inspection tour of factories), in Fujin mondai hen (Women's problems), ed. Meiji bunka kenkyū kai (Meiji Cultural Research Association), vol. 16 of Meiji bunka zenshū (Collected documents on Meiji culture) (Tokyo, 1968), especially "Saikatō no ichi

Strangers from other parts of the country needed housing when they came to Osaka prefecture, but they had to fend for themselves. Following Osaka Cotton-Spinning's budget-minded example, companies in this and other urban centers ordinarily did not provide living quarters until the middle of the 1890s. Exceptions like Kanegafuchi Cotton-Spinning in Tokyo existed, but, as indicated by a newspaper reporter's account of Tokyo Cotton-Spinning's decision in 1891 to close its dormitory for female employees, at that time the company dormitory was not yet a conspicuous part of spinning operations.

I was told that since last year the dormitory has been closed. Presumably, in dormitory accommodations for mill hands strict supervision is essential. Yet there are few individuals available who are suitable candidates for dormitory supervisors. The dormitory was built and a dormitory director appointed. But because they went in and out through the director's entrance, [the sight of the director's superior food and accommodations] encouraged the hands' dissatisfaction with meals and other things and consequently produced that evil, workers' solidarity. It was not just unforeseeable things such as increased charges for a doctor's or a washerwoman's services that caused problems. Because they were separated from their parents they would cunningly stay away from work even when they were only slightly ill. And they would always be going out on what they claimed was family business. Such mischief occurred too frequently, and thus the dormitory was done away with and the switch to commuting [to work] was made.[19]

A few years later, cotton-spinning companies all over Japan would begin constructing dormitories to confine and control female hands from distant villages. These structures sharply curbed the freedom of movement apparently experienced by Tokyo Cotton-Spinning boarders in 1891. The cotton-thread industry, which increasingly included machine weaving among its operations, never completely lost its reserve army of urban and suburban poor. A core of women and girls continued to trudge to the mills each day with their lunches under their arms. As the years passed, however, commuters represented a steadily declining percentage of the mills' work forces.

---

kōjō" (The factory that gets the worst grade), 344–45. This article originally appeared in *Jiji shinpō*, no. 5043, 21 October 1897. Ushiyama's comments are especially interesting because he tended to be highly uncritical of what he saw and presented employers' viewpoints approvingly. His newspaper, *Jiji shinpō*, was the business community's mouthpiece. Sumiya Mikio, *Nihon chinrōdō no shiteki kenkyū* (Historical studies of Japanese wage labor) (Tokyo, 1976), 233.

[19] *Tokyo nichi nichi* (Tokyo daily), 14 February 1892, quoted in Sumiya, *Nihon chinrōdō*, 206.

Competition for Workers

As the 1880s moved on, more and more plants were established. When a new plant opened, it was considered absolutely essential to have a core group of experienced workers able to teach others. At a mill about to open, managers often felt that the only way to acquire the veteran spinners needed to start operations was to lure them away from another company. Even after a mill had been in business for a while, it often continued to recruit by raiding competitors rather than spending time, skill, and money training and maintaining its own work force.

When the Amagasaki Cotton-Spinning Company of Hyōgo began operations in 1890, the company sent ten individuals to Hirano Cotton-Spinning to get some training. Then Amagasaki's management tried to put together a work force by attracting workers employed elsewhere. A technician would be sent as an Amagasaki undercover agent to a rival company, like Hirano, that was far enough away for its workers to know little of Amagasaki. There he would take every opportunity to tell female operatives about "the marvelous treatment" Amagasaki hands received. Eventually, some of the operatives would be persuaded to go back with the technician to his company's mill at Hyōgo. Amagasaki went after workers as far away as Nagoya and Okayama but concentrated especially upon experienced hands in closer Osaka mills. Three neighboring firms, Fukushima, Nihon, and Dōjima, were raided energetically. Amagasaki officials were not able to succeed with a secret agent inside Kanegafuchi the way they had done at Hirano, but they did manage to rope in some Kanegafuchi operatives they met at Oguchi, tucking them away conveniently in rented rooms until the furor caused by their disappearance had died down and they could be quietly brought to the Amagasaki mill. Of course, Amagasaki agents who carefully staked out points along the routes traveled by commuting mill women were not the only company representatives to do so. Wherever current or prospective mill hands walked, got off trains, or got into boats, cotton-spinning company recruiters could be found. On festival days, among the crush of female pilgrims visiting the image of a popular Goddess of Mercy (*Kannon*), company men were awkwardly conspicuous.[20]

As the industry boomed after the Sino-Japanese War of 1894–1895 and had to compete with silk reeling's keen demand for female labor, the fight

---

[20] Kinugawa, *Honpō menshi*, 4:181–85. Even Osaka Cotton-Spinning, which hired its work force before many of the other mills existed, had to fight for operatives. After a number of companies including Settsu and Hirano were established, Osaka Cotton-Spinning found itself shorthanded. Thus it had to enter into the competitive struggle for female operatives around 1890. See Kinugawa, *Honpō menshi*, 2:412–13.

for mill hands became ferocious.[21] Not only experienced operatives became targets of raiding forays; very ordinary workers were also waylaid. As "secret agent" technicians became known, a company would instead send a handsome male clerk or machine operative to work in a rival firm—if necessary under an assumed name. Such "lady-killers" would lure young women as much by capturing their hearts with honeyed words and filling their heads with dreams of romance as by telling them tales of better wages and working conditions.[22] A company would hire recruiting jobbers and pay them so much a head for the human booty they brought in to operate spinning machines. This provided opportunities for enterprising but unscrupulous middlemen who "introduced" the same group of young women to several different companies, pocketing a fee each time.[23] Investigators from the Ministry of Agriculture and Commerce who documented such practices at the turn of the century reported the case of one such jobber who, as an adherent of the Tenrikyo religion, managed to persuade female hands who shared his religion to leave their employers and follow him.[24]

Of course not all hands had to be enticed or persuaded. Individual workers left mills where they were badly treated or underpaid in order to switch to companies that offered higher pay and the hope of better conditions. The company to which such a worker had been contracted to work a fixed period of time might not release her from her contract and might keep the passbook (*tsūcho*) in which her name, domicile, and wage record was entered. A worker theoretically needed it in order to get a job in another cotton-spinning concern, but that proved no barrier. The new employer might provide her with a new passbook, and a worker often carried around a number of different passbooks, sometimes with different names on the cover of each. Her latest employer would turn a blind eye to signs that she was a runaway from another mill.[25] Managers like Osaka Cotton-Spinning's Okamura Katsumasa—who burst into a meeting between a group of his company's operatives and a recruiter from Kanegafuchi to lecture the hands about the evils of continuously changing employers—might admonish and chastise until their faces turned blue. Their own firms rarely

---

[21] Despite the protests of domestic cultivators of cotton, the import tax on raw cotton from abroad was abolished in 1896. With raw cotton from the United States and India freely entering the country, Japan's cotton-thread exports made great strides: soon they were holding their own among British and Indian threads in the Chinese market. Nakamura Masanori, *Rōdōsha to nōmin*, 158.

[22] Ibid., 156; Nōshōmu-shō, *Shokkō jijō*, 71.

[23] Nōshōmu-shō, *Shokkō jijō*, 72.

[24] Ibid.

[25] Kinugawa, *Honpō menshi*, 4:182; Nōshōmu-shō, *Shokkō jijō*, 71: Sumiya, *Nihon chinrōdō*, 195–96.

refused to employ a competent hand who came over from a rival.[26] Attempts to organize an industrywide alliance in 1882 and 1888 failed to stop companies from raiding each other.

Employers who lost contracted employees did not attempt to introduce incentives aimed at retaining their most productive workers. Managers of newly founded companies especially, who were often very inexperienced themselves, appear to have begrudged expenditures for training and maintaining workers and preferred instead to rob other firms when they could.[27] Such an attitude now seems astonishing, particularly when one considers the new technology that workers had to master. Because mechanized silk production involved turning silk reels by steam- or waterpower instead of by hand, the first Japanese machine reelers of silk could use their traditional handicraft skills in the factory. But machine-spun cotton produced on complicated imported machinery was a very different proposition: cotton hands had to learn entirely new processes on willow machines, scutchers, carding machines, drawing frames, slubbers, intermediate frames, roving frames, ring-spinners, and winding machines.[28] Spinners could learn to operate the ring-spinner much faster than the mule it was coming to replace, but even in British mills operators spent about three to four months learning how to manage ring operations properly.[29] That managers did not spend much time formulating plans to keep those they had trained tells us a great deal about their attitude toward their laborers. Despite the need for trained workers in machine spinning, cotton managers continued to view their operatives as dispensable, ever-renewable resources. When companies lost workers, they first sought fresh ones and only second—when the costs of recruiting began to daunt them—thought of ways to retain the workers they already had. And usually they thought of punitive ways to detain employees rather than of incentives to encourage them to stay.[30]

To refill the ranks left by defections and desertions, cotton-spinning companies began to search for prospective employees all over rural Japan, as their counterparts in silk manufacturing were doing. To keep the workers they had already acquired, they took other clues from the silk industry, building dormitories and holding back wages. With less energy they made attempts not only to draw up but also to enforce industrywide agreements

[26] Kinugawa, *Honpō menshi*, 2:412–13.

[27] Fujibayashi, "Meiji nidai bōseki rōdōsha," esp. 154–55.

[28] Yokoyama, *Nihon no kasō shakai*, 157.

[29] In Britain it took from a year and a half to two years for a worker to master mule operations. Murakami Hatsu, "Sangyō kakumei to josei rōdō," 87.

[30] There were a few exceptions to this pattern. Amagasaki, for instance, apparently pioneered policies aimed at providing amenities that might encourage workers to stay with the firm. Kinugawa, *Honpō menshi*," 4:187–88.

regarding employment practices. An important factor in such moves to increase control over cotton hands was a number of wildcat strikes, which struck fear into the hearts of cotton-spinning managers.[31]

Mill Women in Revolt

The Tenma disturbance of 1889 was such a strike.[32] As the depression caused by the Matsukata deflationary policies was ending in 1886, cotton spinning flourished in the Osaka region and elsewhere. Floods in 1889, however, seriously damaged harvests and consequently sent the prices of rice and other commodities soaring. High prices meant widespread hardship in the cities, and the cotton-spinning workers found their low wages even less adequate than usual. The different rates paid by different cotton firms for the same jobs made it even harder for hungry individuals getting the lowest wages to drag themselves to work every day. Wages at the Tenma Cotton-Spinning Company of Osaka were particularly low.

On 30 September 1889 about three hundred women in the winding room at Tenma decided they had had enough. Calling upon their fellows to join them in a strike, they refused to leave the mill dining hall after the noon break. They demanded to talk to managers about their need for higher pay. Supervisors were able to ease the women back to their workplaces by promising to pass on the call for a raise to the company president. But at five-thirty in the late afternoon the women stopped operations again. Gathering in front of the mill gate, they urged women coming in for the night shift to join them. The next day when the cry for higher wages continued, management decided something had to be done quickly. The company's first official response was to discharge those suspected of being leaders and to lecture the others. This was expected to put a swift end to the rebellious rumblings. Yet despite the fact that the superintendent in charge of operatives fired a spokeswoman and chastised her companions severely, the results were not as management had anticipated. Male operatives joined the female workers and, although the company dismissed more individuals believed to be particularly influential activists, the disturbance grew. On 3 October, spinning-room operatives joined the strike.

The strikers added three other sets of demands to the one for higher wages, but the wage demand appears to have been paramount.[33] An immediate wage hike was urgently required by workers, who could not afford highly priced food and other necessities. This demand was also motivated

[31] Sumiya, *Nihon chinrōdō*, 207.

[32] See contemporary newspaper accounts reproduced in Rōdō undō shiryō iin kai, *Nihon rōdō undō shiryō*, 1:132–34, and Kitazaki, "Meiji 22 Tenma sutoraiki."

[33] *Ōsaka asahi shinbun*, 5 October 1889, reproduced in ibid., 133.

by the fact that Tenma paid less than other companies. As the *Ōsaka asahi shinbun* (Osaka morning sun newspaper) of 5 October pointed out, since wages at Tenma were "two or three rin [a day] lower than at Dōjima Cotton-Spinning, this request was not unreasonable."[34] A second demand, that the company pay the overdue half-year bonuses stipulated in their employees' contracts, was also closely related to income needs. (These bonuses had been due on 20 September.) The third demand was for an end to "unfair treatment," practiced by managers and other supervisory male personnel. This "unfair treatment" consisted of favoring some women and penalizing others on a superior's whim. The fourth demand was an attack on the five-year term of the contracts and the company's practice of holding back a portion of wages accumulated during the five-year term, presumably to be returned to the worker when her contracted term expired.

Since Tenma had only begun operations the previous year, no worker was even two-fifths of the way through her or his contract. The fourth demand suggests that there were strong feelings about held-back wages: the workers felt that all earned wages belonged to them and that no part of them should be kept by the company. The practice of holding back a portion of wages earned would soon become widespread, but in 1889 it was still fairly new in the industry. Five-year contracts were not unknown in cotton spinning but they were unusual; the norm for a contracted time period was three years.[35] With the fourth demand, Tenma hands were telling their bosses that they expected standards in the industry to be observed.

Strikers standing in front of the gate when shifts changed in the morning and evening were able to get support to bring about another work stoppage. Although company officers scurried about in rickshaws, visiting the workers' homes to put pressure on their families, about four hundred hands remained out on strike.

Then on 4 October, company officials did what Meiji companies so often did in strikes: they called in the local police. Police broke up the crowd of workers and supporters in front of the mill gate, admonishing the strikers severely. At the company's request, the police next day arrested sixty men and twenty women and took them away for a thorough interrogation. From the company's point of view, a major problem was management's inability to discover who were leaders and who were followers. It was hoped that police questioning would be more effective than the diligent but fruitless probing undertaken by company officials. Company opinion held that if only the "ringleaders" could be identified and dismissed the troubles would be over.

[34] Ibid.
[35] Kitazaki, "Meiji 22 Tenma sutoraiki," 69.

On the same day that the arrests were made, some of the four hundred striking day-shift hands began to succumb under their employer's persistent bullying: they started drifting back to work. Several hundred night-shift workers refused to do so, angrily reminding their comrades that the company "won't hear of a wage hike but doesn't mind paying out loans on our future earnings."[36]

Exhaustive police interviews and company investigations failed to uncover "the ringleaders," and the firm's admonitions began to soften. Veiled hints and vague promises of improvements reached the strikers' ears. Acknowledging that the strike had been caused by high prices and the workers' difficulties in making ends meet, Tenma offered its mill hands a wage raise and promised to pay, by 20 October, the half-year bonuses to all whose company service extended back before June. For their part, the strikers agreed to send the company an apology through the superintendent of operatives. The work stoppage ended on 5 October.

Participation of the police as strikebreakers was backed by powerful legal sanction. Law 270, which became part of the penal code in 1882, facilitated easy introduction of the police into the dispute. This law stated that "all workers engaged in agricultural or industrial labor who, with the goal of increasing wages or changing the conditions of their labor, shall employ stratagem or force against their employers or against other employees in order to hinder the work shall be punished by imprisonment with hard labor for from one to six months and by a fine of from three to thirty yen."[37] Just calling the police to come and disperse gatherings, with violence if necessary, was a powerful weapon for companies. Employers were also able to use Law 270 to prosecute strikers in criminal court. Five years after the Tenma dispute of 1889, the Tenma Cotton-Spinning Company used this law against some of its mill hands who once again were out on strike.[38]

In 1894 Tenma operatives' exasperation was directed as much at individual supervisors as it was toward shortfalls in expected remuneration. Worker discontent with a superintendent of operatives erupted on 26 January of that year. The superintendent in question, a man called Ozaki, was a graduate of Tokyo Kōgyō Gakkō (Tokyo Engineering School) who had joined the firm the previous August. Despite his impressive school credentials or perhaps partly because of them, he was highly unpopular on the factory floor. Workers complained that he demonstrated unfairness in the way he decided increases and decreases in wages for individual workers.

[36] Ōsaka asahi shinbun, 6 October 1889, in Rōdō undō shiryō iin kai, Nihon rōdō undō shiryō, 1:133.

[37] Saitō Isamu, Nagoya chihō rōdō undō shi (History of the labor movement in the Nagoya region) (Nagoya, 1969), 82.

[38] See articles in the Ōsaka asahi shinbun, 24 and 28 January, 1, 3, 4, and 18 February 1894, reproduced in Rōdō undō shiryō iin kai, Nihon rōdō undō shiryō, 1:134–35.

The *Ōsaka asahi shinbun* reported that he did not know how to manage workers.[39] Ozaki was accused of arbitrarily raising the wages of good-looking female operatives while treating plain-looking ones coldly and lowering their wages without cause. It was also Ozaki's job to look after the bonuses workers expected to receive. Workers claimed he had been unfairly lowering the amounts to be paid.

Another complaint concerned the amount of New Year's money that everyone had just received. Since it was the custom for Tenma, like other companies, to celebrate the New Year by presenting a small gift of money to each operative, every January each Tenma hand had been presented with fifteen sen. But the 1894 New Year's envelopes did not contain even one sen; the company gave each hand a measly five rin.

As the shift changed at 6:00 A.M. on 26 January, thirty workers assembled in the mill dining room and urged workers coming off their shift to join them in a strike. As the call went through both the old and new plants, emotions were running high. In the confusion, a glass door was broken, and someone was injured on the broken glass. Company officials found subordinates unresponsive to orders. While some company officers addressed the hands with soothing words, others quietly sent for the police. Constables came, arrested some workers, and ordered the rest to leave the premises, urging them to go home. Some of the rebels, however, did not return to their homes; instead they gathered at a neighborhood café (*nikuya-san*) and talked. When the shift changed again at 6:00 P.M., the group of dissidents from the café were found urging comrades going in for the night shift to stop work. The swift appearance of constables from the local police station soon broke up their demonstration: thirteen were arrested and the others were sent away so night-shift hands no longer met distractions as they filed in to their machines.

Then suddenly, within the factory, something happened. A small group of operatives who had worked the night shift the previous night began to distribute a crude handbill reading, "Stop night work tonight!" Swiftly this message went through the ranks, and soon many workers joined a gathering that earnestly discussed grievances. Those participating agreed that it was essential to get rid of Ozaki and two other technicians who treated hands unjustly. Unhappy voices demanded a strike if the situation in the mill did not improve. Some suggested that moderate demands for higher wages would, at the very least, get the hated supervisors replaced by "normal" ones who would listen to grievances regarding injustice.

This impromptu meeting was the company's cue to call the police. This

[39] Ibid., 134. Andrew Gordon, *The Evolution of Labor Relations in Japan: Heavy Industry, 1853–1955* (Cambridge, Mass., 1985), 38–39, cites cases of workers in heavy industry resenting technicians who were graduates of technical training schools.

time the firm picked out six men from among the throng of male and female workers, had them arrested, and formally charged them under Law
270 of the Criminal Code with using influence to perpetrate a false scheme
against an employer and other employees. Interestingly enough, while the
company prepared a court case against the unlucky six, it also tried to undercut discontent. After a thorough questioning of seven other defiant
workers, Tenma Cotton-Spinning announced that of the twelve hundred
hands (70 percent of whom were female) henceforth men who made less
than thirty-three sen a day would be given another six, while women who
made less than twenty-three sen a day would be awarded an additional
five.[40] The plan was to punish the "ringleaders" severely while rewarding
the rank and file for withdrawing their support from the protest.

Нhowever, there was a great deal of community sympathy for the arrested
strikers, who were tried in Ōsaka Chihō Saiban (Osaka Regional Court).
Volunteering their services, a number of lawyers came to defend the six
men on not-guilty pleas. Workers subscribed to a fund for the expenses of
the six: those who had little gave generously—even children made dona-
tions—until an impressive sum of between sixty and seventy yen was collected.[41] While the six were at court their families were looked after by
workers, and hundreds of others made monetary contributions to the distressed families. The circle of support for the accused and their cause extended far beyond Tenma's employees: the Ōsaka asahi shinbun reported
that the "evil" thoughts that had prompted Tenma workers to raise the flag
of opposition to their supervisors were spreading to hands at other cotton-
spinning plants, where workers were becoming more defiant in their resistance to supervising technicians.[42] Despite energetic attempts to get back
to old routines, Tenma itself was not able to return to normal operations
during the trial and experienced economic losses as a consequence. Some
employees refused to go back to work; more than 120 signed a solidarity
pledge of support for the strike. Among those who did go back to work at
Tenma, there was also much sympathy: hands would go directly from a
shift to a meeting to discuss events and hear the latest news about the arrested men.

On 17 February, the Osaka Regional Court found four of the accused
guilty, fined them three yen apiece, and sentenced them to two months in
prison at hard labor for planning a work stoppage on the morning of 22
January. The court found the other two prisoners innocent. Although the
three-yen fine was a heavy one for workers to pay, it was the lightest monetary penalty stipulated for those convicted under Law 270. With the com-

[40] Rōdō undō shiryō iin kai, Nihon rōdō undō shiryō, 1:135.
[41] Ibid.
[42] Ibid.

pany holding all the cards, the verdict was probably as favorable as the defenders of the six could expect to get. Police, law, and court were always the friends of the company, never of the workers.[43]

With the strike "leaders" convicted, at Tenma it was back to work as usual. Three years later when Tenma operatives struck in protest over a supervisor's discrimination against female operatives from Ishikawa prefecture, an admonitory lecture from the local police sent them back to their machines.[44] In the summer of 1894 a strike by female operatives in Mie Cotton-Spinning in Nagoya, which had been ignited by male supervisors' discriminatory treatment of the women, also failed after five "leaders" were arrested.[45]

Quite rightly, much has been made of the power of Article 17 and Article 30 of the Peace Police Law of 1900 to prevent labor from organizing or striking.[46] But before 1900, Law 270 could be used against workers attempting to negotiate with an employer.[47] With such legislation in the background, just calling for the local constables could effect miracles for a management facing angry workers with serious grievances.

Such magic appears to have been used against employees of the small Ōmi Asaito Cotton-Spinning Company in Shiga prefecture in 1891. At the beginning of that year, Ōmi Asaito mill hands were extremely dissatisfied with what the New Year had brought them. Workers at Ōmi Asaito were customarily raised one grade in the company's salary classification each January, but in January 1891 there came no word of any such promotions. When workers complained to their superiors that they could not help feeling demoralized when even the greatest devotion to output failed to bring any sort of a raise, they were told that this year they could not expect to receive what they usually got. On 16 February, emotions exploded: seething with anger, the mill's sixty hands left their machines and converged on Korinji Temple in a village in Ōtsu to decide what they should do. There they discussed and debated, finally choosing ten representatives to take two demands to the management: (1) that promotions be made according to company rules, and (2) that accumulated wages which the company had held back be handed over to the workers immediately. Accumulated wages were the 1 percent of monthly wages that the

[43] According to Ōsaka shi-yakasho, *Meiji Taishō Ōsaka shi shi*, 4:642–43, only one of the six was found innocent. However, this book was written much later than the contemporary newspaper accounts.

[44] Ibid., 644; Aoki Kōji, *Nihon rōdō undō shi nenpyō* (A chronological table of the Japanese labor movement), 2 vols. (Tokyo, 1968), 1:57.

[45] Ōkōchi Kazuo, *Reimei ki*, 27.

[46] The articles can be found in Sumiya Mikio, *Nihon rōdō undō shi* (A history of the Japanese labor movement) (Tokyo, 1966), 59. An English translation of them can be found in Stephen S. Large, *The Yuaikai 1912–19: The Rise of Labor in Japan* (Tokyo, 1972), 3.

[47] See Saitō, *Nagoya chihō*, 82.

company deducted each month. The group instructed its delegates to tell Ōmi Asaito managers that unless these two proposals were accepted the operatives would not return to work. The demands were not received calmly. Refusing to consider any part of them, management sent word that all hands were to be fired the following day.

When they heard this news, the angry operatives marched to the mill and set about smashing machinery amid a general commotion that grew louder and louder. They only halted when the smooth-talking son of a company official dashed into the middle of the fray and urged them to wait and present their two demands at the following month's meeting of the company's executives. As this young man pleaded, tempers abated and rioters began to leave the mill. The ten chosen as representatives went off to discuss what might best be done. Meanwhile managers sent for the police. After a stern lecture from the chief of the Kuwayama Ōtsu police station, the workers sent an apology to the company and agreed to go back to work. The evening ended with an outwardly civil meeting of workers and bosses, with both sides agreeing that the strike was now officially over.[48]

Even the powers of police and state could not assure the employers all the victories. In a bitter 1896 strike at the Mitsukoshi Kinuito Cotton-Spinning Company in Shinmachi, Gunma prefecture, sixty-four cotton workers successfully resisted measures that lowered wages, imposed harsher fines than before, and introduced a particularly humiliating method of levying those fines.[49] The Mitsukoshi Kinuito hands may have succeeded partly because of the inexperience of their supervisors, newly transferred to the Shinmachi factory. Certainly the strikers' solidarity and militancy were increased by the fact that new, untried, and untrusted managers had introduced the hated measures. But more crafty managers, who exploited their familiarity with their workers' habits and needs, fired workers indiscriminately, or brought in police officers without notice, could prove invincible foes.

Obviously money was a central issue in the work stoppages in cotton mills. As in the case of the hardship brought about by the high prices of 1889, external circumstances could drive workers to aggressive action. But even louder than the clamor for pay raises was the demand for money that female and male workers claimed as rightfully theirs because they had already earned it. Operatives at Tenma in 1889 and at Ōmi Asaito in 1891 demanded that their employers stop holding back a portion of wages each month as forced savings. The operatives needed all of their wages immediately—not at some future date when it might suit their employers, who

[48] *Kyōto nisshutsu shinbun* (Kyoto sunrise news), 17 February 1891, in Rōdō undō shiryō iin kai, *Nihon rōdō undō shiryō*, 1:135–36. Unfortunately there are apparently no records explaining precisely why or how the workers became "amicable."

[49] Rōdō undō shiryō iin kai, *Nihon rōdō undō shiryō*, 2:52–53; Aoki, *Nenpyō*, 1:39.

in the meantime had full use of the money. Similarly, unpaid half-year bonuses, which Tenma workers had already earned according to their contracts, were seen as funds stolen from operatives. Other remunerations, like the contents of New Year's envelopes and raises accompanying annual promotions, were also viewed as portions of wage packets that employers had promised. When Tenma hands in 1894 struck partly because of the almost empty New Year's envelopes and Ōmi Asaito operatives in 1891 objected to suspension of wage-grade promotions, they felt they were claiming wages they had already earned, not asking for more. Unmoved by company pleas of economic difficulties, workers knew—as Tenma employees pointed out in 1889—that a firm which claimed it could not afford to pay its hands what they had already earned could always find the funds to advance loans on future earnings. And such loans would have to be paid back with heavy interest. Fairness and justice required that the workers receive what was theirs, not that they be penalized by being denied what they had already earned.

An even clearer theme was the workers' rejection of unfair or discriminatory treatment. Ozaki was hated because he abused his power to decide who earned more and who earned less. Both male and female hands suffered under Ozaki, and workers of both sexes supported the 1894 protest at Tenma, although the company singled out six men as "the ringleaders." But much of the discrimination protested against was discrimination directed at women. At Tenma in 1889 and 1894, and Mie in 1894, discriminatory treatment of female hands by male supervisors engaged in sexual harassment was a central cause of disputes. Women who found this intolerable felt all females in the mill were entitled to equal pay for equal work. Since their demands included equal opportunity to do equal work, they rose up against discriminatory treatment on the factory floor. Like the silk workers in Kōfu in 1885, they refused to work under male supervisors who favored the fair of face, the unattached, the sexually compliant, while they penalized the less pretty, the married workers, the ones who would not even flirt.

A spontaneous solidarity brought mill women together to resist abusive male supervisors and encouraged them to unite with male workers against employers who tried to chip away at what little the operatives had. This solidarity had its limits and did not always withstand pressure from employers.[50] Still, it could sustain extraordinarily fierce campaigns. With the state and its laws always on their side, companies could quickly get local

---

[50] Yokoyama, *Nihon no kasō shakai*, 199, reports female operatives protesting against the company's hiring a girl who was a member of the former outcaste class, a "new commoner" (*shin-heimin*).

law enforcers to intervene.[51] But bosses who pushed workers too hard in too arbitrary a fashion often found themselves facing militancy serious enough to disrupt production, at least temporarily.

Once a strike was underway, protesters faced the probability of grave hardship. Unless they struck immediately after payday, they might lose wages owed to them. They might be fined heavily, they might lose their jobs, they might be blacklisted by other employers, they might even be arrested and charged with a crime. Yet support from families and neighbors, as well as from fellow workers at their own mill or other mills, was extended to the blacklisted and prosecuted, as the Tenma disturbances of 1889 and 1894 make clear. Observing this, company policymakers increasingly pondered the feasibility of sending out agents to hire large numbers of young women in distant country districts. Strangers in an urban setting, such girls would not be able to draw upon the family and community connections that sustained strikers during a dispute.

A declining number of local workers continued to be hired, but by 1897, forty-eight cotton-spinning firms were routinely recruiting in areas far from their mills.[52] Thirteen years later, as the Meiji period was drawing to a close, more than 66 percent of the individuals leaving their rural homes "to go out to work" (dekasegi) in other places were heading for cotton-spinning mills in the cities.[53]

[51] Saitō, *Nagoya chihō*, 82–83, discusses regulations prohibiting strikes promulgated by the Osaka prefectural administration.

[52] Takamura, *Nihon bōseki-gyō shi josetsu*, 1:303; Nishinarita, "Nihongata chinrōdō no seiritsu," 112.

[53] Sanpei, *Nihon mengyō hattatsu shi*, 388.

7

Cotton: Recruiting in the Hinterland

Recruiting

Male employees, a minority in the work force, continued to be hired from among job seekers who applied directly to the mill, but cotton-spinning companies everywhere were soon engaging professional labor brokers in different parts of the country to recruit female employees. By 1898, employers believed they knew what kind of workers they could expect from recruiting agents active all over Japan. The report of the employers' Greater Japan Cotton-Spinning Alliance (Dai Nihon Menshi Bōseki Dōgyō Rengō Kai) published for its members in that year categorized female hands tersely. Natives of Osaka and Tokyo, living at home with their families, were frivolous, showing poor endurance and perseverance when they met with difficulties. Few of them could be expected to finish their contracts. Women from Kagawa prefecture were similar in character to Osaka and Tokyo folk; they were not able to save money because they squandered it on food. Workers from the prefectures of Hyōgo and Hiroshima were stupid and illiterate, but they tended to be satisfied with simple food and clothing and many of them completed their contracts. Shiga workers were obedient and thrifty rustics. Ishikawa prefecture women were honest, but if they became dissatisfied they united and took action without breaking ranks. Recruits from Yamaguchi were stubborn, but they saved well, sending money home to their parents regularly. Niigata women were avaricious and covetous; they displayed outward obedience, but one never knew what they might do behind one's back. Hands from Okayama and Ehime were inclined toward obedience, but those from the latter prefecture showed poor records of perseverance and endurance. Wakayama workers were insincere and quit readily. Those from Aichi, Gifu, and Fukushima were unsophisticated—simple, honest folk. Those who came from regions in Kyūshū were not clever, but they were straightforward people who obeyed orders, persevered, and put up with more difficulties than all the others. Nevertheless when Kyūshū women were dissatisfied, they formed alliances and went on strike.[1]

---

[1] Uga, *Bōseki shokkō jijō chōsa gaiyō*, 10–11. The statistics in this report done for the Greater Japan Cotton-Spinning Alliance were for the previous year, 1897. The report declared the desired worker to be one who was unsophisticated and honest, and had great powers of endurance. Ibid., 11.

Usually male, although this was not required by law, a recruiting agent was normally a native of the rural region in which he sought potential mill hands. Like the men who gathered young girls for silk mills, these agents would promise the sky to the poor peasant girls they wooed. A labor broker would talk about fixed hours of work with a regular holiday each week for city entertainments and festive excursions. To children who toiled almost every waking hour (except during the rare village festival celebrations) this must have sounded like heaven. The agent described abundant, tasty food—real white rice, not those unhulled grains and rough grasses. He talked about a gleaming company dormitory equipped with hospital and schoolrooms. He might even show a picture of young girls learning sewing in what he claimed was a dormitory schoolroom. The company he represented was so good to its employees, he told his listeners, that it even provided them with clothing—and not just factory uniforms to save wear and tear on their regular clothes. Those who went to work for this company would be presented with a kimono, that graceful, elaborate garment which young female hearts longed for but knew that, as the daughters of poor cultivator-owners or tenants, they could never hope to own. Then, carefully directing his words at the father of the girl he hoped to ensnare, the recruiter would talk of the money to be earned in high wages and generous bonuses by all those who worked hard. Since his audience usually consisted of people who had worked hard all their lives, this proviso did not make them less receptive to what he was proposing. Fathers and mothers thought of the money, usually desperately needed. Their daughters thought of the alluring prospects dangled before their minds' eyes. The timid who hesitated to leave their familiar surroundings or the mother or father who was reluctant to let a young one go were assured that the recruit could come back home to visit or to stay permanently anytime she chose to do so.[2]

Recruiters' lies begot expectations of healthful, remunerative, pleasant employment in cotton spinning, expectations so far divorced from reality that the shock unsuspecting country girls experienced when they reached the mills was enormous. The records left by runaway mill hands, who poured out tales of their shattered dreams to investigating officials of the Ministry of Agriculture and Commerce at the turn of the century, reveal how unquestioningly so many of them accepted recruiters' promises and how unbearable they found the realization that they had been tricked.[3] Employers themselves bitterly complained about the damage recruiting

---

[2] Nōshōmu-shō, *Shokkō jijō*, 69–70; ibid., Appendix 2, 534; Uga, *Bōseki shokkō jijō chōsa gaiyō*, 30–32; Hosoi, *Jokō aishi*, 71–78; Sanpei, *Nihon mengyō hattatsu shi*, 389–90.

[3] Nōshōmu-shō, *Shokkō jijō*, Appendix 2, 534–35.

agents did with their lies. The 1898 report on cotton workers' conditions put out by the Greater Japan Cotton-Spinning Alliance complained that

> there are great abuses in the recruitment of factory workers. If a company official is used as a recruiter he [as a stranger] often has no credibility in the district to which he is sent, and this produces poor results. However, if outside recruiters are used then they do not look to the interests of those who are recruited or who are candidates for recruitment but only go after large commissions. They lie to candidates, talking about easy labor for high wages and so forth because if they inform them of the real conditions no one will be willing to be recruited. Both [types of recruiter] use deception. When the recruited person starts to work, she is shocked because everything is so different from what she expected. So she runs away and the loss is the employer's.[4]

After enumerating "evil practices" of outside recruiters—which included enticing young girls to leave for cotton-spinning employment without their fathers' permission, taking company money advanced to recruits away from the girls by force, pocketing commissions from one company and then delivering girls to another company for a second set of commissions, or placing girls recruited for cotton spinning in entirely different types of employment—this section of the report concluded that it was the malfeasance of commissioned recruiters that caused people to harbor bad feelings toward cotton manufacturers and made it difficult to recruit factory workers: "Each company should endeavor to cease employing commissioned labor brokers and instead hire directly [send company officials to districts to hire] or use established employment agents to recruit."[5]

Alas, "direct hiring" by company officials did not necessarily eliminate the abuses. A dispatched salaried company employee or one stationed in a company's local recruiting branch office would be unlikely to whisk the girls he recruited off to another company, to sell them to a brothel, or to get them jobs as maids—as independent brokers did, simultaneously collecting commissions from several parties. But as the employers' association report noted, company officials also employed the kind of deception referred to as the "sweet words" of recruiters. And it was the difference between what sweet words described and what actually existed in the mills that caused so many new recruits from the country to run away.

The leaflets that companies had printed up for distribution to the families of potential recruits all over Japan contained less blatant lies than those some of the commissioned brokers told, but the pictures they painted did not accurately reflect reality.[6] In *Nihon no kasō shakai* (The lower classes of

[4] Uga, *Bōseki shokkō jijō chōsa gaiyō*, 30.
[5] Ibid., 31.
[6] See Hosoi, *Jokō aishi*, 71–73.

Japan), Yokoyama Gen'nosuke reproduced an information sheet used by a cotton company to recruit in the hinterland during the 1890s. One can see how such brochures would raise hopes.

Information

1. Factory girls are between the ages of twelve and thirty-five and in good health.

2. Contracted term of employment is three years. When entering the company, one's sealed contract must be presented. It is required that one work continuously throughout the term of employment. In a case of absolutely unavoidable need, a leave of absence up to five weeks may be taken, but anyone taking such a leave has to return to the company money spent in recruiting that person. When the individual returns from her leave of absence, this money will be given back to her.

3. After working the full three years of her term of employment, a worker may continue to be employed.

4. Because the work is spinning cotton on large machines, it is not so demanding. Within a daily work shift of twelve hours, one gets one hour of rest. One does one week of day shift and then one week of night shift in turn. With Sundays, festival days, New Year's, and Obon, there are many holidays.

5. The new employee's travel expenses are paid by the company. Upon arrival in Osaka one may stay in a dormitory where bedding and even eating utensils are lent free of charge. The meals provided are cooked by professionals. Even though meals cost eight sen per person, during the probationary period the company provides them for no charge. However, from each worker who earns more than eleven sen a day, six sen daily [toward food] is collected.

6. In the dormitory is a bath, which is also free of charge. One may take a bath in the morning and in the evening.

7. In the dormitory a sermon is given each month. There is also a school where one can be taught reading, writing, arithmetic, and even sewing during nonworking hours every day.

8. There is a sick bay in the dormitory, and individuals who are ill can always get medical examinations. The company provides the medicines.

9. A child is not charged for board during her probationary period. She will also receive a monthly allowance ranging from fifty-four sen to one yen. As she becomes more skillful, she will be able to earn from eleven to thirty-three sen daily. Depending upon where they work, adults will begin at a daily wage of eleven or twelve sen. Those who do piecework are able to make from five or six yen to over ten yen a month.

10. Those who work well and are well behaved may be appointed as room supervisors in the dormitory and receive allowances in addition to their wages.

11. Funds held back [from wages] are security deposits and compulsory savings. From her security deposit, a worker earning more than twelve sen a day

pays board, and 15 percent of the rest of her wages is set aside as savings, which cannot be withdrawn until the end of the contracted employment term. The 15 percent that is compulsory savings may be sent home to parents or handed over on rare occasions when clothing or something else is being made. The remaining 70 percent of the wages is paid to the individual each month.

12. Factory girls paid daily wages receive a bonus of two days' wages for one month's perfect attendance at work. Those absent one day during a month get a bonus of one and a half days' wages; those absent two days during a month and those on night shift away one night during a month receive a bonus of one day's wages. Those probationary workers who are not on daily wages receive a bonus of ten sen if they work a month without being absent. Regarding pieceworkers, those who have perfect attendance during the month get a bonus of twenty sen, while those who are away only one day during the month get a bonus of fifteen sen, and those absent for two days during the month or away one night on the night shift get a ten-sen bonus. In addition, those with more than a year's continuous service receive another fifteen sen each a month, and each year afterward this bonus goes up ten sen a month. Thus those with more than three years' service receive an extra thirty-five sen each month.

13. During each half year, there are bonuses for those with perfect attendance for five months or more and for those who are assigned to important jobs because their work is so good.

14. Those who are conscientious in their work and surpass their assigned quotas receive bonuses according to their output.

15. Those who work faithfully during their contracted term of employment are rewarded with three yen a year in addition to wages and bonuses, and those who work continuously get five yen a year.

16. There are various other rewards, life insurance, and allowances provided according to the company rules.[7]

By the twentieth century, large companies were using plays and even movies to show entertainment-hungry villages "the real conditions" in the mills. But the happy, healthy-looking young faces and figures that appeared in such dramatizations in immaculate white aprons and short *hakama* (divided skirts) were a far cry from what one would see in the actual factories.[8] The gap between what girls and women were told when they were in their home villages and what they found in the factories remained. And this gap continued to cause new recruits to run away.

They were not supposed to run away, because they were legally bound by the agreements their fathers or guardians had signed before they began their journeys to the mills. In fact, fathers often signed "consent documents" even before they put their seals to their daughters' three- or five-

---

[7] Yokoyama, *Nihon no kasō shakai*, 196–98.
[8] Hosoi, *Jokō aishi*, 70.

year contracts. Before 1889, "contracts" in cotton spinning normally had been oral agreements between employers and their hands.[9] But as costs of recruiting rose, legally binding documents came to play an important part in hiring. As soon as a recruiter had talked a farmer into allowing his daughter to be one of the girls taken to the mill, he would get the farmer to put his seal on a "document of consent" (*shōdaku sho*), giving permission for the child to work in a given company for three or five years. Immediately after seals were set to this simple paper, the recruiter would hand the father a sum of money. As in silk-mill recruiting, this transaction went into company accounts as "preparation money," expenses for preparation for the journey to the mill, but the cash usually was spent right away on pressing family needs, perhaps on rent to the landlord or on food. Sometimes the father signed a form promising to repay this sum if his daughter left the firm before she had worked there for six months—surely any sturdy daughter would last six months, no matter what the hardship.

While the recruiting agent efficiently made transportation arrangements for the girl to get to the mill, no mention was made of travel costs to the family. What the girl and her parents often learned after the girl was working at the mill was that money spent on travel was a loan to be repaid with interest out of the girl's future earnings. When the girl made this discovery she was often angry.

> Everything Mr. ——— [the recruiter] said was a lie. The day after I came to — ——— [the mill] a person who looked like an official told me that my travel and lodging fees amounted to so much; the train cost so much; the horse carriage, so much. We said that if we had known from the start that the travel costs would be so high we would not have come. . . . The person who looked like an official said, "It will be taken off your pay, a little each month until four yen have been deducted."[10]

Contracts

The contracts themselves were longer than the documents of consent, and although the wording varied they all contained provisions in the following categories:

1. A fixed period of employment from three to five years in length
2. A prohibition against working for any other employer during this time period
3. The importance of not allowing company secrets about work techniques to become known outside of the company

9 Yokoyama, *Nihon no kasō shakai*, 200.
10 Nōshōmu-shō, *Shokkō jijō*, Appendix 2, 535.

4. The necessity of obeying strictly all company regulations and orders from employer and superiors

5. The impossibility of requesting release from contracted employment in any circumstances except those involving dire calamity

6. The company's unilateral right to lay off workers whenever it saw fit to do so

7. The company's unilateral right to pay wages as it saw fit

8. Infringements of the factory regulations or of the contract leading to forfeiture of wages earned and of other money owing from the company[11]

These one-sided agreements gave even more power to the company than is apparent from the above summary, as the "factory regulations" that the girls were contracted to obey were legion. Spelled out in them were a multitude of requirements and prohibitions. The following are some of the major ones: workers were never to be absent from work shifts; they were always to be punctual, and punctuality meant being on the job at least twenty minutes before the twelve-hour shift began; workers were to spend time cleaning machinery after the twelve-hour shift was over; clothing to be worn on the job was designated; each week when the machinery was halted a general cleaning of it had to be done; male and female workers were not to interact in any way outside of work; in an emergency when release from contract was requested, all proper procedures were to be followed.[12]

For good measure, some companies made the young women and their fathers or guardians, along with third-party guarantors, sign pledges like the following:

Pledge Document (for new employees)

Address _____ Status _____
Employee's Name _____
Employee's Age _____

Upon being accepted as an operative of your company according to the application, the above person hereby pledges, for a period of three years from the present, not only to work industriously in all good faith, abiding by the company's regulations. She also pledges in work and other matters under no circumstances to disobey any of your directives. Moreover, in fulfilling this pledge, not

[11] For precontract documents see Hosoi, *Jokō aishi*, 93–95; for contents of contracts see Nōshōmu-shō, *Shokkō jijō*, 77; Sanpei, *Nihon mengyō hattatsu shi*, 391; and Uga, *Bōseki shokkō jijō chōsa gaiyō*, 33.

[12] See "Matsuyama bōseki kabushiki kaisha kōjō kisoku" (Matsuyama Cotton-Spinning Corporation factory regulations) and "Okayama bōseki kaisha shokkō kisoku" (Okayama Cotton-Spinning Company factory worker regulations), reproduced in *NFMSS*, 3:162–72.

only the employee but also the guarantor and applicant, in all matters concerning the employee's behavior, shall take responsibility so that no difficulties will arise. In witness whereof we set our seals to this pledge.

Year _____ Month _____ Day _____   Employee's Name   _____ [seal]
                                        Address and Status

                                        Guarantor's Name   _____ [seal]
                                        Address and Status

                                        Applicant's Name   _____ [seal]

To the Matsuyama Cotton-Spinning Company Limited.[13]

Many—perhaps most—of the fathers who placed their seals on employment contracts could not read these documents. Illiteracy was often the norm in families with potential mill hands,[14] but recruiters did not have to count on this alone. Unlike the handbills and brochures filled with glowing descriptions of mill life and work, which were written in simple sentences with the phonetic furigana script provided in the margin beside all Chinese characters, legally binding documents were written in difficult, specialized language. Even when such documents were read aloud, neither parents nor daughters understood them fully. This of course gave unscrupulous recruiting agents much leeway to "explain" the contents with very free translations.

Fathers, uncles, brothers, and husbands put their seals to contractual documents both as legal guardians of the newly hired female workers and as legal guarantors that the girls and women would fulfill their contractual obligations. In return for taking on the legal responsibility, often they were to receive sums deducted monthly from the female hands' wages. In order to get this money for themselves, recruiting agents sometimes put their own names down as guarantors. When they did so, illiterate fathers and daughters had no idea that this money was being stolen from them and their families, because they were unaware that they were entitled to it.[15]

---

[13] Ibid., 170.

[14] See Nōshōmu-shō, *Shokkō jijō*, 77; Yokoyama, *Nihon no kasō shakai*, 179–91.

[15] Sanpei, *Nihon mengyō hattatsu shi*, 390. There were many abuses in sealing contracts. *Shokkō jijō* authors describe cases of contract renewal when the worker herself, rather than her parent, put her seal (in all likelihood her family's seal or a facsimile thereof) on the contract. In one instance, a clerk in the factory office asked a girl to lend him her seal for a moment. He took it, affixed it to the contract, and the worker was unknowingly bound over for another time period of mill work. Nōshōmu-shō, *Shokkō jijō*, 77.

Continuing Abuses

Recruiters who enticed girls whose parents had refused to give them permission to go to work in the city mills were in an especially strong position to reap the benefits of acting as guarantors.[16] And persuading a girl to run away from home was just a step short of kidnapping potential workers, which recruiters who had worked in the cities had long been doing, capturing employees of one company when they were walking around town on a rare day off, meeting trains bringing recruits to town in order to carry off the newcomers by force. Recruiters' abuses were so notorious that the prefectural government of Osaka passed bylaws in 1894 to regulate recruitment, and four years later the prefectural administrations of Hyōgo, Kagawa, Ishikawa, Tottori, and Fukui enacted similar bylaws.[17] Such prefectural legislation appears to have had very little impact; abuses continued as before.[18]

Unethical activities raised the costs of recruitment: the employers' survey published in 1898 claimed that recruitment expenses averaged out to six yen, sixty sen per head.[19] This, as Takamura Naosuke points out, was the equivalent of two months' wages for the average cotton-spinning operative.[20] Since these costs were all regained from future wages of those hired, the companies rarely ended up paying for any of them out of profits. Thus there was no great incentive to reform noxious recruiting practices.[21] A company might incur losses when a new recruit ran away soon after she had reached the mill, but the firm more than made up for these when it confiscated held-back earnings left behind by those who ran away after several months, a year, or two years. Legal action could also be taken against an absconding girl's father or guardian who had sealed her contract. There were loud complaints about unscrupulous recruiting agents

[16] See Nōshōmu-shō, *Shokkō jijō*, Appendix 2, 590–91, for cases of girls who went off to work in textile mills in spite of the fact that their parents, who suspected that the recruiters' promises were lies, had refused them permission to go.

[17] Uga, *Bōseki shokkō jijō chōsa gaiyō*, 31.

[18] Nōshōmu-shō, *Shokkō jijō*, 77. See Uga, *Bōseki shokkō jijō chosa gaiyō*, 30–32, for documentation of abuses after municipal bylaws were passed for the Osaka region. The problem continued beyond the Meiji period: in 1925 an ordinance was promulgated to halt continuing abuses. See Yoshisaka Shinzō, "Labor Recruitment in Japan and Its Control," *International Labor Review* (Geneva) 12 (October 1925): esp. 495–96.

[19] Uga, *Bōseki shokkō jijō chōsa gaiyō*, 20.

[20] Takamura, *Nihon bōseki-gyō shi josetsu*, 1:304.

[21] See Uga *Bōseki shokkō jijō chōsa gaiyō*, 22, for acknowledgment of this. According to the survey data in this report, a company only occasionally paid some of the recruiting expenses of a worker. Even when a company did so, its contribution merely involved reimbursing a worker for some of her travel expenses after the worker had fulfilled her contracted term of employment. Ibid.

and rising costs. But since workers, not employers, paid for the expensive system, companies continued to depend on the new batches of girls from the hinterland whom recruitment brokers brought to the mills each year.

Many of those recruited were very young, although contemporary investigators disagreed concerning how many of them were children under fourteen years of age. The age profile in *Shokkō jijō* taken from the cotton-spinning employers' survey published in 1898 is very similar to that of silk workers in *Shokkō jijō*: during 1897, 1.4 percent of female cotton-spinning operatives were younger than eleven years old, 17.1 percent were aged eleven to fourteen, 46.1 percent were aged fifteen to twenty, and 35.4 percent were twenty or older.[22] Yokoyama Gen'nosuke, on the other hand, questioned this profile. Noting that he himself had seen large numbers of juveniles in Osaka area mills, he cited an independent study done of 15,680 cotton operatives in twenty-two mills in Osaka prefecture. This study, done by a private educational society in Osaka, found that 4,290 of these operatives, that is, more than one-quarter of them, were less than fourteen years of age, and Yokoyama felt that the number of such child workers might even be higher.[23] Acknowledging that cotton plants in Tokyo and other regions employed far fewer children than did Osaka mills, Yokoyama was nevertheless suspicious of the employer association's statistics.[24]

Employer Agreements

Like silk employers, cotton manufacturers collaborated on industrywide agreements. A major goal of these was to restrict the movement of workers

Table 7.1
Ages of Male and Female Cotton Workers in 1897 (number and percent)

	Male		Female		Total	
Under 11	254	(1.7)	813	(1.4)	1,067	(1.5)
11–14	1,085	(7.1)	9,559	(17.1)	10,644	(14.9)
15–20	4,090	(26.7)	25,805	(46.1)	29,895	(42.0)
20 and Over	9,870	(64.5)	19,826	(35.4)	29,696	(41.6)
Total	15,299	(100)	56,003	(100)	71,302	(100)

Source: Nōshōmu-shō, *Shokkō jijō*, 45.[a]
[a] Taken from the employers' survey done in 1897 and published in 1898.

[22] Nōshōmu-shō, *Shokkō jijō*, 45.
[23] Yokoyama, *Nihon no kasō shakai*, 159.
[24] Ibid., 161.

from company to company, but since firms continued to raid each others' work forces right up into the twentieth century, the agreements were often ineffective. In 1893 the Greater Japan Cotton-Spinning Alliance drew up an accord that pointedly prohibited a firm from hiring workers who had formerly worked for another employer in the industry. Yet 1894 was a year when luring and kidnapping cotton workers under contract to someone else was particularly widespread.[25] A special article outlawing abduction of workers was added to the industry agreement in 1902, but it failed to stop kidnapping.[26] Although cotton manufacturers seem to have spent more energy on organizing alliances and writing agreements than did their counterparts in silk, the efficacy of such activity appears to have been limited.[27]

Failure to put an end to the raiding (and the heavy turnover of mill hands to which it contributed) did not prevent employers from uniting to undercut workers' protests. Agreements outlined detailed provisions for employee behavior and harsh penalties for workers who did not adhere strictly to regulations. Such provisions included strong measures for strike prevention and punishment for those who might encourage others to strike. An 1888 accord, for instance, called for the names of all workers linked to strike action to be circulated to all companies in the industry. Members of the cotton-spinning alliance were forbidden to hire such workers. In the event of a strike at one company, other employers who were a party to the agreement had to lend workers to the strike-bound firm. This kind of provision appears to have been much more effective than the general prohibitions against engaging a worker contracted to another employer. At the general meeting of the cotton-spinning alliance in 1889, an official from Osaka Cotton-Spinning credited the agreement's section on strikebreaking with enabling his company to put down a strike.[28] Agreements did not stop employers from grabbing workers any way they could, but they effectively united those employees against operatives in all mills through unilaterally imposed working conditions, heavy fines, insecurity of tenure, and low wages paid at employers' convenience.

[25] Hazama Hiroshi, *Nihon rōmu kanri shi kenkyū* (A history of Japanese labor relations) (Tokyo, 1978), 265.

[26] Sanpei, *Nihon mengyō hattatsu shi*, 393–94.

[27] Hazama, *Rōmu kanri*, 274–75; Takamura, *Nihon bōseki-gyō shi josetsu*, 1:311.

[28] Dai Nihon menshi bōseki dōgyō rengō kai, "Dai Nihon menshi bōseki dōgyō rengō kai giroku" (Greater Japan Cotton-Spinning Alliance minutes) (March 1889), cited in Takamura, *Nihon bōseki-gyō shi josetsu*, 1:159.

8

Cotton: Inside the Hateful Company Gates

Prison Life in the Dormitories

Most of the workers in the pioneer mills with two thousand spindles or fewer had commuted to work.[1] A few of these mills, however, had provided dormitories for female operatives, as Mie Cotton-Spinning did for samurai daughters from the former domain of Tsu.[2] When bigger mills were built in Osaka, Tokyo, Nagoya, and a few other urban areas after Osaka Cotton-Spinning's historic breakthrough in 1883, company stockholders and managers felt no compulsion to provide dormitory accommodation. But during the 1890s, as rural recruits were secured in ever larger numbers, employers realized that these young women needed to be housed, preferably where they could be easily influenced by management. Closely supervising employees' movements from living quarters to factory floor, cotton manufacturers hoped to reduce absentee and runaway rates. Executives, who once considered a hostel for female workers like that provided by Kanegafuchi an unnecessary expense, were abuzz with plans to construct their own. Kurashima Cotton-Spinning built a dormitory in 1893, and other firms quickly followed suit.[3] By 1897—when the amount of Japanese cotton thread exported had begun to exceed the amount of foreign cotton thread imported—in the seventy mills operated by the sixty-eight cotton-spinning companies of Japan, fifty-five of the companies (and fifty-seven of the mills) had dormitories filled with women and girls from all over the country.[4]

These dormitories, like those attached to silk mills, were intended to keep female workers from running away. The prisonlike function is clear from the construction: generally two stories high, they were built right beside a mill—either within an eight-foot fence that enclosed both the mill and its dormitory or surrounded by its own equally high fence and connected to the mill by an elevated bridge.[5] On top of the fences were intimidating adjuncts like sharpened bamboo spears and barbed wire.[6] Many

[1] Kinugawa, *Honpō menshi*, 3:178; Sumiya, *Nihon chinrōdō*, 204.
[2] Ibid., 184.
[3] Hazama, *Rōmu kanri*, 269.
[4] Takamura, *Nihon bōseki-gyō shi josetsu*, 1:303; Nakamura Masanori, *Rōdōsha to nōmin*, 155.
[5] Hosoi, *Jokō aishi* 195, offers simple diagrams of dormitory and mill construction patterns.
[6] Ibid.

mills were situated with a water barrier such as an ocean, river, or swamp on one side; others had a moat surrounding the factory building and adjacent dormitory. One dormitory built beside its mill on Nomi Island in Hiroshima prefecture caused Nomi Island to be nicknamed "slave island."[7] "Describe a dormitory for female mill hands in one word and *pigsty* would be the word," wrote Hosoi Wakizō, noting that, daunting as the outside of dormitories appeared, exteriors were beautiful when compared to what one found inside.[8]

Within the dormitory walls were tatami-matted rooms, in which as many girls and women as possible were supposed to sleep. Freezing in winter, such rooms were often unbearably hot in summer. At best a person had one tatami mat of about six by three feet as her living space when she was not working in the mill. But as in the silk-mill dormitories, ten individuals were often packed into eight-mat rooms, and there is a reliable report of a record twenty-six women squeezed into a ten-tatami room— although the count of twenty-six may have included both day-shift and night-shift workers.[9] With the plants on day and night shifts, two girls shared the same space, using the same inadequate wadded cotton sleeping quilts.[10] Sometimes two girls would wear, in turn, the same sleeping garment.[11] With such arrangements, a worker who was ill could not stay in bed. The limited toilet and washing facilities were often in an appalling state: toilets were not kept clean, and with a hundred girls using the same bath water it became grimy.[12]

Yamanouchi Mina, who first went to work in a cotton-spinning mill in 1913 when she was twelve, remembered unsanitary conditions in the large dormitories erected during the mid-1890s: "Usually when I went to the bath it was full and I could not get in. In a bath about twice as big as a normal-sized bath, over a thousand people would bathe. No matter what time you went there it was full. If, after two or three attempts, you got in, the water was always filthy. I don't think I ever even once had a bath in clean water."[13] As in silk-company dormitories, crowded, dirty living quar-

---

[7] Ibid.

[8] Ibid., 194.

[9] Nōshōmu-shō, *Shokkō jijō*, Appendix 2, 616.

[10] According to Uga, *Bōseki shokkō jijō chōsa gaiyō*, 103, usually individuals were assigned to a sleeping space of 1–1½ *tsubo* (1 tsubo = 3.3058 meters). Because of the shifts only one individual was supposed to be sleeping in that space at one time. See also Yokoyama, *Nihon no kasō shakai*, 175–76, and Nōshōmu-shō, *Shokkō jijō*, 115.

[11] Nōshōmu-shō, *Shokkō jijō*, Appendix 2, 594.

[12] Ushiyama Saijirō, "Kōjō junshi ki," esp. 233, 344–45. See also Nōshōmu-shō, shōkō-kyoku, ed., *Kōjō oyobi shokkō ni kan suru tsuhei ippan* (Common evils afflicting factories and factory workers), seven-page pamphlet (Tokyo, 1897), 2.

[13] Yamanouchi Mina, *Yamanouchi Mina jiden: jūni sai no bōseki jokō kara no shōgai* (The

ters ensured the spread of disease. Employers argued, however, that health hazards were caused by the dormitory residents, girls from poor, ignorant families who had not been taught anything about sanitation.[14]

The promise of rice every day brought many to the mills, but food served in the dormitory dining room was far from appetizing. Rice was indeed the mainstay of each of the day's three meals, but it was an inferior grade of rice, sometimes mixed with other coarse grains and often badly cooked. With the rice went a few pickles or a thin soup or a small portion of vegetables. Occasionally, a tiny amount of bean curd or an egg was substituted for the soup.[15] The employers' association report insisted that this food was more than good enough for the daughters of poor farmers and fisherfolk who were not used to anything nearly as fine.[16] Employers argued that dormitories provided better food than was available in the mill hands' homes in the countryside.[17] Yet Ministry of Agriculture and Commerce investigators found the rice and side dishes to be not only of poor quality but badly prepared and so evil smelling as to be quite unappetizing.[18] Hosoi Wakizō, from firsthand experience in the mills, described kitchen workers dishing out food for thousands of factory hands on humid, summer days. Hosoi told of food in the dishes spoiling before the workers had a chance to consume it.[19] Mill girls themselves reported to government investigators that dormitory food was terrible.[20] One runaway told ministry investigators how she had demanded the white rice her contract promised she would be fed. When she did this, police came to inspect the food, which then actually did improve—but only temporarily; in a short while meals were as before.[21]

The mills charged dormitory residents for meals whether or not they were consumed. Companies complained that food cost them more than what they charged their hands for it. In 1897, journalist Ushiyama Saijirō

---

autobiography of Yamanouchi Mina: My career from the time I was a twelve-year-old cotton-spinning factory girl) (Tokyo, 1975), 19.

[14] Uga, *Bōseki shokkō jijō chōsa gaiyō*, 115.

[15] Nōshōmu-shō, *Shokkō jijō*, 115.

[16] Uga, *Bōseki shokkō jijō chōsa gaiyō*, 111.

[17] Nōshōmu-shō, *Shokkō jijō*, Appendix 2, 593.

[18] Ibid., 114.

[19] Hosoi, *Jokō aishi*, 202.

[20] There are many examples of girls complaining thus about the food to government investigators in Nōshōmu-shō, *Shokkō jijō*, Appendix 2. Even as late as the 1920s, cotton-spinning operatives bitterly complained about the food they were fed. In the results of a questionnaire Tōyō Muslin Company put to its female operatives, the second most common reply to the question, "What is the biggest problem you have with dormitory life?" was "the taste of the food." The only answer more frequently given was "illness." See the forty-page pamphlet published by Tōyō Muslin: Tamura Tarō, ed., *Jokō-in kun shiryō* (Materials for the training of female factory workers) (Tokyo, 1922), 21.

[21] Nōshōmu-shō, *Shokkō jijō*, Appendix 2, 526.

reported what employers told him: a woman's board cost a firm about six or seven sen a day, but she was only charged about five sen a day for it.[22] But the companies' self-congratulatory claims regarding their expenditures on food were wrenched from their true context, that is, the low wages dormitory residents were paid for their work in the adjacent factory.

Not only was the quality of food poor and its preparation shoddy, there was not enough of it to fill the stomachs of young women who did more than twelve hours of exhausting work at their machines every day. The employers' association survey published in 1898 reported that daily meals in the dormitories gave workers from four to five bowls of rice a day.[23] This meant that a girl could expect to have a second bowl of rice once or at most twice a day—and the standard-sized bowl would hold roughly a cup of cooked rice. Hunger drove workers to spend most of what little money they had on sweets and other food sold for profit in company stores or by vendors who visited the factories.[24] Itinerant vendors and operators of company canteens often had a captive market. Yet dormitory residents preferred to give their orders to a girl who had permission to leave the factory to bring them back food from town, where the prices were lower and the selection better.[25]

Their families back home might be hungry too and shivering at night in the cold.[26] But the strict regulation of the dormitory workers' lives made many girls and women long for the life back home among loved ones, however harsh it may have been. A key figure in this regulation was the room supervisor. Each dormitory room was headed by such a supervisor, a veteran worker usually older than most of the others in the room and presumably chosen for her job because she displayed dedication to the company's interests. Ideally, a supervisor could read, as part of her job was to check all outgoing mail for any references unflattering to the firm. The supervisor also was supposed to scrutinize all incoming correspondence received by the women and children under her charge. Authority to with-hold incoming parcels and letters was an important source of a supervisor's

[22] Ushiyama Saijirō, "Kōjō junshi ki," 314. Uga, *Bōseki shokkō jijō chōsa gaiyō*, 111, claimed that girls paid two to four sen less than what the food cost the company.

[23] Uga, *Bōseki shokkō jijō chōsa gaiyō*, 111.

[24] See Orimoto Sadayo, "Myōnichi no josei: jokō o kataru" (Women of tomorrow: Talking about factory women), *Chūō kōron* 44, no. 12 (1929), reproduced in *NFMSS*, 3:239–43. Yamanouchi, *Yamanouchi Mina jiden*, 21, recalls a company store located near the entrance to the dormitory.

[25] Uga, *Bōseki shokkō jijō chōsa gaiyō*, 115; Nōshōmu-shō, *Shokkō jijō*, 113. *Shokkō jijō* reported that in one mill in Kyoto the operatives set up a cooperative store to sell clothing and sundries to themselves. They received support from the company, which gave them free use of the store premises and an interest-free loan to get the venture started. Ibid.

[26] See Irokawa Daikichi, *The Culture of the Meiji Period* [*Meiji no bunka*, 1970], translation ed. Marius B. Jansen (Princeton, 1985), 219–44.

power, because the lonely youngsters longed for news from their families.[27] To know or suspect that news had come but was being withheld must have been unbearable. Reliable witnesses have reported that it was common practice not to tell a girl when communication came from her home.[28] "Father came from Nagoya and said that he had sent two letters. I never got them. They [company officials] said that someone had forgotten to give them to me. Then they handed them over."[29]

Why would the companies fail to pass on parcels and letters from home? Perhaps some of the answer lies in the exercise of petty power by supervisors who might confiscate the small edible treats or humble articles a girl received from her relatives. In addition, company policies usually discouraged contact that would make a girl think she had any option other than working in the mill until the end of her contract. A letter from a parent would probably be passed along if it contained something like: "Please work hard and earn all you can. The family is counting on you." One that said "We need you here" would be destroyed. Outgoing letters that contained any uncomplimentary reference to the firm, working conditions, or dormitory life were usually tossed into the wastebasket.[30] If, on the other hand, the letter writer was not conveying negative images of her life in the dormitory, she might be encouraged to contact her parents. Since so many of the girls were illiterate and room supervisors might read and write, supervisors sometimes wrote letters for girls and read them the ones they received. This not only gave supervisors the opportunity to edit and censor mail; it also put operatives under obligation to them.

Room supervisors had other powers that induced operatives to flatter them and wait upon them. Newcomers customarily were not permitted to leave factory and dormitory grounds until they had worked diligently for several months, showing no inclination to run away.[31] Although permission to leave the grounds had to be obtained from the dormitory supervisor as well as the room supervisor, the latter, charged with watching for hints that a girl might be entertaining thoughts of escape, could refuse permission no matter how long or how well a girl had been working.[32] If a woman returned even five minutes late from an outing, not only might

[27] This situation lasted years beyond the Meiji period. In its 1922 survey of its 1,414 female operatives, Tōyō Muslin Company found that by far the largest number of them stated that "the happiest thing" in their cotton-spinning lives was a parcel or letter from home. Tamura, *Jokō-in kun*, 30–32.

[28] Yamanouchi, *Yamanouchi Mina jiden*, 27; Hosoi, *Jokō aishi*, 177–78; Nōshōmu-shō, *Shokkō jijō*, Appendix 2, 593.

[29] Ibid., 540.

[30] Hosoi, *Jokō aishi*, 177–78; Ushiyama Saijirō, "Kōjō junshi ki," 345.

[31] Nōshōmu-shō, *Shokkō jijō*, 70.

[32] Ibid., 118, acknowledged the opportunity for abuse of the power held by room supervisors and other dormitory officials.

she be kept in for months, but all her roommates might be denied permission to leave the grounds.

Sometimes girls were not allowed to leave unless they were accompanied by company officials or by trusted senior workers. Often a mill would let a girl out only if it was just before payday; then she knew that if she ran away she would lose hard-earned wages.[33] Not to be granted permission to get away from the mill and dormitory on one's own time was one of the restraints most resented by dormitory residents. Runaways repeatedly declared how much they were angered and disappointed when the promise of sightseeing in the city turned out to be a lie.[34] This restraint and the resentment it generated continued far beyond the Meiji period.[35] A cotton worker's song captures something of the dormitory inmates' feelings:

The dormitory supervisors strut about,
But look closely at them and you'll see
They are only persimmon seeds.
When the factory shuts down
And you go back to the dormitory,
You think of nighttime in the village
With the frogs croaking.[36]

Bodies were confined but hearts lived elsewhere.

As false as the promise of city sightseeing was the assurance of educational opportunities in the dormitory. Opportunities to learn to read and write had attracted both young girls and their parents, but, glowing descriptions in brochures and recruiters' "sweet words" notwithstanding, dormitory "schoolrooms" were few and small. In a firm that boasted two or three teachers, "teachers" would turn out to be clerical staff asked to give a few lessons in reading or arithmetic in a corner of the dining room. The promised "sewing instructors" were busy dormitory supervisors and room supervisors who might or might not give one a hand with a needle. Yokoyama Gen'nosuke found little evidence of the educational facilities in

[33] Sanpei, Nihon mengyō hattatsu shi, 392.

[34] See Nōshōmu-shō, Shokkō jijō, Appendix 2.

[35] In April 1924, an article written by an anonymous cotton-spinning worker appeared in a special women's edition of Rōdō (Labor). It bitterly complained about dormitory curfews. The author described how, after working conscientiously for three months, she was at last allowed to request permission to leave company premises for a day. When she eagerly presented herself at the mill gates as soon as they opened on Sunday morning, she was told that she must return before 3:00 P.M. Angrily she claimed that employers "don't care how cramped or dirty the dormitory may be. Thinking of factory girls as beasts of burden they hardly even let us leave the grounds." "Watakushitachi no seikatsu" (Our lives), Rōdō (Labor) (April 1924), reproduced in NFMSS, 3:236.

[36] Nakamura Masanori, Rōdōsha to nōmin, 166.

the mills featured in company advertisements.[37] Even in the model Kane-gafuchi Cotton-Spinning Company, which actually did have pupils study-ing in regular classrooms, Yokoyama found the numbers of such pupils much fewer than the company claimed.[38] As Yokoyama, *Shokkō jijō*, and the employer association's report of 1898 all acknowledged, the crux of the matter was that young people who were mentally and physically exhausted after twelve or more hours of hard labor on day or night shift were in no condition to take advantage of two hours of classroom instruction after work.[39] And such instruction was not available in all mills. What is amaz-ing is not that those who went to lessons were few in number. What is astonishing is that there were any students at all in classes at Kanegafuchi and other firms that made some effort to live up to their advertisements. The hunger for education on the part of such pupils was extraordinary. The odds against getting to class—not to mention staying in class day after day—were enormous.[40] As *Shokkō jijō* observed, "For education to be ef-fective, the hours of work must be shortened."[41]

It is certain that among the workers education was lacking. The results of the 1897 survey done for the Osaka Society for Factory Workers' Edu-cation (Ōsaka Shokkō Kyōiku Kai) revealed that only a small percentage of the industrial workers surveyed appeared to have any sort of literacy—only 8 percent of the female factory workers surveyed had finished the or-dinary course of elementary schooling, an achievement that presumably signified basic literacy.[42] But schooling was not among the companies' con-cerns. Many companies (including cotton-spinning companies) did not even bother to respond to the questionnaire sent out by the Osaka Society for Factory Workers' Education.[43]

The one kind of "education" companies were generous with was "moral education." Its content was similar to what silk workers encountered in lectures and texts discussed in chapter 5. At least two "morality magazines" were published for company use. These contained materials that lecturers

[37] Yokoyama, *Nihon no kasō shakai*, 184.

[38] Ibid., 185.

[39] Uga, *Bōseki shokkō jijō chōsa gaiyō*, 119–23; Yokoyama, *Nihon no kasō shakai*, 186; Nō-shōmu-shō, *Shokkō jijō*, 111–12.

[40] Yokoyama found 60 students in the first year of the Kanegafuchi "school," 82 students in the second year, 38 third-year students, and 1 fourth-year student. See Yokoyama, *Nihon no kasō shakai*, 185.

[41] Nōshōmu-shō, *Shokkō jijō*, 112.

[42] There are, of course, problems involved in measuring literacy. Should one use attendance at school rather than completion of a set course as a yardstick? And how did school-leavers retain any literacy skills they may have acquired when they had few opportunities to use these once they had left school?

[43] Yokoyama, *Nihon no kasō shakai*, 179–84; Sanpei, *Nihon mengyō hattatsu shi*, 396.

could use in their talks.[44] Of course there were company songs to teach employees and to inspire and uplift them.[45] Morality magic-lantern shows also became common in the twentieth century.

Japanese Christians or foreign missionaries visited mills to talk to the workers. *Shokkō jijō* notes that after one such visit the women who had heard a missionary lecture petitioned their employer to ban Christian missionaries from their mill.[46] Unfortunately this report does not state the reasons given for the request, but the following account of a visit by Christians to a mill may offer some clues. Yamakawa Kikue, who was to become a prominent feminist-socialist organizer of working women, has described how, as an inexperienced eighteen-year-old from a middle-class home, she accompanied Christians who took their moral message inside a Tokyo cotton mill on Christmas morning of 1908.

> Since the mill was on continuous night and day shifts, the young girls who had done twelve hours on the night shift finished their meal and gradually drifted into the lecture hall. With their hair hanging down in plaits, their cotton, striped, tight-sleeved garments, their bare legs and sockless feet, they looked twelve to fifteen years old. Although these young girls looked like children, there was no liveliness among them. Pale and exhausted with faces like invalids, they came into the room. Near the front, on the cold wooden floor, mats were spread out and there were about fifty or sixty young girls there. On the platform was a charcoal brazier for the benefit of the lecturers. It was so cold [in the room] that it reminded me of one of those gray days just before the snow falls. It was enough to freeze one's very bones. Led by the lecturers and accompanied by an organ, the young girls sang the Christmas song printed on the blackboard. Then Mr. Yamamuro stood up and spoke. "Lord Jesus Christ was a worker like all of you. He was a carpenter. Work is holy. All of you must become good workers like Lord Jesus. If you give thanks to God for being able to get safely through your work each day, God will surely answer this prayer." Such was the gist of his talk. Then Teacher Kawai Michiko gave a similar talk about the holiness of labor. In a voice quivering with emotion she prayed for a long time. The meeting closed with a hymn.
>
> I remember I couldn't stand that room and that platform. I felt my whole body shake with shame and rage. What blessings from God came into the lives of these pale young girls with the lifeblood sucked out of them, who had worked without sleep all night beside roaring machines? What blessings deserved thankfulness? Should their slave labor be treated as holy?
>
> That day we saw the factory workplaces, the dormitory, and where they ate. I wanted to ask the girls how they themselves felt but was not permitted to do so.

[44] Nōshōmu-shō, *Shokkō jijō*, 112.
[45] Hosoi, *Jokō aishi*, 286–91.
[46] Nōshōmu-shō, *Shokkō jijō*, 112.

Surely this kind of Christianity is just to keep management happy. . . . Right after the meeting, Mr. Yamamuro and his colleagues left. I never wanted to do anything with those people again.[47]

This mill at least had a room for instruction even if it lacked desks or other amenities. It is highly unlikely that the girls ever used it for their own entertainment. Entertainment or recreational facilities were even more rare than schoolrooms: a track meet once or twice a year was generally the only organized play activity for dormitory workers other than rare festival celebrations.[48]

The other major amenity featured in company brochures was health care. This too was minimal. Clinics existed in the mills, but even in the large plants where they were staffed by a doctor and one or two nurses, they were usually very rudimentary. All but the smallest mills had a quarantine room for victims of contagious disease, but only Kanegafuchi had built facilities especially for quarantine use. Simple treatment and medicine were administered to dormitory residents free of charge and to commuting workers and their family members at prices lower than those in town. For other treatments and medicines there were fees.[49]

Company doctors undoubtedly treated some operatives successfully, but for many of the seriously ill there was little or no effective medical treatment.[50] For one thing, it was difficult for a girl to get permission to be seen by a physician: both her room supervisor and the dormitory supervisor had to authorize a visit to the doctor, and supervisors were under pressure to ensure that all their charges worked a full shift every day or night. Those who obtained permission to go to the clinic tended to be very ill indeed. Moreover, when a physician did examine a girl, he was likely to remember he was the company doctor and as such to understate her illness. The sick were urged to think positively and were sent back to work. The hopelessly ill were sent home to their families. These were obviously in late stages of extremely serious, often fatal, illnesses. As in silk factories, tuberculosis, beriberi, and a host of respiratory, gastrointestinal, ophthalmic, and neurological diseases were rampant in the cotton mills.[51]

---

[47] Yamakawa Kikue, *Onna nidai no ki*, 140–41. Since to a female factory hand a carpenter's status was so much higher than her own, one wonders if the statement that "Jesus Christ was a worker like all of you" held any meaning for the operatives. To the middle-class evangelist of the Meiji era, however, carpenters and factory hands were all lower-class workers.

[48] Nōshōmu-shō, *Shokkō jijō*, 112–13.

[49] Hosoi, *Jokō aishi*, 226–27. Hosoi gives good marks to Kanegafuchi.

[50] Ushiyama Saijirō talked to the father of a girl working for Mie Cotton-Spinning and heard that the father was happy with the medical treatment his daughter had received for her diseased uterus. Ushiyama Saijirō, "Kōjo junshi ki," 317.

[51] Murakami Nobuhiko, *Onna no shokugyō* (Women's occupations), vol. 3 of *Meiji josei shi* (A history of Meiji women) (Tokyo, 1971), 169–70.

Brutality on the Factory Floor

The factory was no more comfortable than the dormitory. Ventilation was poor and workers were known to pass out from the heat. Winter was hard enough, but with windows tightly shut, the hot humid days in summer were hell. Dust and noise reached intolerable levels. In roving and spinning sections especially, cotton fluff flew about everywhere, getting in eyes, noses, mouths, and ears, entering the pores of the skin exposed to it. In constant motion, spinning machines made such a loud clamor that operatives had to scream to make themselves heard. With such a racket it was even hard to hear the mill whistle blowing. After a few years, workers became partially deaf. If the mill contained a weaving section—and many spinning mills did—that section was deliberately kept damp to ensure the quality of the cloth being produced. As a result, weaving rooms were filled with steam and had water dripping from the ceiling. The hair and clothes of workers there were always wet, and the cotton fluff clung tenaciously to their damp faces.

Employers claimed that cotton-spinning operatives only worked eleven hours a day because they received two fifteen-minute breaks and a thirty-minute meal period during each twelve-hour shift. They claimed that an eleven-hour workday was rather short for poor people at the bottom of society.[52] But much of the work that "poor people" in Japan had traditionally done, including agricultural work, permitted changes in tasks and routines and was not performed under the rigid assembly-line conditions of the cotton factory. Stockholders and managers themselves rarely had personal experience of any kind of manual labor. Thus it is quite possible that the fact that there were differences between agricultural labor and factory work, for instance, never occurred to them. Like Yamamuro Gunpei, to whom carpenters and mill hands were equally humble and equally laborers, to men who toiled neither in field nor in factory and had little direct contact with those who did, manual work was all of a piece. The cotton hands themselves made distinctions. Within the mills they found some jobs far more exhausting than others. They sang

The spools are heaven
The ring is hell,
And the roving frame
Carries a wheel of fire.[53]

At any rate, eleven hours of daily work was the "official" time worked, not the actual hours put in. As the authors of *Shokkō jijō* discovered, shifts

[52] Uga, *Bōseki shokkō jijō chōsa gaiyō*, 57.
[53] Nōshōmu-shō, *Shokkō jijō*, Appendix 2, 617.

scheduled from six o'clock to six o'clock were changed to suit a firm's convenience. For two or three hours after the shift ended, operatives could be kept busy at cleaning and machine maintenance or in preparing materials to be used during their next shift. When these hours were added, the result was sometimes eighteen rather than eleven hours of labor. Absenteeism was high on the night shift, so day-shift workers were co-opted to fill vacancies. For those co-opted, it meant working a twenty-four-hour shift. *Shokkō jijō* claimed that some of those who did so were put back on their regular shift after working through the night: these unfortunates worked an unbelievable thirty-six hours straight.[54] Factory rules authorizing two fifteen-minute rest breaks and one thirty-minute meal break were often ignored. Machines were run during official rest periods, so all or some of those who worked them were unable to rest.[55] Operatives often had to eat while their machines were running.[56] Since so many of the hands were paid according to how much they produced, there was great pressure to keep working during breaks. If an exhausted novice paused when the morning whistle blew signaling a "rest period," her mates would scream at her to keep on going—the experienced hand's piece-rate pay depended upon everyone's part in the production process. And of course work supervisors were always on the floor urging everyone to keep on producing, producing, producing. When the machines were finally silent on Sunday at the end of a week, exhausted operatives still had no real "free day" to look forward to: a woman whose term on the day shift was over after 6:00 P.M. Saturday had to begin a week of night shift before 6:00 P.M. Sunday.[57] Bodies damaged by the drastic changes in sleep patterns that accompanied alternating shift work were never given time to heal. The only real holidays observed in most mills were during New Year's and the midsummer Obon festival, when machines stopped running for a few days.

Most workers dreaded the night shift. In the early days the industry had acknowledged this dread by paying slightly higher wages for night work, but in 1890, when all companies had gone over to twenty-four-hour operations, extra payment stopped.[58] Night work thereafter became a routine part of mill work for all hands. Absenteeism was greater on the night shift: while room supervisors escorted their charges to work, it was easier for commuting workers not to appear. When the places of absent workers were not taken by substitutes, those who were present had to do more than their usual share of the work. As a former spinner told government inves-

---

[54] Ibid., 53.

[55] One suspects that, as in Japanese-owned cotton mills in Shanghai two decades later, rest periods were often for supervisory personnel only. See Emily Honig, *Sisters and Strangers: Women in the Shanghai Cotton Mills, 1919–1949* (Stanford, Calif., 1986), 144–45.

[56] Nōshōmu-shō, *Shokkō jijō*, Appendix 2, 550.

[57] Ibid., 49–51.

[58] Hazama, *Rōmu kanri*, 293.

tigators, "Those who were absent got no pay while those who were present did the work of two or three operatives for no more pay than usual."[59]

In chapter 9, Ishihara Osamu's findings regarding the health hazards of night work are examined in detail. According to tests Ishihara did, young girls did not tend to regain weight lost while working the night shift, even after they went back on a day shift.[60] Since those coming off the night shift did not get to sleep until about 10:00 or 11:00 A.M. and were out of bed by 4:00 P.M., many young bodies got only five or six hours sleep a day. Government investigators described the girls who came off the night shift as particularly pale and sickly-looking. An engineer in one mill suggested that few of the women who worked the night shift would have to worry about getting pregnant because those who did night work usually stopped menstruating.[61] A male worker remarked that the only male operatives who liked night work were those with "poor morality," because on the night shift there were fewer supervisors and more opportunities for sexual harrassment.[62] A great many girls and women described the night shift as the most hateful, bitter experience they had to endure.[63]

Often those who worked at night could not sleep in the daytime because it was too light. Many of them endured chronic headaches and stomach pains, often becoming gravely ill. Crying children had to be bribed with sweets to get them down to the factory floor in the evening.[64] Operatives regularly fell asleep on the job. Struggling to keep themselves awake at their machines, they sang:

At two and three in the middle of the night,
The grass and the trees get to sleep.
Is it too much that I should be sleepy?
If the cotton-spinning maids are human beings,
Then the dead trees in the mountains are blooming.[65]

Not all workers dreaded the night shift, however. A few told government investigators that sleeping only four or five hours a day gave them time to do other things. "At first I found the night shift hard, but when I got used to it then it became easier than the day shift. When you are working on the day shift there is no time to do laundry and such or to look after yourself. But on the night shift you can do things in the morning or before you go to work in the evening. . . . However, the night shift is very hard

[59] Nōshōmu-shō, Shokkō jijō, Appendix 2, 616.
[60] Ishihara, Jokō to kekkaku, 180.
[61] Nōshōmu-shō, Shokkō jijō, Appendix 2, 557.
[62] Ibid., 55; ibid., Appendix 2, 565–66; Yokoyama, Nihon no kasō shakai, 178.
[63] Nōshōmu-shō, Shokkō jijō, Appendix 2.
[64] Children of seven to ten sorted cotton dropped on the factory floor and did cleaning. Ibid., 499.
[65] Yamanouchi, Yamanouchi Mina jiden, 20.

for people at first."[66] Another reported that, because she had a husband, she had lots of chores to do and could not manage to do them all when she worked day shift. Thus she found night work convenient.[67] Another married worker agreed: "When I work night shift I can go home early in the morning and do laundry and housework. And if in the afternoon I get a little sleep it's enough. The day shift is not as convenient so I came to like the night shift."[68]

The authors of Shokkō jijō took a strong stand against the night shift, devoting passages to arguments in favor of abolishing it to save health and lives.[69] Aware that employers were united in their opposition to abolition because double shifts increased profits, the authors contended that in the long run abolition would greatly reduce expenses and thus net profits would not be reduced. With just one shift, machinery would last longer, they pointed out. Since night work was a major reason for the high runaway rate, without it, companies would spend less on recruitment and be able to retain larger numbers of experienced workers with training and skill. Healthier workers would be more productive. Yet even as they advanced these arguments, the authors must have known that employers would not be convinced.

As in the silk mills, sexual harassment on the cotton-factory floor was common. A supervisor could assign difficult jobs and other harsh penalties to a girl who resisted his advances. A night-shift overseer could summon a girl and force his attentions on her by rape if inducements failed.[70] Very young and far from home, with beatings and brutality all around them, some girls hungrily responded to any show of affection. Those who feared punishment or had little confidence in their skills were particularly vulnerable to the overtures of seduction-minded male superiors or co-workers. Over and over again the songs of factory women warned their sisters against becoming victims of predatory males.[71]

> If you're taken in by sweet talk
> Your money will be swiped and you'll be abandoned.
> In the end you'll suffer undreamt-of hardships,
> Blown hither and thither like a drifting weed.
>
> Don't become infatuated.
> The male workers in this company

[66] Nōshōmu-shō, Shokkō jijō, Appendix 2, 518.
[67] Ibid., 520.
[68] Ibid., 531–32.
[69] Ibid., 62–69.
[70] Hosoi, Jokō aishi, 267.
[71] See ibid., 331, for the following three verses and the rest of the verses in the songs they were taken from.

Will throw you out afterward
Like used tea leaves.

It's no good to fall in love.
The winding boss only
Cares about wound thread.
He's heartless.

The women knew they were being treated as playthings and resented this even when they could not resist it.

The boss and I
Are like spinning-machine thread;
Easily tied but easily broken.[72]

Again and again many fell into the trap, only to be discarded when they became pregnant or the seducer (or rapist) found new prey. Some of the victims ended up as prostitutes or semiprostitutes.[73]

Sometimes pregnancies led to marriages or at least to common-law relationships, with the man and woman moving to company lodgings (or company-approved lodgings) to live as a couple. One operative reported that in such a case the woman would usually quit work—at least temporarily—in her seventh or eighth month of pregnancy.[74] On the other hand, a man might just "pay off" the woman with a small sum, and for him that would be the end of the matter. Sometimes a man refused all responsibility, claiming it was not his child. "My friend—when she was three months pregnant her man ran away. . . . She was going to be laid off because she was pregnant. She couldn't go home to her parents and she was saying she was going to kill herself. I was worried about her. Fortunately she wasn't laid off. Luckily a man working day and night shifts had feelings for her. He took her as his wife with the baby in her belly."[75]

In her autobiography, Yamanouchi Mina related a less happy result. She described a beautiful young spinning hand from Akita prefecture who

[72] Ibid., 333.

[73] According to Hosoi, official statistics declare that the previous occupation of 11 percent of Japan's licensed prostitutes in the early 1920s was "cotton-spinning factory operative." His own educated guess put the percentage at 30. He argued that cotton-spinning factory girls who became prostitutes did not do so of their own volition but were usually seduced or forced into the profession—often by company recruiters. Ibid., 332. Nōshōmu-shō, *Shokkō jijō*, 72, mentions cotton-spinning recruiters selling girls into prostitution. When government investigators interviewing individual female operatives in cotton-spinning factories asked, "Do some factory women prostitute themselves?" the answer was, "You couldn't say that they prostitute themselves, but there are many who sleep with male workers at the male workers' lodgings. There are those who find the [factory] work hard and thus quit and become prostitutes. They join a brothel in the vicinity of the company." Ibid., Appendix 2, 498.

[74] Ibid.

[75] Ibid., 530.

had been seduced by a male co-worker. When this girl became pregnant, her lover dropped her. Lacking money to return to her home in Akita, she continued working until the ninth month of her pregnancy. She had visited her lover's wife, begging her to take in the child when it was born, but this hope had been bluntly dashed. Finally she managed to get to her family in Akita, just as she gave birth to a dead child. Within a month, she was back in Tokyo working in the cotton industry again.[76]

Workers tended to be driven rather than encouraged to work well and hard. In addition to a continual stream of verbal abuse—operatives reported they were scolded for countless deficiencies—women and girls were subjected to a great deal of corporal punishment.[77] It was not unusual for a room supervisor to beat sick or slow workers who did not get out of bed quickly enough. Room supervisors were allowed a fairly free hand with corporal punishment, but occasionally extremely brutal treatment got them into trouble. "At the end of last year a room supervisor stripped a female operative naked and beat her severely with a broom stick. The next day the girl's mother came and took her away home. Then the room supervisor was roundly scolded by the dormitory supervisor."[78] But of course most dormitory residents' mothers were far away, unable to appear at the company gate and demand their daughters, even if by some miraculous chance the mothers learned of their suffering. Overseers hit people for errors, sleepiness (children sometimes fell asleep by their machines), slowness, lack of skill. New hands might be beaten because they had not yet learned procedures. Company officials freely admitted that routinely thrashing female operatives was part of lower management's job.

The punishment could be severe. Hosoi relates a tragic incident that occurred in the Nishinari mill of Mie Cotton-Spinning near the end of the Meiji era.[79] According to Hosoi, a young woman named Nishihara Iku from Saga prefecture was reprimanded at the Mie mill for dozing on the night shift. She was made to stand holding a stack of bamboo poles high in her arms. After ordering her to keep the bamboo well above her head, her boss went off for a rest break. Nishihara tried to keep her heavy bundle high, but she could not prevent her arms from dropping lower and lower. After a long while the boss returned and, since she was not in the exact posture that he had ordered, he loudly cursed her as a useless idler and struck her across the face. The startled girl staggered under the blow and dropped her bundle—and two or three of the poles landed on the overseer's foot. Since the sticks were tipped with metal they hurt the man. Out-

[76] Yamanouchi, *Yamanouchi Mina jiden*, 23.

[77] Nōshōmu-shō, *Shokkō jijō*, 90–91 and Appendix 2; Hosoi, *Jokō aishi*, 153–55; Hazama, *Rōmu kanri*, 274.

[78] Nōshōmu-shō, *Shokkō jijō*, Appendix 2, 593.

[79] With the details he provides, Hosoi appears to be repeating well-known hearsay.

raged, he pushed her hard just as the spinning machinery was turning, and the exhausted girl fell into the metal teeth of the machinery, where she was crushed to death. In the company statistics the cause of her death was recorded as carelessness at work.[80]

Extreme punishment for major offenses was routine. A worker caught stealing something from her workmates or the company was harshly treated.[81] She was stripped naked, beaten severely, and paraded around the mill with a sign reading "I am a thief" hung on her back. Humiliation was as important in this punishment as physical pain: the offender was often forced to stand on a stool before everyone with the sign on her back, and all the other workers were invited to hit her or pull her hair. Frustration and rage accumulated during the hands' wretched working lives was thus vented upon one of their hapless fellows—not upon the company.

An even worse crime than stealing was running away. Chastising runaways returned by the police, company officials pulled out all the stops. A girl who tried to escape might be shut up in a dark cupboard for days, deprived of food, stripped naked, and thrashed mercilessly. Occasionally extreme physical brutality could get a company officer into trouble: in 1901 government investigators heard that a work supervisor who beat an escaping hand so badly that she had to be hospitalized was arrested and apparently served time in prison.[82] But this was exceptional. Usually when someone from the mill went to prison it was an operative arrested for stealing a bit of thread.[83] There was no mention of physical punishments in company rules and regulations. Nevertheless, such brutal penalties were as real as the monetary and other punishments that were listed in regulations. One historian of labor relations has gone so far as to call practices connected with corporal punishment "the informal punishment rules" that supplemented the "formal punishments in the regulations."[84] Beatings and humiliations ground down bodies and minds; as we shall see below, "formal punishments" shrank the workers' already-small wage packets.

The Wage System

As is illustrated in table 8.2, female wages in cotton spinning were less than male wages, although for much of the Meiji period female cotton spinners'

---

[80] Hosoi, *Jokō aishi*, 154–55.

[81] In the Shanghai mills Emily Honig studied, workers were searched as they left the mills after work. There was no need for daily searches of most of the Japanese workers who lived in dormitories with few places to hide anything.

[82] Nōshōmu-shō, *Shokkō jijō*, Appendix 2, 551.

[83] Ibid., 550–51.

[84] Hazama, *Rōmu kanri*, 274.

real wages, including so-called bonuses, were higher than female wages in other important employment sectors for women.[85]

There were two basic components in the cotton-spinning wage system: daily wages according to wage classification and piecework wages according to the quantity and quality of work produced.[86] Most male workers were paid set daily wages; most female workers were paid piecework wages. The results of a survey of sixteen mills in the Kansai area given in table 8.1 illustrate this. Women who were paid daily wages were usually beginners, paid at the lowest classification rates. Once they had acquired some skill, females were usually put on piecework.[87] Other women who tended to be paid day wages were those relatively few females in the lowest supervisory jobs.[88]

But payment according to day wages or piecework was only half of the wage story. Administration of "rewards and punishments"—of monetary bonuses and fines—was closely related to the wage-payment system. In fact, it would be more accurate to assert that "rewards and punishments" accounted for an important portion of the wage packet paid to each operative at the end of each month, twice a month, or every ten days.[89] In recognition of this, workers doing piecework were given a wage classification corresponding to classifications set for employees on day wages. This was necessary because the "bonus," or *teate*, parts of the "rewards and punishments" were paid according to each worker's wage classification.[90] A wage classification entitled a worker to a fixed amount of wages, not a sliding amount as was common in the silk industry.[91]

There were about half a dozen different types of bonuses paid to operatives who achieved continuous attendance for various periods of time, who completed their contracted employment terms or portions of them, whose production was qualitatively or quantitatively outstanding, whose inventions increased profits.[92] These bonuses were very similar to what was promised in sections 12 through 16 of the company information sheet for recruits presented in chapter 7.

Monetary punishments were much more numerous than such "rewards" for good service. One could be punished by fines for tardiness, absentee-

[85] Nakamura Masanori and Molteni, "Seishi gijutsu," 62, show female cotton-spinning workers' wages exceeding female agricultural workers' wages in 1902 and female silk-reeling workers' wages in 1903.

[86] Uga, *Bōseki shokkō jijō chōsa gaiyō*, 65–82.

[87] Nōshōmu-shō, *Shokkō jijō*, 80.

[88] Hazama, *Rōmu kanri*, 291.

[89] See Uga, *Bōseki shokkō jijō chōsa gaiyō*, 76–77, regarding when and how often wages were paid.

[90] There were usually about ten wage classifications. See Nōshōmu-shō, *Shokkō jijō*, 80–81.

[91] Ōishi Kaiichirō, ed. *Nihon sangyō kakumei no kenkyū* (A study of Japan's industrial revolution), 2 vols. (Tokyo, 1975), 2:163.

[92] Uga, *Bōseki shokkō jijō chōsa gaiyō*, 54–56; Nōshōmu-shō, *Shokkō jijō*, 86–87.

Table 8.1
Wages according to Sex and Payment Method in Sixteen Kansai Cotton-Spinning Mills in 1901 (number and percent)

Wage-Payment Method	Male Workers		Female Workers		Total Workers	
Day wages	4,780	(80)	6,295	(30)	11,075	(41)
Piecework wages	1,244	(20)	14,910	(70)	16,154	(59)
Total	6,024	(100)	21,205	(100)	27,229	(100)

Source: Nōshōmu-shō, Shokkō jijō, 81.

Table 8.2
Daily Wages at Sixteen Cotton-Spinning Mills in Kansai in 1901

	Male	Female	Total Workers	% of Total Workers	% of Female Workers
10 sen or less	58	169	227	0.92	0.90
11–15 sen	313	2,825	3,138	12.70	14.61
16–20 sen	536	5,306	5,842	23.64	27.50
21–30 sen	2,374	8,524	10,898	44.10	44.10
31–40 sen	1,220	2,153	3,373	13.65	11.16
41–50 sen	530	322	852	3.45	1.70
51–60 sen	216	43	259	1.05	0.02
61–80 sen	96	2	98	0.40	0.01
81 sen–1 yen	19	0	19	0.07	0.00
More than 1 yen	6	0	6	0.02	0.00
Total	5,368	19,344	24,712	100.00	100.00

Source: Nōshōmu-shō, Shokkō jijō, 81–82.

ism, negligent work, accidentally damaging goods or machinery, "stealing" waste materials or thread, or for any minor infraction of the mills' endless rules—or for "inappropriate conduct." Inappropriate conduct was very vaguely defined, but needless to say it included any word or action critical of the company. In addition to fines, one could be punished by being forced to work extra time—at cleaning jobs, for instance—for no pay. Another monetary punishment was demotion to a lower wage classification. One of the most severe monetary punishments was to be fired by the company, which then confiscated all one's forced savings and other back wages.

Table 8.3
Female Cotton Workers: Wages and Productivity, 1889–1900

Year	Total Workers	Females as % of Total Workers	Avg. daily Female Wage as % of Avg. Daily Male Wage	Female Workers' Avg. Real Daily Wage (in sen)	Est. Avg. Thread Production (momme) per Spindle per Hr. (Ring)	Est. Thread Production (momme) per Worker per Hr.	Est. Spindles per Worker
1889	8,174	68.2%	48.1%	17.50			28.4
1890	12,409	70.2	47.7	16.67			26.5
1891	16,206	74.8	50.3	18.49	3.60	80.5	28.2
1892	22,562	75.2	49.1	17.01	3.70	80.3	23.6
1893	24,290	76.4	50.4	17.11	4.03	75.7	22.7
1894	30,936	76.5	52.4	16.94	4.08	96.0	24.6
1895	38,642	76.2	55.7	17.58	4.10	96.1	22.8
1896	42,928	76.2	58.4	18.71	4.02	98.5	23.5
1897	52,582	76.9	59.8	19.61	4.23	100.8	24.5
1898	60,568	77.4	60.4	21.50	4.45	114.2	25.6
1899	62,951	77.1	58.3	23.25	4.72	130.8	27.4
1900	58,440	77.3	62.8	23.90	4.98	148.9	30.8

Source: Takamura, *Nihon bōseki-gyō shi josetsu,* 1:302.
[a] Average thread production per spindle and per worker were estimated for thread count of twenty.

Mie Cotton-Spinning Company's rewards and punishments are outlined in detail in the 1898 report of the Greater Japan Cotton-Spinning Alliance.[93] In replying to the alliance's survey of the previous year, Mie reported four categories of "bonuses." The first was a bonus to dormitory residents who worked for a month without absence. The second was a similar bonus to commuting employees who were absent no more than three days during a month. The third bonus was to workers whose production exceeded—qualitatively and quantitatively—standards of production set by the company. The fourth was to employees who had worked continuously over various periods of time: different amounts of money in this category went to workers who had completed half of their contracted working period, to workers who had done so with few or no daily absences, to workers who continued to work up to and after contracts had been completed. It also included awards to workers who had worked hard during extraordinary circumstances and to workers who had made improvements in machinery or contributed inventions.

Mie's list of punishments was much longer. The company had a list of nineteen offenses that might incur fines deducted from wages. They were:

1. Tardiness
2. Disobeying company rules or orders
3. Improper behavior
4. Bad conduct stemming from laziness
5. Smoking in unauthorized areas or using materials that could lead to a fire
6. Complaining or inciting others [to complain]
7. Obscene behavior
8. Lying
9. Pretending to be ill and not coming to work
10. Negligence or lack of endurance at work
11. Being one whose frequent absence hinders the work
12. Lack of attention to detail that sets a bad example for others
13. Selling or buying property belonging to the mill
14. Reading while working a shift
15. Carelessness regarding machinery that causes a blast of hot air to be released or contributes to occurrence of an injury or impedes the working of machinery
16. Loss of tools or injury caused by loss of tools
17. Damage or loss of attendance sheet [of factory record book]
18. Hiding offences 15 or 16 when they occur
19. In the case of 16, if the circumstances are unclear all or part of the compensation money due to the injured person may be paid in equal shares to all of the operatives.

[93] Uga, *Bōseki shokkō jijō chōsa gaiyō*, 156–57, 168–69.

Management and supervisory personnel had a great deal of discretionary power with which to enforce regulations—improper behavior could be the way a girl looked at her boss. Fining was frequent and harsh. It was a major means by which companies avoided paying wages that were due.

Women who rose to junior supervisory positions told of company pressures upon them to punish the women under them. If they fined and struck and scolded those assigned to them into ever greater production, they were hated by their subordinates. But if they did not do so, those above them would make their lives miserable and they might lose their positions.[94] In the words of a woman who was no longer a floor supervisor: "The job of supervisor may be easier on the body, but in order to be praised by your superiors you have to make the people under you hate you. If you treat those below you well you are scolded by your superiors."[95] There is no evidence in these mills of the solidarity that sometimes existed between the lowest-ranking, often female supervisors (called "Number Ones") and female workers in cotton mills in pre-Liberation China. Emily Honig has described examples of this solidarity in Shanghai mills:

> Sometimes, . . . when women workers needed to rest, the Number Ones collaborated with the operators. In all Japanese[-owned] mills the overseers retired to the tearoom at 9:00 A.M. for an hour break. If the Number One in her department was sympathetic, a piecer could take advantage of the overseer's absence and rest. The worker walked to the aisle as soon as the overseer was gone and turned off the motor running the spindles on her frame. The bobbins of roving instantly stopped whirling and the thread feeding the spindles froze in place. Either the Number One or one of the other operators would stand guard, watching for the overseer to return, and then signal the workers to resume production. They knew that if they were caught they would be fined or fired.[96]

It is hard to imagine something like this ever happening in a cotton mill in Japan—and not only because of the imperatives of piecework. The Number Ones studied by Honig sometimes fought the Chinese, British, and Japanese owners and managers of their cotton mills fiercely: for instance, when managements tried to set new procedures for hiring workers, the Number Ones insisted that they should decide who got jobs in workshops under their supervision.[97] Any of their counterparts in Meiji Japan who might try to resist company policies would soon lose her or his job.

Unquestionably the results of the wage system with its few monetary bonuses and many monetary penalties were low wages for most workers in cotton spinning. Ōishi Kaiichirō's comparison of cotton-spinning workers' monthly wages in Japan and in India during 1890 in table 8.4 under-

[94] Nōshōmu-shō, *Shokkō jijō*, Appendix 2, 497, 519.
[95] Ibid., 497.
[96] Honig, *Sisters and Strangers*, 144–45.
[97] Ibid., esp. chap. 4, "Making Connections," 79–93.

Table 8.4
Average Monthly Wages in Cotton Spinning in India and
Japan in 1890 (in yen)

	Male Workers	Female Workers
India	4.50–9.00	2.70–4.50
Japan	4.80	2.32

Source: Ōishi, Nihon sangyō kakumei kenkyū, 2:162.

lines this conclusion. The comparative cost to Japanese employers of wages
was even lower than this table would indicate, because in 1890 almost 70
percent of the cotton-spinning workers in India were male, while the
higher-paid males accounted for slightly less than 31 percent of Japanese
cotton-spinning workers.[98]

Another important aspect of the wage system was "forced savings." As
in the silk industry, employers deducted amounts from the hands' wages
each month to be held back by the company. Amounts deducted would be
one or two days' wages each month. Sometimes the company would give
interest on this money; when this was done the interest might be higher
than contemporary bank rates. But sometimes there would be no interest.
In both cases, these funds might be kept entirely by the company until a
worker's contracted term of employment was completed, or a part might
be kept by the company and part sent home to the worker's father or husband.

A worker could forfeit the forced savings portion of her wages for a
variety of reasons. If she was fired or ran away before her contract was over,
the company routinely confiscated her savings. If, through illness or other
cause, a worker was absent for substantial periods of time, her savings
might be confiscated. If she found employment elsewhere without the permission of her employer, or if—this provision was deliberately vague and
was used against workers who showed any kind of defiance up to and including taking part in strike action—a woman "knowingly harmed her employer," she could forfeit her savings.[99]

In addition to fines and forced savings, there were a host of other deductions taken from mill women's wages. Dormitory residents had fees to
pay, and those who lived in company boardinghouses had to pay rent.
There were charges for some of the medicine distributed to the sick. Many
operatives were paying off the interest and the principal of "travel expenses" and advances against future earnings. When payday came around
and many workers received little or no money, a company might loan small
amounts against future earnings. While charging interest on such loans,

[98] Ōishi, Nihon sangyō kakumei kenkyū, 2:162.
[99] Hazama, Rōmu kanri, 285; Sanpei, Nihon mengyō hattatsu shi, 409.

the company kept, for its own use, the "forced savings" portions of wages already earned by those who were borrowing money.

Running Away

The wage system, like its counterpart in silk reeling, was intended to keep the girls in the mill. Notwithstanding heavy penalties for leaving a mill without permission, cotton workers absconded in droves. Leaving behind hard-earned wages, they leapt over walls in the middle of the night, crept away in the hubbub of shift changes, disappeared while outside the factory walls. Commuting workers simply stopped showing up for work. The survey undertaken by the employers' association in 1897 and published in its 1898 report estimated that of 71,002 cotton-mill workers, 45 percent of the females (26,470) and 42 percent of the males (6,486) left their jobs before a year was up.[100] *Shokkō jijō* painted a similar picture a few years later, as we see in table 8.5.

Table 8.6, also from *Shokkō jijō*, illustrates the fact that leaving the mill before one's contract was finished usually meant running away. Although this mill is not named, it is probably the Hyōgo mill of the Kanegafuchi Cotton-Spinning Company, a firm that had better working and dormitory conditions than most of its rivals.[101] At this mill, at this time, more than 52 percent of all female operatives and more than 53 percent of all male operatives left their employer by running away.[102] It was harder for the women, who were locked up in the dormitory, to escape, but locks and walls failed to contain 2,800 of them. This pattern of flight would remain typical of the industry as a whole until after the end of the Meiji period.[103] The percentage of runaways was even higher at other companies.[104] Of course those who ran away before they had worked for six months had not yet accumulated much in the way of forced savings. But many of those who left after one, two, or more years were abandoning substantial amounts of hard-earned wages.

Mothers and Young Children

It was hard enough for a girl in her teens or early twenties to endure the cotton-spinning life; women who had to bring their little children with

[100] Uga, *Bōseki shokkō jijō chōsa gaiyō*, 43.

[101] See Gary R. Saxonhouse, "Country Girls and Communication among Competitors in the Japanese Cotton-Spinning Industry," in Patrick, *Japanese Industrialization*, 97–125.

[102] Nōshōmu-shō, *Shokkō jijō*, 79.

[103] See Saxonhouse, "Country Girls," 101.

[104] Ibid.

Table 8.5
Turnover in Sixteen Cotton-Spinning Mills in Kansai in 1901

Length of Time Worked	Male Workers	Female Workers	Total Workers	% of Total Workers
Less than 6 months	1,568	5,281	6,849	28
6 months to 1 year	1,054	3,960	5,014	20
1 to 2 years	945	3,507	4,452	18
More than 2, less than 3 years	644	2,294	2,938	12
More than 3, less than 5 years	680	2,643	3,323	13
More than 5 years	477	1,659	2,136	9
Total	5,368	19,344	24,712	100

Source: Nōshōmu-shō, Shokkō jijō, 79.

Table 8.6
Modes of Departure from a Cotton-Spinning Mill in Hyōgo in 1900

	Commuters		Dorm Residents (Female)	Total
	Male	Female		
Dismissal	397	292	400	1,089
Escape	1,475	2,046	2,800	6,321
Illness	5	30	225	260
Death	0	0	31	31
Total	1,877	2,368	3,456	7,701

Source: Nōshōmu-shō, Shokkō jijō, 78.

them, and those children themselves, had an even worse time. The companies tried to hire workers who were at least fourteen years old, but mothers and elder sisters sometimes brought young children to the mill because they had no other place to leave them while they worked. The very young played as best they could among the machines, while their mothers or elder sisters worked the frames and spindles. As soon as little ones were old enough to be useful, they were given tasks. They would sort the waste cotton that dropped on the factory floor, do cleaning, and run errands until they were old enough to learn regular jobs. About the time of the Sino-Japanese War of 1894–1895, companies started to use young children on the night shift.[105] Children often fell fast asleep and had to be continually scolded awake.[106] Working youngsters of tender years were paid very low wages—about eight sen a day at the turn of the century.[107] Sometimes child workers were only paid what they were charged for meals: males of any age were not permitted to stay in the dormitories, but little girls were charged less for dormitory food than were adults.[108]

A mother who brought a little girl with her to the dormitory had to pay for the child's food whether or not the child worked for wages. Starting on the lowest rung of the wage ladder herself, the mother was under a great deal of pressure to get her daughter working as soon as possible.

> A woman who was separated from her husband brought her eleven-year-old child into the factory. Since the child was charged a full seven sen [a day] for her board, she had to work on the ring for twelve sen a day. The child had to work the night shift but she cried and wanted to go back to her old home. But she was told that if she did not work she wouldn't be able to eat. The mother had to go get the child and scold her down to work. The child, who had had three years' of primary school, had been told that there was a school in the factory, and she had even brought her school things with her. It was so sad.[109]

A widow with three children told her sad tale to government investigators. After her husband died, she left her village home and went with her eight-year-old daughter, five-year-old daughter, and three-year-old son to a city mill. Because she had a male child, she could not get into the dormitory, so she rented a four-and-a-half-mat room from the company at fifteen sen a month. She and her eight-year-old daughter were put to work in the spinning department, working on a ring. The woman's starting wage was nine sen a day, although she received two addition sen a day because she had children. Her eight-year-old made six sen a day. During the day, her two youngest could play in the mill, but when she worked the night shift, she had to leave them alone in the rented room. Sometimes she brought them to the mill at night. Every day her children cried, wanting to go back to their village home. Finally, after about four months when she was making twenty-two sen a day, she was able to send the younger two to her sister's home in the country. Then she and her eight-year-old moved into the dormitory.[110]

Cotton manufacturers and their management staff felt that female operatives should be satisfied with their dormitory facilities, working conditions,

[105] Sanpei, *Nihon mengyō hattatsu shi*, 385.
[106] Nōshōmu-shō, *Shokkō jijō*, Appendix 2, 499.
[107] Ibid.
[108] Ibid., 502.
[109] Ibid., 540.
[110] Ibid., 547.

and wages. They pointed out that cotton workers were daughters of the country's poorest families, the members of which often worked longer hours elsewhere for even lower pay. They argued that dormitory meals were better than those served in many poor homes. Calling their employees self-indulgent, lewd, homesick, too willful to follow regulations, unable and unwilling to master machine skills, easily enticed by recruiters for rival companies, they searched for explanations of what they saw as the unreasonable and ungrateful attitudes of the women and girls in the mills. Employers were often puzzled and irritated by their operatives' discontent, but they had to acknowledge that cotton workers were far from satisfied. What employers did not seem to understand or acknowledge was that their own picture of working life in the mills was much brighter than that of the women and girls they employed.[111]

Some operatives managed to adjust to mill demands and to endure with relatively few complaints, but many others found the life sheer hell. In the endless verses of the songs they made up as they worked their machines, they told each other about their discontent.[112]

Song of the Living Corpses

My family was poor,
At the tender age of twelve
I was sold to a factory.
Yet though I work for cheap wages,
My soul is not soiled.
Like the lotus flower in the midst of mud,
My heart too
Will one day blossom forth.

I was carried away by sweet-sounding words.
My money was stolen and thrown away.
Unaware of the hardships of the future,
I was duckweed in the wind.

Excited I arrived at the gate,
Where I bowed to the doorman,
I was taken immediately to the dormitory,
Where I bowed to the room supervisor.
I was taken immediately to the infirmary,
Where I risked my life having a medical examination.
I was taken immediately to the cafeteria,
Where I asked what was for dinner.
I was told it was low-grade rice mixed with sand.

[111] Uga, *Bōseki shokkō jijō chōsa gaiyō*, 15–16.
[112] The songs that follow are found in Hosoi, *Jokō aishi*, 409–12 and 413–14.

When I asked what the side dish was,
I was told there weren't even two slices of pickle to eat.
Then I was taken immediately to the factory,
Where I donned a blue skirt and blue shirt,
And put on hemp-straw sandals and blue socks.
When I asked where I was to work
I was told to fasten threads on the winder.

Because my parents were good-for-nothings,
Or, because my parents weren't good-for-nothings
But I was a good-for-nothing myself,
I was deceived by a fox without a tail.[113]
Now I'm awakened at four-thirty in the morning;
First I fix my face, then go to the cafeteria;
Then it's off to the factory
Where the chief engineer scowls at me.

When I return to my room,
The supervisor finds all manner of fault with me,
And I feel like I'll never get on in this world.
When next I'm paid
I'll trick the doorkeeper and slip off to the station,
Board the first train
For my dear parents' home.
Both will cry when I tell them
How fate made me learn warping,
Leaving nothing but skin and bone on my soul.

We friends are wretched,
Separated from our homes in a strange place,
Put in a miserable dormitory
Woken up at four-thirty in the morning,
Eating when five o'clock sounds,
Dressing at the third bell,
Glared at by the manager and section head,
Used by the inspector.
How wretched we are!

Though I am a factory maid,
My heart is a peony, a cherry in double blossom.
Though male workers make eyes at me,
I'm not the kind to respond.
Rather than remain in this factory,
I'll pluck up my courage,

[113] The fox is a cunning deceiver in Japanese folklore.

And board the first train for Ogawa;
Maybe I'll even go to the far corners of Manchuria.[114]

Like silk workers, cotton operatives thought of their homes and loved ones, often far away.

In the Midst of Mountains Everybody Knows

In the midst of mountains everybody knows,
Where the sound one hears is the sound of waterfalls
One finds the Fuji Cotton-Spinning Company of Suruga

I came here as a punishment for defying my parents.
Now I toil at Suruga,
Never to defy my parents again.

People come to Suruga,
Thinking they will save money,
But one cannot make any money here.

We don't sleep at night, we work the evening shift.
Our life spans are shortened.
All of us are wretched, all.

Someday I'll tell my parents back home
The bitter tale of the factory;
And move us all to tears.

Though the regulations are unjust,
This factory was built on regulations.
And if they are broken it's an offense.

I long to quit and go home,
But there is no return without train fare.
With tearful eyes I watch the railway line.

Stealthily I creep to the gate
To be abused by the gatekeeper.
Weeping, I flee to the dormitory.

The full moon is in the shadow of the clouds,
My parents in the shade of the mountains;
And I in the shadow of the factory's cotton.

Employers either knew nothing about the feelings expressed in such songs or cared nothing for them. Tamura Masanori, head of Shimano Cotton-Spinning Company, had his own version of how employees felt—a

---

[114] For many Japanese of that time, "Manchuria" had the kind of connotation that "Siberia" had in mid-twentieth century North America.

version that was not untypical. "From ancient times in our country there have been warm feelings [*onjō*] between·employer and employee. It has been a relationship similar to that between the [feudal] lord and his retainer. The lord treats the retainer like one of his own children. The retainer, besides performing his duties in return for his sustenance, has every intention of giving up life [for his lord] without regret if the occasion should arise."[115] How much time did cotton manufacturers like Tamura spend in their mills? Did employers—employers who assured themselves that the material rewards their mill hands received were good enough for them—often walk across the factory floor from the roving frames to the spinning machines to the winding room to the weaving workshop? Had they ever heard mill women singing? Investigators sent into the mills by the Ministry of Agriculture and Commerce heard some of the cotton operatives' songs. Among the verses they transcribed in their notebooks was this:

> Go up to the gate
> Of that hateful company,
> And you'll hear the voices
> Of fiends and demons.[116]

[115] Marshall, *Capitalism and Nationalism*, 58.
[116] Nōshōmu-shō, *Shokkō jijō*, Appendix 2, 617.

9

Comparative Perspectives: Factory and Countryside

WERE the difficulties endured by the girls and women who went to the textile mills greater than those experienced by relatives and neighbors who remained behind in the villages? Unfortunately the nature of the question and the quantity and quality of the evidence do not permit a straightforwardly tidy conclusion. Nevertheless, no serious attempt to understand the position occupied by female textile workers within the larger context of Meiji society and other comparable industrializing societies can ignore this question. Thus this chapter compares the environment of women and girls who remained in the countryside with conditions in mills in Japan and, to a lesser extent, elsewhere. Thanks to the comparative focus of the astonishingly sophisticated research on health and mortality of kōjo in the textile mills done by Ishihara Osamu near the end of the Meiji period, we can also evaluate the differing degrees to which farm women and factory women faced life-threatening health risks. Ishihara's findings show us that although silk workers and cotton workers shared many experiences, their respective chances of contracting or surviving serious illnesses were not necessarily identical.

Sisters (and brothers) who stayed behind in the impoverished villages often lived very hard lives. In the villages of northeastern Japan, home to so many of the textile factory women, bad harvests during the Meiji era reduced farmers to severe chronic poverty. In *The Culture of the Meiji Period* (*Meiji no bunka*), Irokawa Daikichi writes about poor farmers in Miyagi prefecture. One of his cases concerns the fate that in January 1906 befell the family of fifty-three-year-old Endō Hisaharu, a farmer of Hitotsuguri village, Tamatsukuri district. Endō

> had lost his means of livelihood due to poor crops. He and his family of four had been without food for days. On this particular evening, a neighbor passed in front of his house and heard a pitiful moan, "I think I'm dying." The neighbor immediately brought some rice cakes and tried to feed them but it was too late. Hisaharu was too weak to eat and died the next morning. His wife, Matsu, 56, had lost the use of both arms through rheumatism; the following day she, too, died. The only survivors were his sickly eldest son and his small grandchild. The cause of the deaths was reported as chronic bronchitis, but it is said that at the

village office they admitted that the cause of death had been a "prolonged lack of food."[1]

Other cases Irokawa describes are equally grim:

> Ujiie Tomosuke, 51, also a farmer in Hitotsuguri-mura, and his family of five, lived in a small rented house. The walls had completely disintegrated, and they had hung up straw mats instead. These did not, however, keep out the icy wind. The roof, too, was so dilapidated that the sky showed through; it afforded no protection from rain and snow. "Even during the coldest season," the account goes, "the family wore thin rags for clothes. Their sleeves did not even reach their elbows and their pant legs came to their knees. The shirt of the baby, Tosuke, was so short that his stomach was not even covered." Of course there was no bedding. "They sat around the fire for warmth, spread straw on the ground, and slept with straw mats covering them."[2]

Such "horror stories," as Irokawa rightly calls them, may have been extreme cases, but cold and hunger in prefectures like Miyagi were ever-present possibilities for many. In Miyagi, before the wounds inflicted by the poor crops of 1902 could heal,

> the Russo-Japanese War started. Just at the time the war required sacrifices of many kinds, people were affected again by unprecedentedly bad crop conditions. Even middle-class farmers, who owned part of their land but also rented some, experienced economic difficulties; many dropped down a peg, losing what they owned. . . . Many lower class farmers had neither rice to harvest in the autumn nor any means of work, and when starvation loomed, those living in the mountain villages gathered nuts and dug wild plants for food. But when winter snow arrived, even this became impossible.[3]

The poorly prepared and spoiled food that Hosoi Wakizō and investigators for the Ministry of Agriculture and Commerce saw in the textile factory dining rooms would have seemed a splendid feast to starving Miyagi farm families, shivering at night in shelter so much worse than a drafty dormitory. Contemporary scholar Mikiso Hane, comparing hardships of the countryside to hardships of the textile factories, concluded that the factory food was better than that eaten by girls and women who stayed behind in the villages.[4] Much earlier, the cotton employers' survey published in 1898 had reached the same conclusion, further arguing that mill working hours (after twelve or thirteen of them, an operative's time was her own) were

---

[1] Fujiwara Ainosuke, ed. *Meiji 38 nen Miyagi-ken kyōkō shi* (A history of the 1905 crisis in Miyagi prefecture), 1916, quoted in Irokawa, *Culture of the Meiji Period,* 220.

[2] Ibid.

[3] Ibid., 219–20.

[4] Hane, *Peasants,* 180–81.

shorter than the laboring time of poor people generally. The survey authors pictured farmers as working every waking hour.[5]

How adequate the workers themselves judged the food is debatable. Retired silk and cotton workers interviewed late in life did not usually recall bad food in the mills; some of them remembered factory food as better than what they had eaten at home.[6] Nostalgia may have colored survivors' memories of their youth. On the other hand, since the earliest experiences about which most of these veterans were talking occurred at the end of the Meiji era, it is also possible that by 1910 or 1911 factory food had improved. However, the partially rosy recollections of elderly women stand in stark contrast to the stories runaway mill girls told police officers and government investigators at the turn of the century. These were full of bitter complaints about mill food, which apparently played a central part in desperate decisions to run away.[7] The cotton employers' report of 1898 noted that mill hands were very unhappy with company food. This puzzled and angered the employers on behalf of whom the report was written. The employers felt they were already providing better food than the poor should expect to consume.[8]

There is also the question of the amount of food provided. Was it enough to fuel bodies that worked long hours at very intensive labor? A comparative study of quantities and kinds of food eaten by mill operatives and quantities and kinds of food consumed by farm women continuously working with silkworms during the busiest part of the silkworm season might be a more relevant comparison than a general one of factory-dormitory food and farm-household food. Unfortunately, such a comparative case study is beyond the scope of this investigation. Certainly there is much evidence to suggest that dormitory food did not satisfy workers' appetites. Operatives tended to spend whatever cash they possessed on "extra" food. And of all the illnesses from which dormitory inmates suffered, digestive diseases were more prevalent than any other kind of ailment.[9]

---

[5] Uga, *Bōseki shokkō jijō chōsa gaiyō*, 57, 109–11. Patricia Hilden found that French textile employers during the same period took a similar attitude regarding needs of their factory hands: "According to the government's own estimate, . . . a textile family never earned enough for its members—or even one of them—to 'eat normally.' This fact aroused little concern from most mill owners. When one *bobineuse* told a factory director that her 1888 wage—10 fr. a week—did not allow her to 'butter her bread' he replied, 'Use lard. It's cheaper and good enough for an *ouvrière*.' " Patricia Hilden, *Working Women and Socialist Politics in France, 1880–1914: A Regional Study* (Oxford, 1986), 97.

[6] Yamamoto Shigemi, *Aa nomugi tōge*, 328; Shimonaka Kunihiko, ed., *Nihon zankoku monogatari* (Tales of Japanese cruelty), 5 vols. (Tokyo, 1972), 5:115–16.

[7] See Nōshōmu-shō, *Shokkō jijō*, Appendix 2.

[8] Uga, *Bōseki shokkō jijō chōsa gaiyō*, 111.

[9] Ishihara Osamu's "Eisei-gaku jō yori mitaru jokō no genkyō" (Present conditions of hygiene among factory girls), originally published in 1914, was based on data concerning com-

Strict confinement and other unpopular aspects of dormitory accommodation have been discussed at length in earlier chapters. A textile dormitory did, of course, provide a roof overhead such as a family like the
Ujiie of Hitotsuguri village did not have. And the experience of boarding
with other young women could mean companionship and support within
one's own age group.[10]

A simple comparison cannot be made between factory work and farm
work in the Meiji period. As we have seen, farm work was extremely demanding for women, who worked alongside their menfolk and also bore
the extra burdens of "women's work," which frequently kept them busy far
into the night. Since their tasks were performed within the economy of the
farming family, the work of farm women and girls was not usually done as
part of a group of age peers. Yamamoto Shigemi's informants did not remember mill work as harder or less pleasant than farm work.[11] Nevertheless, there was considerable variety in the long hours of farming, and tasks
changed with the seasons. Many chores were done outdoors in the open
air. A great deal of the work was accomplished without a "boss"—certainly
without a highly critical boss closely monitoring one's every move.

Laura Strumingher has described nineteenth-century French peasant
women who, after reeling silk independently, alone or with other women
in their own homes, moved into the filatures of Lyons to reel under the
watchful eyes of male supervisors.[12] The work was not significantly different from what they had done before, but the setting in which they did it
had changed drastically. The same sort of change was experienced by Japan's first machine reelers of silk in Tomioka and other plants.[13] Even when
tasks done in the factory technically resembled handicraft procedures followed earlier, close supervision changed the nature of the work, generally
making it harder and more unpleasant. Certainly factory routines meant
much less control of the work by the person who performed it. A radical
adjustment was demanded even of the early operatives who came to the
mills with a reeling or hand-spinning background. How much more difficult it must have been for the vast majority of the machine-textile workers

parative disease rates among dormitory women working in cotton spinning, silk reeling, and
weaving between 1889 and 1902. Digestive diseases was the most common type of ailment
among them. Ishihara, *Jokō to kekkaku*, 77–171.

[10] One could also argue that dormitories provided by the company saved the workers from
having to find their own living accommodations as did the silk workers of Lyons. See Strumingher, "Les canutes de Lyon."

[11] Yamamoto Shigemi, *Aa nomugi tōge*, 328.

[12] Strumingher, "Les canutes de Lyon," 62.

[13] A greater gap separated hand spinners of cotton in the Osaka area from machine-spinning operatives beginning in 1883. Yet to a certain extent they also experienced a change in
setting rather than in the kind of work they did. On the other hand, unlike the first machine
reelers in the silk industry, they also had to master totally new techniques.

of the Meiji era who learned their reeling and spinning skills after they began work in the factories!

In the villages, youngsters might work under mothers, older siblings, other intimates. Done by strangers, factory supervision was always alien. It never included anything like the worker-supervisor solidarity Emily Honig discovered among "Number Ones" and the women who worked under them in Shanghai cotton mills. It never tolerated the informal work sharing that enabled a physically absent operative in the cotton mills of Lowell, Massachusetts, to earn almost a full day's pay as other women tended her machines while she took a short respite or recovered from an illness.[14] (When others tended the machines of an absent worker in a Meiji cotton mill, the absent one received no wages at all and those who did her work received no more than their ordinary pay.) In textile mills in antebellum southern states in the United States, with work forces of slaves, supervisors who were themselves slaves were sometimes able to protect those who worked beneath them.[15] A Japanese supervisor who tried to protect subordinates was likely to lose his (or, at the lowest level of supervision, her) job. It is significant that the woman quoted in chapter 8 about the impossibility of treating "those below you well" was no longer a floor supervisor. At best the Japanese foreman or forewoman was relentless; often he or she was cruel. The songs the operatives sang are full of negative images of the supervision they endured.

> The demon supervisor,
> The devil from the office,
> They're no help at all.
> Come on, silkwork![16]

Overwhelmingly the evidence suggests that physical punishment was an accepted part of supervision.[17] Factory girls may have been familiar with blows and brutality before they reached the mill. Yet when a supervisor chastised one of them, the humiliation of public shame inflicted by a stranger must have added greatly to the very real bodily pain of the beating.

Although rape and other forms of physical assault were not unknown in village life, in the mills women and girls were especially vulnerable to sexual attack or seduction. Away from supportive families and familiar surroundings, often lonely, disciplined harshly, caught up in the dehumanizing rou-

---

[14] Thomas Dublin, "Women, Work, and Protest in the Early Lowell Mills: 'The Oppressing Hand of Avarice Will Enslave Us,' " in *Class, Sex, and the Women Worker*, ed. Milton Cantor and Bruce Laurie (Westport, Conn., 1977), 46.

[15] Randall M. Miller, "The Fabric of Control: Slavery in the Antebellum Southern Textile Mills," *Business History Review* 55, no. 4 (Winter 1981): 489.

[16] Nakamura Masanori, *Rōdōsha to nōmin*, 98.

[17] Hazama, *Rōmu kanri*, 274.

tine of racing machinery, youngsters were hungry for any sign of affection or gesture of kindness. Company regulations, especially in cotton firms that employed substantial numbers of male operatives, might stress strict separation of female and male workers, but among the latter were plenty of successful sexual predators.

Such "success" was probably facilitated by the lack of solidarity between female and male operatives.[18] Nevertheless, as we have seen in chapter 6, before dormitories became a familiar part of textile factory premises, male and female hands could and did unite to present shared grievances to their employers. Firmly established by the mid-1890s, the dormitory system did not preclude sexual exploitation by individual male workers and supervisors, but it did reinforce the general separation of the sexes desired by employers. In silk filatures ordinary male workers were scarce; any men or boys in the plants were usually supervisors or potential supervisors. On the cotton factory floor, male workers generally did different jobs from those performed by their more numerous female counterparts, but they were paid higher wages for comparable work.[19] Usually it was males, not females, who rose from the ranks of ordinary workers to become supervisors, and always it was men who rose from the ranks to become technicians. The way for a technician or supervisor to pursue a successful career was to identify completely with the company and not at all with the men and women toiling under him.

Many males in the factory girls' world were supervisors, technicians, or owners with almost life-and-death powers over female operatives; a superior could ease one's tasks considerably or he could make one's working days a living hell. There is much evidence to suggest that superiors used their powers extensively.

Sexual harassment, as predictable as the daily blasts of the mill whistle, was an experience Japanese mill women shared with female factory workers in other industrializing settings. Meiji textile women would have sympathized with Harriet Robinson who, sometime during the 1840s, was dismissed from her position in a Lowell cotton mill after she spoke to an overseer about his familiar manner with her and with other operatives.[20] They would have recognized the nineteenth-century supervisors in the textile mills of Lille, Roubaix, and Tourcoing who fined operatives who resisted their advances.[21] Japanese mill hands would have understood the

[18] For a thoughtful discussion of male-female solidarity in the cotton industry of industrializing Britain, see Neil J. Smelser, *Social Change in the Industrial Revolution: An Application of Theory to the Lancashire Cotton Industry, 1770–1840* (London, 1959).

[19] Hosoi, *Jokō aishi*, esp. 35–45; Yokoyama, *Nihon no kasō shakai*, 167–68.

[20] Harriet H. Robinson, *Loom and Spindle or Life among the Early Mill Girls* (1898; Kailua, Hawaii, 1976), 35.

[21] Hilden, *Working Women*, 111–12. For the same problem in a British context see Jan

Russian cotton worker's complaint about her foreman to a St. Petersburg factory inspector in 1901: "If a woman worker pleases him, he calls her to his office and is not shy about making the most foul propositions. If she refuses she is subjected to pressure, oppression and even firing. Once a girl ran out of his office screaming, and the very next day she was fired."[22] The Japanese workers would not have been surprised by the choices facing cotton-mill women in Tianjin in pre-Liberation China: "There were people who played up to the foremen, and people that the foreman took a fancy to. If you didn't go along, he would always pick on you. Some people couldn't take it and had to leave. There were some the foreman fired if they didn't consent. It was a common thing."[23]

Another disadvantage familiar both to Meiji textile operatives and to their counterparts elsewhere was illiteracy and lack of schooling. Educational authorities in the silk-producing prefecture of Nagano fought a losing battle to set up effective elementary-school programs for Meiji factory girls. Yokoyama Gen'nosuke was shocked at the degree of illiteracy among cotton operatives in Osaka. Even in companies like Kanegafuchi that did try to offer after-work classes, operatives were too exhausted to study when they finished their twelve-hour shift. Like those factory women who attended the Sunday schools for the urban poor in turn-of-the-century Russia, the textile women in Meiji Japan who got any schooling at all had to be exceptionally determined.[24] In nineteenth-century France the story was similar. In 1880 the prefect of Lille, Roubaix, and Tourcoing reported that in these three textile centers only one in three of those under the age of twenty could read, and "it is likely that even fewer girls could read than boys."[25] In these cities literacy among mill women improved only slightly toward the end of the century.[26]

Factory children were probably one of the last groups to be drawn into the universal public education system being so carefully constructed by the nation-building rulers of Meiji Japan. But were female mill hands any less literate than females in peasant households who, after a few years in elementary school tackling a difficult written language, wrote little and read less throughout their subsequent adult lives? As late as 1935, in the village of Suye in Kumamoto prefecture Ellen Lury Wiswell found that "the

---

Lambertz, "Sexual Harassment in the Nineteenth Century English Cotton Industry," *History Workshop* 19 (Spring 1985): 29–61.

[22] Quoted in Rose L. Glickman, *Russian Factory Women: Workplace and Society, 1880–1914* (Berkeley, 1986), 142.

[23] Gail Hershatter, *The Workers of Tianjin, 1900–1949* (Stanford, Calif., 1986), 161.

[24] Glickman, *Russian Factory Women*, 132–41, discusses Sunday schools and Russian factory women.

[25] Hilden, *Working Women*, 49.

[26] Ibid. Hilden also notes that in France there existed other textile districts with higher literacy rates among female operatives. Ibid., 51.

women over fifty were functional illiterates, and many younger women had only the most tenuous control over the complex universe of written characters and syllabary."[27] If functional literacy rather than years of schooling is used as a yardstick, factory girls and women of the Meiji period were probably not much worse off than their sisters in the villages when it came to reading and writing.

Occupational hazards did differ for factory girls and their rural counterparts. Accidents that occurred within the mills could mean injury or death. In both silk and cotton plants fear of fire was perennial. Because girls and women were locked in their dormitories at night and the few emergency exits in the workshop areas were often locked and bolted, fire was especially terrifying.[28] Earthquakes, like the one in 1901 that killed three hundred employees at the Naniwa Cotton-Spinning Company, could also bring tragedy.[29] Accidents involving machinery routinely maimed and killed. In cotton companies especially, such accidents—which might have been reduced in number and severity if safety equipment had been installed or safety procedures had been taught—were commonplace. Hosoi Wakizō offers a breakdown of a total of 451 accidents that occurred in a seventeen-month period in a mill employing approximately eight thousand workers. He found that fingers were the most common casualties but that injuries to hands, heads, faces, and feet were also frequent.[30] In this respect the environment of farm workers was safer. It should also be noted, however, that the danger from accident in textile production was less than that experienced by industrial workers in other trades. In coal and metal mining, for instance, where a large proportion of the workers was female, cave-ins, explosions, flooding, poisonous gas, and fires repeatedly caused mass fatalities.[31]

Exceeding the damage from accidents in the silk and cotton factories was the havoc caused by epidemics of killer diseases like cholera and dysentery, which could swiftly wipe out all or a large part of a company's work force.[32] Yet tragic as such epidemics were, nonepidemic disease was a greater threat to the lives of Meiji silk- and cotton-factory girls and women.

[27] Robert J. Smith and Ellen Lury Wiswell, *The Women of Suye Mura* (Chicago: 1982), 10.

[28] See Hosoi, *Jokō aishi*, 245, for examples of mills with three hundred to five hundred employees but only one or two emergency exits, which were often locked and bolted. These doors were probably sealed—as were dormitories—to keep workers from running away.

[29] Ibid., 240.

[30] Ibid., 358–60.

[31] Hane, *Peasants*, 229; see also Morisaki Kazue, *Makkura* (Pitch dark) (Tokyo, 1977).

[32] Hosoi, *Jokō aishi*, 245–47, describes a horrible incident that he claims took place at an unnamed mill in Osaka during a cholera epidemic. Hosoi states that a deliberate decision was taken by company management not to make strenuous efforts to save all the female factory hands who contracted cholera, because to do so would have involved a high expenditure of money and energy. According to his account, some girls were actually given poison to drink

Grave illness and early death from nonepidemic maladies were more common among female operatives in silk and cotton mills than among the population at large, which included large numbers of urban and rural poor.[33] The high incidence of serious illness among female textile workers was made very clear by Ishihara Osamu's extensive study of 1909–1910, which drew on earlier collections of health data as well as upon the year-long efforts of his many researchers.[34] While factory owners and managers might worry more about cholera or dysentery, pulmonary tuberculosis, tuberculosis, and beriberi less dramatically but more thoroughly sickened and killed not only the girls and women in the factories but the relatives and neighbors who contracted the diseases that infected operatives brought back to their villages.

Conscious of the importance of the countryside as well as the factory in the lives of female textile operatives, Ishihara knew that he had to study the health of returning and returned workers as well as the statistics on factory health presented to him by mill owners and managers.[35] Approximately 200,000 women and girls who "went out to work" (dekasegi) were surveyed by Ishihara and his researchers. Within a year, about 13,000 of these 200,000 were returning to their villages seriously ill.[36] Among these 13,000, 12.3 percent had pulmonary tuberculosis, 21.6 percent had "tuberculosis-type illnesses," 17.5 percent had beriberi, and 18.1 percent stomach and intestinal diseases.[37] Among such returnees who died from illness, causes of death were estimated by Ishihara and his colleagues as follows: 39 percent from pulmonary tuberculosis, 31.5 percent from tuberculosis-type illness, 6.4 percent from beriberi, 6.6 percent from stomach and intestinal diseases.[38]

---

with their medicine to hasten their deaths, and those who resisted were forced to drink the poison. Since police instructions required all bodies of cholera victims to be burned, by the time parents inquired about their daughters' deaths all evidence had been destroyed.

[33] As late as 1930, rural families "constituted 10.6 million out of 12.6 million families, but . . . were the recipients of only half of the country's household income." Mikiso Hane, *Japan: A Historical Survey* (New York, 1972), 409.

[34] See Ishihara, *Jokō to kekkaku*.

[35] It was the influence of Miyairi Keinosuke, Ishihara's professor at Fukuoka University Medical Faculty, that convinced Ishihara of the importance of the countryside. Miyairi, while doing research in Fukuoka prefecture regarding schistosomiasis, put great effort into surveying rural areas where incidence of this disease was high. Twenty-five-year-old Ishihara grasped from the professor he so respected the importance of the countryside in understanding communicable disease. See Kagoyama Takashi, "Kaisetsu: jokō to kekkaku" (Female factory workers and tuberculosis: A commentary), in Ishihara, *Jokō to kekkaku*, esp. 20–21.

[36] Kagoyama, "Kaisetsu," 24. One male worker of the Mie Cotton-Spinning Company contracted tuberculosis and then went back to his village (where no one had ever had this disease before) and infected thirty people. Ibid., 24–25.

[37] Ibid., 31.

[38] Ibid., 32.

Although in early childhood the death rates of Meiji boys and girls were almost identical, after the age of about ten more females than males died. In the general population, female deaths seem to have been heavily related to reproductive, but in the factory population the higher rates of female death were closely connected to diseases like tuberculosis.[39] Among female factory workers who returned home exhausted or ill, death took the young especially. As table 9.1 illustrates, young factory females who returned to the countryside—especially in the sixteen-to-nineteen age bracket—died at greater rates than did females of corresponding age in the general population. Ishihara argued that when the statistics of those who died while working in the mills were added to statistics recording deaths of workers who expired after they returned home, the death rates of factory women were actually two to three times greater than death rates for their counterparts in the general population.[40] He found operatives' deaths from various forms of tuberculosis to be about 10 percent higher than deaths from the same illnesses in the general population—and the latter category included many victims who contracted tuberculosis from returning factory workers.[41]

If Ishihara's study concluded that it was more hazardous to a girl's health to go out to work in a factory than it was to stay home in her village, it also demonstrated that work was more dangerous in cotton spinning than in silk reeling or other trades. Cotton workers died at higher rates than did silk operatives or weavers, the third major group of dekasegi females Ishi-

Table 9.1
Female Death Rates per 1,000 by Age Group among the
General Population and Returning Factory Workers in 1910

Age	Deaths in General Population	Deaths among Returning Workers
Under 12	4.36	6.08
12–13	4.39	5.73
14–15	5.00	7.58
16–19	6.85	14.86
20–25	9.17	11.67
Over 25	10.12	8.35

Source: Ishihara, Jokō to kekkaku, 166.

[39] Nōshōmu-shō, kōmu-kyoku, "Kōjo eisei chōsa shiryō" (Data on factory sanitation) (Tokyo, 1910) in Ishihara, Jokō to kekkaku, 68.
[40] Ibid., 171.
[41] Ibid.

hara found to be at grave health risk. Of 1,000 female factory hands in all three trades who returned to the countryside during one year, 172 were estimated to be seriously ill or dying.[42] Yet out of 1,000 returning female cotton operatives in a year, 271 were ill or dying compared to 177 ill or dying weaving returnees and 125 returning silk operatives.[43] In silk mills, beriberi was common among those under sixteen, and stomach and intestinal maladies were more prevalent in other industries. But cotton workers contracted the three major killers, beriberi, pulmonary tuberculosis, and tuberculosis, at much higher rates than did operatives in other industries. Teenaged girls working in cotton mills were especially susceptible to killer diseases.[44]

Since night-shift work (long campaigned against by some of the bureaucrats in the Industrial Bureau of the Ministry of Agriculture and Commerce who had engaged Ishihara's services) was suspected of being an important factor in cotton operatives' vulnerability, Ishihara carried out some detailed case studies of cotton workers' physical fitness, paying particular attention to the effects of night work. In these studies, the weight, height, and chest girth of females working in cotton mills was repeatedly measured over extended periods of time, and the results were compared to measurements of girls of the same ages in the public and private school populations of Japan.

Weight loss observed among those who worked the night shift was dramatic. As Ishihara illustrated in the tables he gave members of the National Medical Association (Kokka Igaku Kai) at their conference in 1913,[45] cotton operatives who worked a week of night shift lost substantial amounts of weight that they did not regain during the following week of day-shift work. In the examples he gave the assembled doctors were two groups of female workers in two different cotton mills. Among the first group of eighty-one workers monitored, the average weight loss during a seven-day stint on the night shift was 170 monme or 637.5 grams. During the subsequent week of day work an average of 69 monme or 258.75 grams were

[42] His estimate here included those who died before they reached their home villages.

[43] Ibid., 160.

[44] The susceptibility of teenaged girls to killer diseases is a strong theme running through all of Ishihara's writings.

[45] Ishihara failed to get his research results accepted for publication in scientific journals when he had them ready in 1910, and he did not have the funds to publish them privately. Therefore he reluctantly sought the help of lay journalists to communicate his findings beyond the Industry Department of the Ministry of Agriculture and Commerce: newspaper reporters were invited to attend his guest lectures on legal medicine at Tokyo Imperial University, and news of his findings consequently appeared in influential periodicals. Articles about his work and the good offices of a sympathetic professor at Tokyo Imperial University enabled him in 1913 finally to address the National Medical Association members and to publish his work in the association's journal and later in another scientific journal. See Kagoyama, "Kaisetsu," 25–28.

regained, but this still left the average operative 101 monme or 378.75 grams lighter than she had been before she began the night shift two weeks earlier. In the other group, an average of 154 monme or 577.5 grams was lost during a week of night work, while an average of 135 monme or 506.25 grams was gained during the next seven days of day shift.[46]

As Ishihara told the physicians, the tendency was for the weight of workers to decrease gradually but steadily until the operatives, "were nothing but skin and bones."[47] Since this was happening to youngsters whose bodies were supposed to be growing, the health implications were grave. He concluded that among female cotton workers there was indeed a close connection between the harm done to bodies by night work and the high incidence of death by tuberculosis.[48]

With its extensive documentation, Ishihara's research challenged the claims of employers and their apologists in government and elsewhere that the hardships of factory life could be easily endured by female operatives because they were young and strong and only worked for a short period before they went home to the countryside and got married. The year Ishihara began his research, Kuwada Kumazō of the Association for the Study of Social Policy was arguing:

> When making comparisons with factories in Western countries, one must take into consideration certain unique facts regarding the extremely long working hours in factories in our country. In our country's factories, many women are employed. Single, they stay at the factories several years before marriage; but when they wed they leave the factories. Thus for them factory labor is only temporary employment; it is not work done throughout their lives. Moreover, since they do it while in the lusty vigor of their youth, they can endure what by comparison are extremely long working hours. In the countries of the West, however, since factory labor is a lifetime job done both before and after marriage, they [female workers] cannot possibly endure extremely long hours of labor.[49]

Kuwada may have been so sure that factory women only worked for a while before marriage because marriage was the career that most adult peasant women pursued. Yet it is clear that few female textile workers left the factories in order to get married. Nakamura Masanori's findings illustrated in table 9.2 reveal the reasons given by almost seven thousand dekasegi workers for returning home in 1909.

While much more comparative research must be done before firm con-

---

[46] "Furoku: jokō to kekkaku" (Appendix: Female factory workers and tuberculosis), in Ishihara, *Jokō to kekkaku*, 180.

[47] Ibid.

[48] Ibid., 181.

[49] Quoted in Nakamura Masanori, *Rōdōsha to nōmin*, 168.

Table 9.2
Reasons Dekasegi Female Operatives Returned Home in 1909.

	Number	Percent
Illness[a]	1,677	24
Related to work	393	5
Released from employment[a]	1,001	15
Family reasons	2,041	29
Marriage	438	6
Blood relations' illness	413	6
Other reasons	983	15
Total	6,946	100

Source: Nakamura Masanori, *Rōdōsha to nōmin*, 172.

[a] "Illness" includes those who died of serious illness after they returned home. "Released from employment" probably included some who were released by employers because they were too ill to work.

clusions can be drawn, the brief exploration in this chapter does offer a beginning. In the countryside there were frequent cases of extreme poverty: farming families perished without the food and shelter that sustained those able to work in the mills. Farm work was hard and heavy and during certain seasons endless. Schools existed for farm children, but given the conditions of their lives many of them had as few real opportunities to gain or maintain basic literacy as did textile workers.

In the thread factories some of the work may have been less arduous, but the worker had less flexibility and variety in her routines and she was closely controlled by superiors who were often hostile. She was more vulnerable to persistent sexual harassment. While danger from accidents and epidemic disease was far greater in the mills, nonepidemic diseases made textile work even more risky. The latter maimed and killed factory girls at rates significantly higher than those experienced by other Meiji Japanese, although as kōjo returned to their homes country people also became exposed to killers like tuberculosis. The chance of death from factory disease was higher among cotton-spinning operatives than among silk-reeling employees.

10

Alternatives: The Loom and the Brothel

THERE were other destinations for dekasegi women and girls than the silk-reeling company or the cotton-spinning mill. Two major ones will be considered in this chapter as part of our quest toward comprehension of "options" available to the female factory workers of the Meiji era. These two are the weaving firm and the licensed brothel. With some knowledge of working and living conditions in and perceptions regarding weaving and prostitution, two conspicuous occupations for rural daughters of the poor during the Meiji period, we may better understand the situation of their contemporaries who became kōjo in the cotton-spinning and silk-reeling mills.

Hundreds of thousands of young women who went out to work became apprentices in small and middle-sized weaving businesses that flourished during the Meiji decades. The Ministry of Agriculture and Commerce reported that by 1900 there were in Japan 371, 780 weaving establishments housing a total of 773,412 looms. According to ministry statistics, during that year 40,137 males and 828,407 females worked in these establishments.[1]

As Ishihara discovered, in weaving plants and workshops—which employed about four times as many females as cotton spinning and silk reeling combined—there was much malnutrition, stunted growth, eye infection, and respiratory disease. Although the women and girls there were more at risk from deadly disease than silk operatives, they were less susceptible than cotton workers. Because so many of the looms were hand-powered in the small workshops and sheds, bodily damage from serious accidents was less than in the silk or cotton trades. In all other respects, however, wages included, living and working conditions in weaving establishments were at least as harsh and often worse than those in machine reeling or spinning.

In pre-Meiji days, a young woman might be apprenticed to a weaving master and his wife to learn skills she would take back into her natal family and eventually into her husband's family; in her adult life she would weave at home for domestic needs and market sales. With the weaving boom of Meiji that accompanied the expansion of silk and cotton thread production, weaving houses were more inclined to hire girls whose families desperately needed wages or had more children than they could manage to

[1] Nōshōmu-shō, *Shokkō jijō*, 165.

feed rather than youngsters from families that could afford looms. Thus more and more of those who joined weaving establishments came simply to earn a little money for their families. Such recruits were rarely able to use weaving skills they acquired once they had finished their apprenticeships and had returned to homes that could not afford looms.[2] A weaving master and his wife with a small operation began to employ three or four girls as "cheap labor" rather than as apprentices to be taught prized skills. Those who continued to come with hopes of becoming full-fledged weavers were often disappointed.[3]

Conditions were so well known in weaving districts that local families refused to allow daughters to work in a weaving household. If a neighboring family could not teach daughters at home, those daughters probably would not learn to weave. According to *Shokkō jijō*, in weaving districts parents would frighten little girls with threats to apprentice them to a weaving house.[4] Thus recruiting agents were called upon to bring in youngsters from district rural parts—youngsters who knew nothing of the realities of weaving employment. Recruiters persuaded them and their parents of the desirability of weaving employment just as recruiters offered enticements to prospective silk- and cotton-mill hands.

Abuses by recruiters for weaving firms reportedly were even greater in number and more outrageous in kind than were those practiced by recruiters working for cotton- and silk-thread companies.[5] Yokoyama Gen'nosuke described some of the tricks weaving recruiters used.

There are people in the countryside known as go-betweens [*sewa-nin*] who conspire with employment agents [*keian*] in Kiryū and Ashikaga. They say things that are sure to gladden the hearts of young girls—such as promises of being able to wear fine clothes if they go to Ashikaga. Go-betweens even strongly tempt the girls' fathers and mothers with their clever talk. These go-betweens usually accompany the girls to the weaving districts. Go-betweens and employment agents, however, pocket part of the contract money while pretending they are getting advance-loans [for the girls]. The female operatives are completely unaware of what is happening. The go-betweens who brought the girls soon leave and the girls are shocked to learn from the master that money advanced to them

[2] Sanpei Kōko, *Nihon kigyō shi* (A history of Japan's weaving industry) (Tokyo, 1961), 464–65.

[3] In the weaving districts of Kiryū and Ashikaga, after apprentices had mastered the basics of reeling or winding thread on spindles, they were often kept at such tasks rather than being taught weaving proper. If they were allowed to work the looms, they might be restricted to simple patterns. Yokoyama Gen'nosuke cites a case of fourteen girls in one weaving house running away together because they were not permitted to learn advanced weaving skills. Yokoyama, *Nihon no kasō shakai*, 101.

[4] Nōshōmu-shō, *Shokkō jijō*, 180.

[5] Ibid., 178–83.

went to the go-betweens and employment agents. It is not unusual in Kiryū and Ashikaga to see such wretchedly helpless girls sorrowing. Of the twenty yen contracted for seven years of work, half of the money might be stolen by the go-between and employment agent.[6]

Even if a girl's father did receive the full advance-loan to which he was legally entitled, it was often quite a small sum. The following contract, signed late in the Meiji era, provided the father of the contracted weaving apprentice, Sekine Hisa, with only twenty yen advanced against a four-year working commitment.

Apprenticeship Employee Contract

Mishina Major Section, Orihara Village,
Ōsato District, Saitama Prefecture
The Second Daughter of the Householder, Sekine Yokichi
Sekine Hisa, Born July, Meiji 30 [1897]

For 20 yen.
The aforementioned person, in order to become proficient at the trade of weaving, shall be treated as the employee of your good selves for a fixed term of years according to the following conditions.

1. For a period of time up until 10 November, Meiji 47, a full four years from now.

2. Remuneration to be paid [by the employer] is 20 yen the first year, 5 yen the second year, 10 yen the third year, 15 yen for the fourth year, for a total of 50 yen.

3. The employer will provide clothing twice a year, summer and winter.

4. During her term of employment she will obey and preserve the rules of your house and of course will diligently learn the weaving trade.

5. During the period of the contract she will not request to be released.

6. In the unlikely event of her running away or other dereliction of duty, there must be appropriate reimbursement for the employer's losses, and also in case circumstances make it necessary for her to request release from employment before the contracted time has elapsed there must be the same aforementioned reimbursement for losses incurred by the employer.

The guarantor as well as the parent/guardian shall ensure that the above articles of the contract, as well as any other conditions that may be forthcoming, shall be obeyed so that no losses whatsoever shall be incurred by yourself. The contract, as herein set forth, is to be kept for future reference.

---

[6] Yokoyama, *Nihon no kasō shakai*, 104.

ALTERNATIVES 177

22 November, Meiji 43 [1910]
Person Concerned: Sekine Hisa
Father: Sekine Yokichi
Guarantor: Kuramoto Itō

Kasahara Kensaburō, Employer
Shinazawa Major Section, Ota Village, Chichibu District

However, the payment of wages to the said worker shall be in the form of clothing and expense money from the first to the second years, 10 yen in the third
year, and twenty yen in the fourth, with the 20 yen advance-loan money making
up the total of 50 yen.[7]

Other girls, engaged as apprentices for a fixed sum or sums to be paid to
their parents, not themselves, worked for years for room and board and
occasional clothing. Those who did not become skillful enough to satisfy
their masters within the contracted time period might be required to stay
on after the contract was finished in order "to pay back" the advance-loan.

For my parents,
I worked a ten-year term;
For the master
I did another two years.[8]

Yokoyama described the situation in the Ashikaga and Kiryū weaving districts.

Generally speaking, female operatives do not receive definite amounts of wages,
because they are apprentices. They are only to receive bonuses on completion of
term, five yen for those with three-year terms, ten or twelve yen for those with
five-year terms, and twenty yen for those with seven-year terms. However these
[bonuses] turn out to be in name only. . . . In actual fact, when the female operatives joined the workshop substantial sums of money went to their parents
and intermediaries. When they finish their contracts they do not receive even one
sen. Some even work half a year or a year after their contracts are finished in
order to pay back advance-loans.[9]

Those who apprenticed daughters in such a fashion tended to be very
poor or to be parents who placed a very low value upon their daughters.
The girls soon learned that they had been sold cheaply by their needy fam-

[7] Inoue Mitsusaburō, *Orimono uta no onnatachi* (Women of the weaving songs) (Tokyo,
1980), 72–74.
[8] Ibid., 55.
[9] Yokoyama, *Nihon no kasō shakai*, 102. There were, however, some variations in remuneration received. Skilled workers received more, as did those who stayed on after their contracts
were finished.

ilies. The following song recalls some of the versus cotton- and silk-mill
women sang.

> If the girls in the weaving shop
> Are human beings,
> Then butterflies and dragonflies
> Are birds.[10]

> When the thread breaks
> It's so hard.
> Today again I was
> Scolded by the master.

> Speedily I want to go
> And climb that mountain
> To be at the side of
> My loving parents.[11]

Employers, of course, encouraged weavers to sing different kinds of
songs—singing was often encouraged as song was seen as "the helpmate
of work" (*uta wa shigoto no tsuma ni naru*) while conversation was discouraged because "chattering slows the work" (*oshaberi wa shigoto no noritsu ga
ochiru*).[12] The following verses were popular with the weaving masters.

> For the sake of my parents
> Night and day are the same to me;
> Weaving by day and weaving by night
> Is how I want to live!

> If you cry,
> Long are the days and the months;
> If you sing,
> It goes by like a dream.[13]

The majority of Meiji weavers were fourteen to twenty years old, but
Shokkō jijō investigators found significant numbers of younger workers: in
the Osaka region 10 percent of the weavers were under the age of ten,
while another 40 percent were between the ages of ten and fourteen; in
silk-weaving areas of Fukui prefecture, 33 percent of weavers were
younger than fourteen, among Kasuri weavers of Kurume, Fukuoka prefecture, about fifty percent were under fourteen.[14]

[10] Nagoya josei shi kenkyū kai, *Haha no jidai*, 71.
[11] Inoue Mitsusaburō, *Orimono uta*, 55.
[12] Ibid., 18.
[13] Ibid.
[14] Nōshōmu-shō, *Shokkō jijō*, 167–68.

The normal working day for a weaver was from five to six in the morning until nine or ten at night, with very short, if any, breaks for meals; meals might instead be consumed by the girls as they worked. Before market days, a normal routine was to work until two or three in the morning. Holidays were usually restricted to Obon, New Year's, and local festivals. Meals were as plain and meager as those eaten in silk and cotton mills. Yokoyama, visiting working premises in the weaving districts of Kiryū and Ashikaga, heard girls singing this song:

> Bring the rice bowl closer.
> Look at the mixture of rice and barley.
> What, no rice?
> Eyes fill with tears.[15]

When government investigators talked with girls and women in weaving houses at the turn of the century, they often noted that a girl was in her middle or late teens but her growth had been so stunted that she looked about twelve or thirteen years old. In addition to complaints about dreadful food, they heard about lack of sleep, working and sleeping in the bitter cold, rough treatment for the less skilled and those who were ill, painful punishment for runaways. Many spoke of cruel employers.

> In 1899 when I was fourteen I came to ——— and in ——— village took fixed contract service in a weaving plant called ———. After one and a half years my health gradually became poor. Nevertheless, from about 5:00 A.M. until twelve at night I had to wind thread on the spindles. If one lost even a little of it [the thread], one was beaten with a rod, hit with an empty spool, or stripped naked and flung out into the freezing cold.[16]

The following story, which a weaving operative told to a government investigator in October 1902, describes deprivation familiar to those who worked in the industry.

> I was born in Ota town. At age thirteen I first went into service at the weaving house in Ashikaga town called ———. It is a weaving house that has a bad reputation around here. One gets out of bed between three and four in the morning and the earliest one stops working is around eleven in the evening. . . . Other than the guardian deity's festival, Obon, and New Year's, you don't get half a day off all year. As for the food, you get soup in the morning, pickled radish at noon, the same soup again at night. You don't see fresh fish from one end of the year to the next. . . . It's three parts rice to seven parts barley. . . . Because the

[15] Yokoyama, *Nihon no kasō shakai*, 99.
[16] Nōshōmu-shō, *Shokkō jijō*, Appendix 2, 611. See ibid., 605–7, for an interview with an employment agent substantiating girls' claims of ill-treatment.

food is bad everyone gets diarrhea—me too. . . . All the female operatives here
are from distant districts. . . .

I also worked at ———— but the days off, work hours, and food were just as
bad as at ———— [place described above]. I didn't even earn one rin. If you were
not a highly skilled worker you would weave from 5:00 A.M. to 10:00 P.M.
Those who cannot do a full quota of work don't even get pocket money. . . . I
was ill-treated only twice. The angry mistress pulled me around by my hair and
abused me when I damaged some material slightly. And once when I had trouble
with the frame she beat me. The master is a good person but the mistress is
terrible. One day an employment broker came and said that at Kiryū conditions
were better, over there the money is sweet, the treatment is mild, why not go
there. I began to want to go. I was taken there. A five-year contract. . . . It is out
of bed at three in the morning, working until eleven at night with no rest days—
same as the other place. . . . It is the worst food I ever had while working. Almost
no taste of bean paste in the bean-paste soup.[17]

Conditions were much like those endured in small silk-thread operations,
especially in zaguri plants. A kind and patient master and mistress could
make life easier, but considerate employers appear to have been scarce.
Weaving novices would have understood well the silk workers' song:

The machine is frightening,
But the supervisor is more frightening;
The owner is frightening,
But the owner's wife is more frightening.[18]

Weaving apprentices did not suffer tragic accidents with machinery; nor
did they face as great danger from fire as did those who worked in the
thread factories. They were less likely to die of tuberculosis, pulmonary
tuberculosis, or beriberi than were cotton workers but were more at risk
from these than were silk workers. The ill-treatment weavers received at
the hands of both recruiters and employers was at least as bad as that encountered in the mills. As in the filatures and cotton plants, physical brutality was meted out unevenly: those who quickly achieved the skills that
brought profits were treated better than others and the inept were often
severely abused. In the cramped quarters of the small weaving houses, girls
spent nearly all their waking and sleeping hours in close proximity to their
employers. The master or his deputy was almost always within striking
distance of slow learners. In the weaving establishments, working conditions, living arrangements, hours, and wages were, on the whole, markedly
worse than in the cotton and silk factories.

[17] Ibid., 609–10.
[18] Yamamoto Shigemi, *Aa nomugi tōge*, 386.

While one can trace weaving back into ancient times, what is supposedly the world's oldest profession, was another "option" for Meiji daughters of the poor. If a contract to labor in a factory meant hard years and a document binding one to a weaving house meant harder years still, the fate of those whose parents contractually committed their daughters to work in prostitution was much worse. At the very bottom of the social pyramid, prostitutes faced a more difficult work world than weavers or machine-textile operatives. Although thousands of daughters of the poor were sold to licensed brothels, fewer entered this kind of employment than went to the textile mills or the weaving houses. In 1897 national records listed 49,108 licensed prostitutes; fifteen years later there were 50,410 registered women in public brothels.[19] Such figures do not, of course, include the unlicensed prostitutes, entertainers, or women in eating and drinking establishments who worked the sex trades.[20] Nor do they include the girls and women who were kidnapped or otherwise procured for shipment to brothels overseas, especially in East Asia and Southeast Asia.[21] Unlicensed sex workers, including those shipped overseas, may have endured even more hardships than did their sisters in the licensed brothels, but the latter labored in an environment much more trying than that of the textile mill.

In the major cities, land was set aside for licensed brothels, a practice originating in pre-Meiji times. Before 1868, however, brothel districts were not found in the castle towns of every domain, because a number of the feudal lords had banned brothels.[22] After the Meiji Restoration, when all of Japan came directly under the rule of one central government, the practice of public prostitution spread everywhere.[23] Although an international incident involving a Peruvian ship in 1872 moved Japanese authorities to officially prohibit the buying and selling of girls and women—and thus officially made employment in the brothels "voluntary" on the part of the individuals working in them—the change was but cosmetic.[24] When

[19] Yoshimi Kaneko, "Baishō no jittai to haishō undō" (Actual conditions of prostitution and the movement for abolition of prostitution), in *Nihon josei shi 4: kindai*, 228, and Hane, *Peasants*, 210.
[20] Sexual-service workers include such a wide range of individuals in different jobs that they cannot all be considered here.
[21] See Yoshimi, "Baishō no jittai," esp. 234–36, regarding the kidnapping. Regarding the prostitutes who served in Japanese brothels overseas, see Yamazaki Tomoko, *Sandakan hachiban shōkan* (Sandakan brothel number eight) (Tokyo, 1975); *Sandakan no haka* (The graves of Sandakan) (Tokyo, 1977); *The Story of Yamada Waka: From Prostitute to Feminist Pioneer* [*Ameyuki-san no uta: Yamada Waka no sūki naru shōgai*, 1978] (Tokyo, 1985); Morisaki Kazue, *Karayuki-san* (Tokyo, 1976).
[22] Yoshimi, "Baishō no jittai," 225.
[23] Murakami Hatsu, "Sangyō kakumei to josei rōdō," 15.
[24] In 1872, "A Peruvian vessel, the *Maria Luz*, engaged in transporting kidnapped Chinese coolies to South America, had docked for repairs in Yokohama. Some of the coolies jumped ship and asked the Japanese authorities for help. The Japanese complied and condemned the

the distinguished statesman Itō Hirobumi was asked in 1896 what he thought of Japan's system of public prostitution, he replied that it was a splendid arrangement which, among other things, enabled filial daughters to help their poverty-stricken parents.[25]

Certainly daughters of economically distressed families made up most of the workers in the trade. Inmates of the brothels of Tokyo, which housed the heaviest population of licensed prostitutes in the land, came in largest numbers from the capital and from the poorer agricultural provinces.[26] Overwhelmingly, girls became prostitutes because their parents were ill, threatened with loss of livelihood, or dead—although since parents had the "right" to sell their daughters (supposedly with the daughters' permission after brothel service was made "voluntary"), parental greed landed some girls in red-light districts.[27]

Although employment agents (keian) recruited large numbers of prostitutes ostensibly as "maids" or "waitresses," the real destination of such recruits was not hidden. Urban employment agents erected large signs in front of their premises advising, "People wishing to sell their daughters please inquire within."[28] While many people in the cities knew what work in a brothel involved, countryfolk who lived far from the urban entertainment districts were not equally knowledgeable. Thus in the villages agents used the same "sweet words" that fooled generations of female factory recruits. Girls and their parents would be told colorful lies about life in the brothels. They would hear that the city food and accommodations were luxurious, that the girls would get beautiful kimonos to wear, that they would handle many customers but in most cases would just pour drinks of sake, that they would do so well that in two or three years they would be able to go back home.[29] But to an urban or rural family, the coveted prize

Peruvians for running what was, in effect, a slave trade. The Peruvians countered by pointing out that slavery, in the form of girls sold to brothels, was practiced in Japan too. This forced the Japanese government to ban the buying and selling of girls and women, but it did not prohibit 'voluntary' service in the brothels." Hane, *Peasants*, 208.

[25] *Fujin shinpō* (Women's news), no. 20 (September 1896), reproduced in Yoshimi, "Baishō no jittai," 246, and Murakami Hatsu, "Sangyō kakumei to josei rōdō," 6–7.

[26] In 1902, out of 5,531 licensed prostitutes in Tokyo, the largest number, 1,628, came from Tokyo, and the next largest, 776, came from Niigata. (Mie provided 598 and Aichi 366.) By 1907, Niigata was sending more licensed prostitutes to Tokyo than any other area—1,449 out of Tokyo's total of 6,705 licensed prostitutes were from Niigata. Yoshimi, "Baishō no jittai," 228–29.

[27] Yoshimi, "Baishō no jittai," 228; Murakami Hatsu, "Sangyō kakumei to josei rōdō," 34. Murakami Hatsu cites the case of a prostitute who worked in a brothel after her parents' death in order to support the nine-year-old brother her sister was raising. Ibid., 42–43.

[28] Tsurumi Shunsuke, Hashikawa Bunzō, Imai Seiichi, Matsumoto Sannosuke, Kamishima Jirō, and Sugai Junichi, eds., *Nihon no hyakunen* (A hundred years of Japan), 10 vols. (Tokyo, 1961–1964), 4:35.

[29] Yoshimi, "Baishō no jittai," 220–31.

that brought the reluctant around was usually the loan advanced against a girl's future earnings.

These loans were much higher than those made to parents of silk- or cotton-factory recruits. According to national statistics, the average amount of such a loan was 40 yen in 1877, 75 yen in 1887, and 270 yen in 1912.[30] Such countrywide averages do not of course reveal the wide range among districts and individuals hired. In 1900 the *Mainichi shinbun* (Daily newspaper) reported that loans advanced could be as much as 600 yen or as little as 50 yen for contracted terms which were usually six but never shorter than three years.[31] Such advance-loans were extremely difficult to pay off because brothel owners collected most of the money the girls earned, and the enormous expenses prostitutes incurred also kept them in debt. Out of what little was left of a woman's earnings after the owner took as much as 90 percent for his share and for payments on the advance-loan (such payments often covered only the loan's interest charges) she would have to pay inflated prices for bedding and other furnishings and for lodging and food. She had to purchase clothing, cosmetics, treats to serve her guests and charcoal to warm them; she had to spend money on hairdressing, visits to the bathhouse, and doctor's fees. Many a brothelkeeper deliberately ordered expensive items to keep his workers in debt. Right up until the end of World War II, licensed prostitutes were forced to continue working after their contracted periods of time had elapsed in order to pay off their loans.[32]

Only a limited portion of the costly loans ever reached the pockets of parents; deductions for employment agents' services, travel expenses, and the like reduced the sums parents received. Murakami Nobuhiko describes the case of a 100-yen advance loan "paid" to the parents of a girl recruited to work in the Yoshiwara district in Tokyo. Of the 100 yen, 65.46 were deducted to pay for the employment agents' fees and travel costs to Tokyo, leaving the parents with 34.54 yen.[33]

Often girls were very young when they were recruited. A child might be sold to a house when she was ten or eleven—or even as young as three.

---

[30] Chūō shokugyō shōkai jimu-kyoku (Central Bureau of Employment Recruitment), *Gei shōgi shakufu shōkai-gyō ni kan suru chōsa* (Survey of employment recruitment of Geisha, licensed prostitutes, and barmaids) (1926), cited in Yoshimi, "Baishō no jittai," 230. Average advance-loans made to recruited geisha were thirty yen in 1877, fifty yen in 1887, and two hundred yen in 1912. Ibid.

[31] Cited in ibid.

[32] According to the Central Employment Bureau's survey of January–March 1926, of 1,602 women who contracted to become licensed prostitutes, 872 did so in order to "settle their advance-loan debts." In other words, these women were recontracting after their terms had expired because they owed money on loans advanced at the beginning of their previous terms and on loans advanced while they were working their previous terms.

[33] Murakami Nobuhiko, *Meiji josei shi*, 36.

The understanding was that she would begin working in the trade when she reached puberty. Recruiters went after young women, especially good-looking young women. In 1895 in the prefecture of Tokyo more than 83 percent of the 5,456 licensed prostitutes were under twenty-four years of age and 33.5 percent of the total were in the fifteen-to-nineteen age bracket.[34]

In the brothel hard, hard work was the norm. The women was driven not only by her own financial requirements but by a brothel operator's ruthless attempts to maximize profit from his human machine before that machine deteriorated or broke down completely. The food licensed prostitutes were fed was neither tasty nor plentiful. Customarily they were served only two skimpy meals a day: they would eat at about 3:00 or 4:00 P.M., and although they might work all through the night they would not be entitled to another meal until the following morning. When they complained of hunger, they were urged to persuade their customers to buy food for them from the house—at prices five times higher than food costs outside the red-light districts. Even if a customer fell asleep, the rules prohibited the working women from sleeping beside him: she was constantly checked to see that she was not "sleeping on the job." If she was caught doing so she received a stiff fine. Even those who were not chosen by customers got little sleep; wallflowers remained on display as the long night wore on. Eventually they might be sent in disgrace to sleep not in their rooms but in filthy quarters, and the following morning they were given little or no food to eat. The women who were popular with customers were expected to work unceasingly as long as there was a client desiring their services. When trade was brisk, the women had to work around the clock. Brothel owners kept a strict watch on their "property" because despairing prostitutes would sometimes run off with customers—usually to commit suicide with them.[35]

Suffering from a chronic shortage of sleep, poor and sometimes scanty food, and nervous strain from long hours of frantic overwork, it is not surprising that licensed prostitutes succumbed to a host of illnesses. Run-

[34] Matsunaga Shōzō, "Shakai mondai no hassei" (Genesis of social problems), in *Nihon rekishi* (Japanese History), ed. Iwanami kōza (Iwanami lectures), 26 vols. (Tokyo, 1975–1977), 16:248.

[35] Information about working conditions and treatment of women in the brothels is taken from Murakami Nobuhiko, *Meiji josei shi* 4:39–40, esp.; Yoshimi, "Baishō no jittai,"; Yamamoto Shun'ichi, *Nihon kōshō shi*; Hasegawa Ken'ichi, ed., *Kindai minshū no kiroku 3: shōfu* (Records of the people in the modern period 3: Prostitutes) (Tokyo, 1971); Takahashi Keiji, *Monogatari*. Sometimes such a customer would seek suicide with a prostitute because he was hopelessly in love with her but lacked the funds to buy her out by paying off the debts she owed the brothel owner. On the other hand, a man who (for a number of different reasons) desired to commit suicide but was reluctant to do so alone was often able to find a licensed prostitute willing to die with him.

down bodies contracted colds, digestive ailments, and tuberculosis, as well as the venereal diseases that plagued women in the sex trades. Licensed prostitutes were required to be examined weekly by doctors in the venereal disease clinics of which Itō Hirobumi and other prominent apologists for Japan's system of public prostitution were so proud. Yet regular examinations probably did little to protect the women's health. In the first place, although prostitutes were required to submit to weekly examinations, they risked contracting or passing on infection every day of the week—sometimes every hour of the day or night. Second, examinations tended to be primitive, and in those days before antibiotics there was often little aid for sexually transmitted diseases. Third, it was an open secret that the brothel keepers made arrangements with clinic doctors: examinations were often perfunctory, intended only to fulfill the letter of the law. A woman would have to be gravely ill to be ordered not to work for a week.[36]

Yamamuro Gunpei, a tireless campaigner against public prostitution, published the contents of a 1910 letter sent to the Kyoto prefectural office by a licensed prostitute suffering from tuberculosis.

> Recently I went to the police to get permission to leave the brothel. For some reason the police did not allow me to leave. The reason I want to leave the brothel is my poor health. For this reason, I cannot please the customers or satisfy my master. . . . I do not have any parents or brothers. I am all alone, so my master treats me brutally. Recently one of my co-workers, Yuki, was kicked downstairs from the second floor. She died as a result of that fall. Because of this I have come to fear my master even more than before. So please, please allow me to quit the brothel. You can verify the truth about my master's cruelty by asking around.[37]

Despite illness and cruel treatment, many filial daughters, like those who went to the thread mills and weaving sheds, did try to carry on for the sake of the families they were helping. The following prostitute's love song shares much with verses sung by female textile hands.

[36] Murakami Nobuhiko, *Meiji josei shi*, 4:44–50 esp. According to the diary of a nurse who worked at a Tokyo clinic for prostitutes, about 260 prostitutes were examined in her clinic daily between 11:00 A.M. and noon. If a woman had a wound, it would be disguised with cosmetic coloring. Before New Year's, the busiest season of the year in red-light districts, everyone examined was given a clean bill of health. Ibid., 47. Government and other apologists for Japan's system of licensed prostitution insisted that the clinics with doctors and nurses controlled transmission of venereal diseases and protected the health of the brothel inmates, hence ensuring "safe" prostitution as opposed to the illegal and "unsafe" prostitution of unlicensed prostitutes who, along with their procurers, were subject to fines and terms of imprisonment. Since the clinics clearly did not guarantee safe sex, it was undoubtedly monetary, not sanitary, reasons that gained tax-paying licensed brothels government approval.

[37] Yamamuro Gunpei, *Shakai kakusei ron* (On cleansing society) (Tokyo, 1977), 30, quoted in Hane, *Peasants*, 216.

I parted from my beloved man
For the sake of my parents;
I was sold to another province,
Whether north, south, east, or west, I do not know.
I have these painful duties to perform
But it's for my parents and it can't be helped.
Though I don't begrudge my duty,
I may be hurt having private parts
Examined by cold-hearted doctors;
A treasure box that I wouldn't even show my parents
I hate to have examined.[38]

Even daughters who vowed to endure for their parents' sakes or were passively resigned to what they accepted as their fates might become too ill to work.[39] The tendency of most licensed prostitutes to be young, as well as other circumstantial evidence, suggests that girls and women did not last very long in this occupation. Some prostitutes were helped to leave the brothels by social reformers who campaigned for abolition of public prostitution. But despite ingenious efforts by reformers to use legal loopholes to free brothel inmates, the courts would not allow women in debt to quit the service.[40] Running away was often next-to-impossible: a red-light district was enclosed by barriers, and its only gate was patrolled by alert guards who made sure no women left without permission from her master. Those who did manage miraculous escapes found it extremely difficult to earn a living away from the districts.[41] Suicide was a way out for some; a

[38] Irokawa, *Culture of the Meiji Period*, 226–27, analyzes this song in a different context. It is longer than the portion quoted here.

[39] Murakami Nobuhiko reports stories about brothel keepers killing prostitutes who could no longer work. Murakami Nobuhiko, *Meiji josei shi*, 4:44.

[40] Journalists like Shimada Saburō and Kinoshita Naoe and Christian crusaders like Yamamuro Gunpei and the U.S. missionary U. G. Murphy spoke out loudly against public prostitution. They had some limited success using the courts to help individual prostitutes give up employment in the brothels. It has been argued that such reformers' efforts were actually responsible for a decrease in the number of prostitutes at the turn of the century: in 1899 there were 52,274 registered prostitutes in Japan, but by 1901 that number had been reduced to 40,195. Yoshimi, "Baishō no jittai," 255–56. However, this trend was short-lived, as the courts refused to allow women who had debts to leave the brothels.

[41] None of the reform leaders had concrete, practical agendas for dealing with problems encountered by ex-prostitutes who left the brothels. In Gunma prefecture, which abolished public prostitution in 1893 and remained the only prefecture without licensed brothels until nationwide abolition in 1956, only 30 percent of the licensed prostitutes were bought out or returned to their parents when the brothels closed. The rest presumably moved to houses in other parts of the country. To free 30 percent of the prefecture's licensed prostitutes was an outstanding achievement. Still, the fate of the other 70 percent reminds us of the dimensions of the problem. Reformers found that the women and girls they helped to escape from the

researcher who studied love suicides in 1910 found that in that year only 0.4 percent of the women who took part in such suicides were "ordinary women" (*ippan josei*) while 99.6 percent were prostitutes.[42]

Cotton-spinning and silk-reeling operatives paid a high price for the help they tried to give their families. But other dekasegi girls and women of the poorer classes also paid dearly. Adolescent years spent in a weaving house could be harder on the mind and body than time spent in a large textile mill. The life of those girls and young women sold to the brothels was harsher still and entailed little chance of leaving the trade after the contracted term of employment was over. For all its dangers then, life in the Suwa filatures or Osaka mills was generally not as difficult and unrewarding as that endured in the weaving houses of Ashikaga and Kiryū or in Yoshiwara or other red-light districts. Yet many experiences were shared by the daughters of the poor who "went out to work"—whether they went to factory, weaving master, or brothel.

In the first place, all three—factory hands, weaving apprentices, licensed prostitutes—were "sold" by their parents. In the case of prostitutes the transaction was most blatant, but in all three cases written documents legalized the handing over of a girl in exchange for money that her father would receive both on the spot and later. People spoke of poor farmers "selling their daughters to the mill or the brothel," as if the two were the same fate. As a verse of a cotton-worker's song lamented:

Because my family is poor,
At the age of twelve
I was sold to this company.[43]

The unscrupulous recruiting agent, operating in an area far from the textile factory, weaving shop, or brothel he worked for, played a key role in the "sale." The choice of a distant recruiting ground was no accident. Recruiters and employers counted upon ignorance of conditions in the occupations among the peasant families they wooed. They also counted upon a lack of sophistication that would enable them to hide the fact that high recruiting fees and travel expenses would be deducted from the moneys the families were supposed to receive. In the minds of girls brought to factory, shop, or brothel, false promises and recruiting agents were closely associated.

Once at her place of employment, the mill hand, the novice weaver, and the licensed prostitute all lived highly supervised lives, strictly confined to designated quarters when they were not working. In the dormitory, the

brothels managed at best to find employment on the fringes of the red-light districts and often were drawn back into the profession they were trying so hard to leave. Hane, *Peasants*, 214.

[42] Cited in Murakami Nobuhiko, *Meiji josei shi*, 4:40.

[43] Hosoi, *Jokō aishi*, 407.

weaving master's home, or the house of prostitution, girls lost the freedom
of movement they had taken for granted at home in the village. Literally
locked up, they were surrounded by ever-watchful guardians and supervisors. They were all urged by their employers to work extremely hard and
perform their tasks well. They were strongly discouraged from having any
activities apart from those connected with the enterprises in which they
worked. Runaways from mill, weaving shop, or brothel were all treated
brutally.

Like the purchased commodities they were to their employers, they were
thrown away if they became worn or useless. Silk workers who were so
sick they could hardly walk were sent to struggle homeward across the
mountains. As the account books of the Yamanoue Kairyō Company presented in chapter 4 remind us, those same silk workers had been kept at
their posts profitably producing for the firms during earlier stages of their
illnesses. Cotton-mill hands received little aid from their companies when
accidents maimed them; any compensation they received usually came
from fellow workers' earnings.[44] Cotton-firm employers may not have
been above hastening the death of cholera-ridden operatives, since nursing
the sick back to health entailed expense.[45] Ailing weavers, often treated
with much less care than the looms they worked, were turned out when
they could no longer make a profit for the master.[46] Women who toiled in
the red-light districts were treated as the chattels of the proprietors of the
houses to which they "belonged." Hearsay evidence has it that brothel
keepers went so far as to kill prostitutes in their houses who did not bring
in any money.[47] Not only were the girls and women used as money-earn-
ing machines; factory women, apprentices, and prostitutes were also commodities used as private sexual objects by the men who controlled them.

Unfortunately, this objectification of the female worker is not a vanished
part of Japan's early industrializing past. In the 1980s, Japanese media began focusing upon the significant numbers of young women being
brought to Japan from neighboring Asian countries to work as *Japayuki-
san* (literally, in a corruption of Japanese and English, "person going to
Japan," a play on the designation *karayuki-san*, meaning "person going
abroad" or literally "person going to China," applied to those Japanese
prostitutes who went overseas) in circumstances that would have been all
too familiar to textile and other female workers of the Meiji era. The newspaper *Fujin minshu shinbun* (Women's democratic newspaper), for example, on 12 December 1986 reported details regarding the case of two
young Filipino women, aged eighteen and twenty-one, who, with the help

[44] Nōshōmu-shō, *Shokkō jijō*, 100–110; Murakami Nobuhiko, *Meiji josei shi*, 3:172.
[45] See n. 39.
[46] See for instance Nōshōmu-shō, *Shokkō jijō*, Appendix 2, 611–13.
[47] Murakami Nobuhiko, *Meiji josei shi*, 4:44.

of Japanese lawyers, were bringing charges against the employer who had hired them to work as hostesses and forced them to work as prostitutes at a "night pub" (*naito pabu*) in the town of Misato, in Kodama district, Saitama prefecture. Persuaded by recruiters in their own country to go to Japan to work as hostesses, they had both signed a contract in which their occupation was given as hostess, their monthly wages were fixed, and their food, clothing, and accommodation were specified as the employer's responsibility. The reality was that they had their passports taken from them, they were confined to their living space on the second floor of the night pub, they were not allowed to leave the premises, and they were forced to work continuously as prostitutes for men who paid about 40,000 yen (out of which the girls received one thousand) each time they utilized the girls' services. The two reported that when they strenuously protested doing such work the manager told them that if they raised objections they would be killed. Somehow they managed to steal back their passports and flee for their lives to the Philippine embassy. There they had a meeting with a caseworker who introduced them to sympathetic lawyers.[48]

Such stories are far from rare. In May of 1986 a shelter for runaway Asian dekasegi females was established in Tokyo, and by early December its staff and facilities had aided about one hundred women.[49] Since such women are often carefully guarded captives and are threatened with torture or death if they try to escape, the ones who do run away probably represent just the tip of the iceberg. As a staff member at this safe house noted, those who try to escape have to be very brave: "With no money, not knowing the language, not knowing where to escape to, they run away—even when running away itself is a great risk."[50] To a defense lawyer who, hiding her identity, managed to talk to him, the owner of one establishment that employs such women explained that of course he would try to hang on to the goods he had purchased from international recruiters: "If they run away it is only natural that we search for them. . . . We already paid the promoter 500,000 yen for each one of them. . . . The police don't scare us one bit. We use gangsters to hunt them down."[51]

The plight of the Japayuki-san today is disturbingly like the lot of many Meiji dekasegi women. During the Meiji period, ugly treatment of working women was often justified as part of the sacrifices needed directly or indirectly by a young nation struggling to become industrialized. Directly, sacrifices by factory operatives and other women were to help finance the

---

[48] "Tsumi serareru no wa itsumo kanojotachi: Japayuki-san" (It's always the women who are the sinners: Japayuki-san), *Fujin minshu shinbun* (Women's democratic newspaper), no. 2018, 5 December 1986, 1.

[49] Ibid.

[50] Ibid.

[51] Ibid.

modernization efforts that would make Japan great.[52] Indirectly, their sacrifices for their families meant that the state could continue to ignore the
deep poverty that remained the fate of many and became the fate of so
many more during the "shining era" of Meiji. Itō Hirobumi was surely
thinking of the budget problems of nation builders and not of Confucian
morality when he argued that public prostitution in Meiji Japan was "beautiful" because it enabled filial daughters to make sacrifices for poverty-
stricken parents.[53]

Today, the deep poverty is gone but tolerance of such abuses lives on.
Exploitation of the Asian dekasegi women may be illegal, yet it engages a
network of active conspirators and passive participants in Japan; business-
men, travel agents, gangsters, customers, and others keep it going. The
strength of this tolerance was unconsciously revealed by the newspaper
reporter who, at a news conference about the Japayuki-san, wondered
aloud if the Filipino women had any right to protection of their human
rights, since they had entered Japan illegally.[54]

Because from premodern times Japan's daughters of the poor worked
long and hard for their families, they were vulnerable to exploitation. During the Meiji period employers found profitable ways to exploit them, and
because they were at the bottom of the social pyramid such exploitation
was widely accepted. In today's affluent times the mentality that condoned
harsh treatment of female workers is, one hopes, weaker, but it is still alive.
Currently the exploited daughters of the poor leaving their homes for work
elsewhere may be foreigners coming to Japan from countries like Thailand
and the Philippines. Yet what Hosoi Wakizō and other pioneering social
chroniclers called Japan's "pitiful history of female workers" continues—
even if the pitiful female workers are no longer Japanese.

[52] See chapter 5 and Ronald P. Dore, "The Modernizer as a Special Case: Japanese Factory
Legislation, 1882–1911," *Comparative Studies in Society and History* 11 (1969): 433–50.
[53] Yoshimi, "Baishō no jittai," 245–46.
[54] "Tsumi serareru no wa itsumo kanojotachi," 1.

Conclusion

Textile Women and Their Families

In some ways, girls and women who trekked to the silk and cotton mills were following in the footsteps of the dekasegi sojourners of the Edo period. After the Meiji Restoration as before, they left their villages not only to reduce the number of mouths their families had to feed but also to give vital economic assistance to those families. Individuals continued to go out "in service" to traditional occupations after 1868. For instance, a young peasant girl often went off at a very young age to be a child minder in a household that provided her room and board and little or nothing else for taking care of young children, doing housekeeping tasks, and working at the side jobs done by women in peasant families—jobs like winding cotton thread or weaving cloth for home consumption or market.

> How well I've minded the crying child.
> Please master, give me some free time.
> Where do I go if I get free time?
> I go to the weaving shed to weave.
> Without high clogs on my feet
> I can't reach the frame of the loom.[1]

There were, of course, important differences dividing dekasegi patterns before and after the Restoration. In pre-Meiji times a girl who went off to spin or weave in a regional textile business may have been sent mainly to learn techniques that only much later, after she returned home as a skilled spinner or weaver, might earn cash for the family. The dekasegi worker of the Edo period did not usually leave her local district; certainly she seldom traveled beyond her fief. During Meiji it was often an immediate need for a substantial sum of cash that precipitated a country girl's departure. The dekasegi movement was on a much larger scale during Meiji, with hundreds of thousands of young people going out to work in other districts and other prefectures. As in premodern times, after the restoration "going out to work" was one of a number of significant economic contributions girls and women made to families that respected and appreciated them as workers. It is not surprising that they were asked by their parents nor that they were themselves willing to go to the new mills of Meiji.

Although they left their villages to become Japan's first industrial work-

[1] Nagoya josei shi kenkyū kai, *Haha no jidai*, 21.

ers and played a central part in the country's transformation from a feudal land to a modern nation-state, their motives for leaving home were more closely connected with propping up the old society than with building the new one. Since Japan's industrialization was carried out within the framework of the traditional order, it preserved rather than dissolved many premodern structures.[2] Certainly traditional arrangements in the countryside, involving heavy financial burdens for most of the peasantry, were kept more or less intact. Poor tenant farmers were able to stay on the land because of wages their daughters earned in the textile mills. By helping desperate families to pay the tax collector and the landlord, girls and women in the textile plants helped perpetuate the hierarchical and exploitive relationships of the pre-Meiji countryside. Their labor in the factories also supported the general expectation that women would work long and hard for the families.

 Mill women and girls' assisting their families at home in the countryside has been a major theme in this study. However, although farm women generally went to the mills for their families' sake, not all who went still had families to save. Sometimes daughters went to the mill (or the brothel, or the weaving shed, or the mine) because their families were breaking up. Sometimes they went because their parents were dead. Irokawa Daikichi paints a bleak picture of rural life in the fourth decade of Meiji:

> Village societies had changed; the community no longer constituted a body that guaranteed the security of life and equality among its members. It had become instead a fictive communal village, an organization based in part on compulsion and dominated by landlords. As a result poor people had no means for help, either within or without their village. The "family" would have been their last hope, but that family was often destroyed as a result of continuous years of crop failures, as family members had to go off and seek help on their own.[3]

In the mills, wives who were separated from husbands, widows on their own or with children, and daughters who ran away from home all worked beside girls whose parents had put their seals to their contracts.

Not all of those girls who had parents returned home to them after the contracts had been fulfilled. In Tokyo, a cotton-spinning veteran told government investigators in 1900 that about 10 percent of the mill workers remained in Tokyo after their contracts had ended, and among them were female workers who married and continued to work in the industry after marriage.[4] And in the demimonde of the cities and towns there were al-

---

[2] See Ōtsuka Hisao, "Modernization Reconsidered with Special Reference to Industrialization," *Developing Economies* 3, no. 4 (December 1965): esp. 400.

[3] Irokawa, *Culture of the Meiji Period*, 222.

[4] Nōshōmu-shō, *Shokkō jijō*, Appendix 2, 505.

ways former mill women who had lost their jobs or had run away.[5] The family back home was a dominant concern of machine reelers and spinners. Nevertheless, it must also be remembered that for some girls and women textile factory work came during and after the dissolution of their families.

Textile Women and Industrialization

Although their intention was to contribute to their families' welfare rather than to the new nation's, the contributions made by female textile workers of the Meiji period to Japan's first wave of industrialization were enormous. Beginning in the 1880s, the chief weapon in the arsenal of Japanese silk manufacturers waging economic war in international markets was the low wages they paid their operatives. It was the fingertip skill of the young women bending over the cocoon basin, not efficient machinery or a high grade of raw materials, that made possible the silk manufacturers' profits.[6] Similarly, the low cost of labor in the Meiji cotton mills was central to the cotton industry's rapid rise to prominence in both domestic and foreign markets.[7]

As we have seen, both silk and cotton workers paid dearly for their contributions. We know that they paid more heavily than did the managers who ran the mills, or the government policymakers and enforcers who facilitated establishment and development of silk-reeling and cotton-spinning industries. Middle-class Japanese who had firsthand awareness of work and life in the mills acknowledged this. Those few who visited the factories were, like Yamakawa Kikue, often shocked by what they saw. Iwamoto Zenji, a Christian intellectual and educator, wrote in 1898: "I saw the factories. I saw the factory girls' dormitories. And I saw the factory girls who worked the night shift completely exhausted, stark naked, over-

[5] Nawa Tōichi, *Nihon bōseki-gyō no shiteki bunseki* (A historical analysis of the Japanese cotton-spinning industry) (Tokyo, 1948), 401–2; Margaret E. Burton, *Women Workers of the Orient* (West Bedford, Mass., 1918), 64–65.

[6] See Ishii, *Nihon sanshi-gyō*. Of course the banking arrangements made available to silk producers by the Meiji government also helped maintain the silk manufacturing industry. Ibid.

[7] This was acknowledged by Mutō Sanji, general manager of the leading cotton-spinning company, Kanegafuchi (later named Kanebō) from 1894 to 1930, quoted in Nawa, *Nihon bōseki-gyō*, 369–70. Both Freda Utley and Sung Jae Koh have demonstrated that computation of comparative labor productivity and costs in the cotton industries of Japan, India, and Great Britain is an extremely complicated task. But their thoughtful estimates support general conclusions drawn by Yamada Moritarō that Japanese wages in cotton were lower than those of other countries, including India. See Freda Utley, *Lancashire and the Far East* (London, 1931), 76–108, 189–229; Sung Jae Koh, *Stages of Industrial Development in Asia: A Comparative History of the Cotton Industry in Japan, India, China, and Korea* (Philadelphia, 1966), esp. 74–82.

come by sleep, with no other luxury than lying with their eyes shut."[8] Textile-factory workers were not, however, the only daughters of the poor to make heavy sacrifices during the Meiji period. We know that other working women in the agricultural villages, the weaving houses, the brothels, and elsewhere also paid dearly.[9]

Textile Workers' Consciousness and Identity

E. P. Thompson has suggested that class comes to exist when some people, "as a result of common experiences (inherited or shared), feel and articulate the identity of their interests as between themselves, and as against" others.[10] This the textile women did, although not necessarily in ways that would fit into conventional theoretical or empirical expectations regarding "class consciousness."[11] Before compulsory residence in dormitories and long delays between earning and payment of wages became norms, united efforts by mill women to assert their interests against "unfair" employers met with some success. In such confrontations economic interests were primary, but protesters were concerned about their human dignity, too. Even after employers enforced measures that made strikes almost impossible to sustain, factory girls sometimes defied their bosses with spontaneous work stoppages. A women in an Osaka cotton mill told government investigators about a wildcat strike that occurred in 1899 when a company official showed prejudice toward workers from Ishikawa prefecture. Hands quickly passed the work on the factory floor and in the dormitory corridors, and production was halted for two days. It began again when the company got rid of the offending official.[12]

With important exceptions, as I have suggested, girls and women in the mills saw themselves primarily as defenders of their absent families' inter-

[8] Iwamoto Zenji, "Osaka no kōjo" (Factory girls of Osaka), *Jogaku zasshi* (Women's education magazine) 469 (10 August 1898): 30.

[9] For instance, women in the metal and coal mines and in the match factories endured terrible working conditions. See Idegawa Yasuko, *Hi o unda hahatachi* (Mothers who gave birth to fire) (Fukuoka City, 1984), and Yokoyama, *Nihon no kasō shakai*.

[10] E. P. Thompson, *The Making of the English Working Class* (Harmondsworth, Middlesex, 1968), 9. Thompson's sexist language and conceptualization mar his splendid work and make it very difficult to quote directly from this book.

[11] In my opinion, Emily Honig in her otherwise excellent book, *Sisters and Strangers*, missed an opportunity when she limited her examination of the class consciousness of the female cotton-mill workers of Shanghai, in the period 1919–1949, to conventionally theoretical definitions of class consciousness articulated earlier by Jean Chesneaux and Chinese historians of labor in Shanghai. See my review of her book in *Social History* 13, no. 1 (January 1988): 117–19.

[12] Nōshōmu-sho, *Shokkō jijō*, Appendix 2, 500.

ests. Despite divisions due to strong regional ties, the needs and problems of poor families all over rural Japan were very similar. Shared concerns, both economic and emotional, about their families played a large role in the textile women's sense of themselves as a distinct group.

Patriotism, on the other hand, did not play a large role. Calls by employers and government for female textile workers to identify with the Meiji nation were largely ignored after the 1870s. During that decade the first machine reelers of silk at Tomioka and elsewhere often responded positively to the government's challenge to "reel silk for the nation" as class solidarity cut across gender. These early machine reelers were, of course, girls and women from the ex-samurai class and their allies, well-to-do commoners. People of these classes not only tended to support the government's national aims ideologically; some were also in a position to reap profits as sericultural or thread entrepreneurs from the silk production the government was encouraging. And these first factory girls were seen as semiprofessionals; they were called "trainees" and "worker-teachers." They were treated with respect and dignity, enjoyed considerable freedom of movement, and labored in working conditions much better than those in both silk and cotton mills from the 1880s on. After that first optimistic decade of Meiji, the textile operatives—whose ranks were overwhelmingly composed of daughters of the poor, especially rural daughters of the poor—showed little inclination to reel or spin for the sake of the nation. By the twentieth century, employers' lectures, lessons, specially published textbooks, and company songs were repeatedly exhorting their mill hands to sacrifice for the good of the country. Yet despite systematic indoctrination by management and government enthusiasts, who argued that national interests were not only of utmost importance in themselves but also happened to be identical with company interests and those of the factory women's families, the textile workers appeared to be interested only in their families. The factory owner claimed to have inherited the patriarchal mantle of his operatives' fathers, but the women who worked for him were not fooled. The songs they chose to sing were not nationalistic company songs. Those who, even for their families' sake, could not bear to stay in the mills, "voted with their feet" and ran away. The nation and the companies had much more success in capturing bodies for mill work than they did in capturing hearts and minds.

The kōjo's identification of herself as a member of a distinct group was both positive and negative. The pride that an operative felt because she was able to make important contributions to her appreciative family empowered her to throw back her head and sing, "Don't scornfully call us kōjo!" Pride in earning skill was coupled with the knowledge that employers belonged to yet another separate group that appropriated that skill to serve their own interests: "Kōjo are treasure chests for the company." But those operatives who, through illness or lack of skill, were not able to earn for their families or for the company, were more likely to internalize employers' abased views of themselves. In addition, the lowly position in society as a whole assigned to factory girls weighed on the negative side of their ambivalent self-assessment.

There is nothing surprising about the textile workers' negative images of themselves. So much of what they encountered in their working lives conspired to keep them in their places. They were bound—usually by others and not themselves—to contracts that gave all "rights" to employers. There were daily humiliations for the unskilled worker worrying about disappointing needy parents back home. For many there was sexual exploitation by managers and male workers who took no responsibility for the consequences of their actions. Unhealthy working and dormitory conditions loudly proclaimed worker dispensability. Respectable people looked down upon daughters of the poor; in the popular mind, being "sold" to a textile mill was akin to being "sold" to a brothel. In the face of all this, what is surprising is the strength of the positive images of self-worth that emerged among machine operatives in the cotton and silk mills.

The sense of belonging to a group that was indeed worthy was articulated in various ways. Among the stories Yamamoto Shigemi was told about silk workers' lives was one about four sisters who had returned to their village in the snowbound Hida hinterland after working in a silk mill in Shinshū. The local notable, a powerful landlord, asked their parents if he could "borrow three of their daughters for the evening." Although he "requested" the girls' presence at his house, given his position in a neighborhood where everyone bowed low before him his request was really a command. He had engaged skilled workmen to rethatch the roof of his house during the cold month of December and had promised them that if they completed the job before the year's end he would provide each of them with the sexual services of "a fine girl." Since the craftsmen had managed to complete the job, the landlord had come "to borrow" three of the four returned daughters. Angrily refusing for them all, one of the daughters told him that if he wanted prostitutes he should go to the town of Furukawa and get them, because she and her sisters, "superior factory girls" who had been praised by the president of a big silk company as "treasures of that silk company," would not go to his house. Furious, the landlord left, declaiming ominous threats. The girls' father knew that as a consequence of his daughter's bold action he would lose his tenancy of both wet and dry fields, a fate that spelled ruin in his village of tenant farmers. But his daughters were sure that with their earning power the family would not starve.[13]

These silk workers' sense of worth and pride as members of a group

13 Yamamoto Shigemi, *Zoku aa nomugi tōge*, 102–12.

worthy of respect is closely aligned with their earning power and the confidence it gave them. The employer who recognized their value was an ally, but if he ceased to recognize it he could well become an enemy, regardless of his high position. As one of these young women told the landlord, the four of them knew they were the silk company's profit-making "treasures." But the story (told by a younger sister of the four when she herself was an old woman) focuses upon the fearless resistance of a factory girl, who is also a humble tenant farmer's daughter, to powerful, male authority.

The defiant factory girl appears elsewhere as a heroine—for instance, in tales told about a silk worker in Nagano named Iwataru Kikusa. On 15 August 1907, while on her way home from shopping, thirty-two-year-old Iwataru fought off a murderous attack by a man who had already killed several women in the Suwa silk district. She seized her assailant's testicles and pulled them so hard that he lost his stranglehold on her and revealed his face. Since she escaped not only with her life but also with the knowledge of his identity, the police, who for almost a year had been searching in vain for the perpetrator of a series of ghastly murders, swiftly captured him. As a result, Iwataru Kikusa became famous in the silk district as a courageous factory girl triumphantly resisting the powerful male. As we see in the following verses of a song popular among Suwa area kōjo in 1907, Iwataru was transformed into a fighter against male oppressors met every day within the factory:

Don't scornfully say,
"Factory girl, factory girl."
Iwataru Kikusa is
A real factory girl.

Iwataru Kikusa is a shining
Model of a factory girl.
Let's wrench the balls
Of the hateful men!

Mr. Overseer, Mr. Supervisor,
You'd better watch out!
There is the example
Of Iwataru Kikusa.

Who dares to say that
Factory girls are weak?
Factory girls are the
Only ones who create wealth.[14]

[14] Yamamoto Shigemi, *Aa nomugi tōge*, 142–49.

The women and girls of Suwa sang about Iwataru Kikusa because she, like themselves, was a factory girl. Unlike themselves, she had risen to heroics. It was not hard for them to imagine the feats they would have liked her, and perhaps themselves, to perform.

The girl or woman in the silk or cotton factory of Meiji was often "an arm of the family economy,"[15] as indeed her dekasegi mother or grandmother may have been before the Restoration. That family economy she worked so hard to maintain was part of an exploitive rural economic system, also dating from pre-Restoration days. While she helped keep landlord-tenant farming alive in the countryside, her contributions to the new industrializing economy were of great significance. Like other daughters of the poor working elsewhere, she made her contributions at considerable economic, social, physical, and emotional cost. Whether she made these contributions gladly or grudgingly, in her own mind she made them for her family and herself, and not for the country or company. Together with her sisters in cotton and silk mills all over Japan, she came to identify herself as a factory girl and, defying others' disparagement, wore the label with pride.

[15] This is how young women factory workers in industrializing Europe were described by Louise A. Tilly and Joan W. Scott, *Women, Work and Family* (New York, 1978), 109. There are many similarities between the women in the family wage economy in nineteenth-century Europe as described by Tilly and Scott and the factory women of Meiji Japan.

Sources Cited

Abe Tomio. "Kinsei nōson no josei" (Rural women in the late feudal period). *Nihon rekishi* (Japanese history) 213 (February 1966): 18–29.

Adachi Masao. *Kinsei zaigō shōnin no keiei shi* (Business history of late feudal village merchants). Tokyo: Yūkonsha, 1955.

Allinson, Gary. *Japanese Urbanism: Industry and Politics in Kariya, 1872–1972.* Berkeley: University of California, 1975.

Aoki Kōji. *Nihon rōdō undō shi nenpyō* (A chronological table of the Japanese labor movement). 2 vols. Tokyo: Shinseisha, 1968.

Ariyoshi Sawako. *The Doctor's Wife [Hanaoka Seishū no tsuma].* Translated by Wakako Hironaka and Ann Siller Kostant. Tokyo: Kodansha International, 1978.

Bowen, Roger W. *Rebellion and Democracy in Meiji Japan: A Study of Commoners in the Popular Rights Movement.* Berkeley: University of California Press, 1980.

Burton, Margaret E. *Women Workers of the Orient.* West Medford, Mass.: The Central Committee of the United Study of Foreign Missions, 1918.

Chūbachi Masayoshi and Taira Koji. "Poverty in Modern Japan: Perceptions and Realities." In Patrick, *Japanese Industrialization*, 363–89.

Cole, Robert E., and Ken'ichi Tominaga. "Japan's Changing Occupational Structure and Its Significance." In Patrick, *Japanese Industrialization*, 53–95.

Crawcour, Sydney. "Changes in Japanese Commerce in the Tokugawa Period." In *Studies in the Institutional History of Early Modern Japan*, edited by John W. Hall and Marius B. Jansen, 189–202. Princeton: Princeton University Press, 1968.

Davin, Delia. *Woman-Work: Women and the Party in Revolutionary China.* Oxford: Clarendon Press, 1976.

Dore, R. P. *Land Reform in Japan.* London: Oxford University Press, 1959.

——. "The Modernizer as a Special Case: Japanese Factory Legislation, 1882–1911." *Comparative Studies in Society and History* 11 (1969): 433–50.

Dublin, Thomas. "Women, Work, and Protest in the Early Lowell Mills: 'The Oppressing Hand of Avarice Will Enslave Us.'" In *Class, Sex, and the Woman Worker*, edited by Milton Cantor and Bruce Laurie, 471–90. Westport, Conn.: Greenwood Press, 1977.

Fujibayashi Keizō. "Meiji nidai ni okeru wa ga bōseki rōdōsha no idō genshō ni tsuite" (Changing phenomenon of Japanese cotton-spinning workers during the second decade of Meiji). In Meiji shiryō kenkyū renrakukai, *Meiji zenki no rōdō mondai*, 137–76.

Furushima Toshio. *Edo jidai no shōhin ryūtsū to kōtsū* (Commodity circulation and transportation during the Edo period). Tokyo: Ochanomizu shobō, 1951.

——. "Seiritsu jinushi no rekishiteki seikaku" (The historical characteristics of landlordism in its formative stage). *Nōgyō keizai kenkyū* (Journal of rural economics) 26, no. 3 (October 1954): 1–16.

Gammon, Vic. "Folk Song Collecting in Sussex and Surrey, 1843–1914." *History Workshop* 10 (Autumn 1980): 61–89.

Garon, Sheldon. *The State and Labor in Modern Japan*. Berkeley: University of California Press, 1988.

Glickman, Rose L. *Russian Factory Women: Workplace and Society, 1880–1914*. Berkeley: University of California Press, 1986.

Gordon, Andrew. *The Evolution of Labor Relations in Japan: Heavy Industry, 1853–1955*. Cambridge: Harvard University Press, 1985.

Halliday, Jon. *A Political History of Japanese Capitalism*. New York: Pantheon Books, 1975.

Hanai Makoto. "Seishi jokō to gakkō kyōiku" (Silk manufactory girls and school education). *Nihon shi kenkyū* (Journal of Japanese history) 19 (July 1978): 25–47.

Hane, Mikiso. *Japan: A Historical Survey*. New York: Charles Scribner's Sons, 1972.

———. *Peasants, Rebels, and Outcasts: The Underside of Modern Japan*. New York: Pantheon Books, 1982.

Hasegawa Ken'ichi, ed. *Kindai minshū no kiroku 3: shōfu* (Records of the people in the modern period 3: Prostitutes). 5 vols. Tokyo: Shinjinbutsu ōraisha, 1971.

Hauser, William. *Economic Institutional Change in Tokugawa Japan: Osaka and the Kinai Cotton Trade*. Cambridge: Cambridge University Press, 1974.

Hazama Hiroshi. *Nihon rōmu kanri shi kenkyū* (A history of Japanese labor relations). Tokyo: Ochanomizu shobō, 1978.

Hershatter, Gail. *The Workers of Tianjin, 1900–1949*. Stanford: Stanford University Press, 1986.

Hilden, Patricia. *Working Women and Socialist Politics in France, 1880–1914: A Regional Study*. Oxford: Clarendon Press, 1986.

Hirschmeir, Johannes. "Shibusawa Eichi: Industrial Pioneer." In Lockwood *State and Economic Enterprise*, 209–24.

Honig, Emily. "Burning, Incense, Pledging Sisterhood: Communities of Women Workers in the Shanghai Cotton Mills, 1919–1949." *Signs* 10, no. 4 (Summer 1985): 701–14.

———. *Sisters and Strangers: Women in the Shanghai Cotton Mills, 1919–1949*. Stanford: Stanford University Press, 1986.

Horie Yasuzō. "Modern Entrepreneurship in Meiji Japan." In Lockwood, *State and Economic Enterprise*, 183–208.

Hosoi Wakizō. *Jokō aishi* (The pitiful history of female factory workers). Tokyo: Iwanami, 1954.

Idegawa Yasuko. *Hi o unda hahatachi* (Mothers who gave birth to fire). Fukuoka City: I-shobō, 1984.

Inoue Kiyoshi. *Nihon josei shi* (A history of Japanese women). Tokyo: San'ichi shobō, 1967.

Inoue Mitsusaburō. *Orimono uta no onnatachi* (Women of the weaving songs). Tokyo: Tōsho sensho, 1980.

Irokawa Daikichi. *The Culture of the Meiji Period [Meiji no bunka, 1970]*. Translation edited by Marius B. Jansen. Princeton: Princeton University Press, 1985.

Ishihara Osamu. *Jokō to kekkaku* (Female factory workers and tuberculosis). Vol. 5 of *Seikatsu koten sōsho* (Classics of everyday life). 8 vols. Tokyo: Kōseikan, 1970.

Ishii Kanji. *Nihon sanshi-gyō shi bunseki* (An analytical history of the Japanese silk-reeling industry). Tokyo: Tokyo Daigaku shuppan kai, 1972.

Iwamoto Yoshiteru. "Suwa seishi dōmei no seiritsu ki ni okeru katsudō" (Activity during the period of establishment of the Suwa Silk Manufacturers' League). In *Nihon kindai ka no kenkyū* (Studies in Japanese modernization), edited by Takahashi Kōhachirō, 1:349–70. 2 vols. Tokyo: Daigaku shuppan kai, 1972.

Iwamoto Zenji. "Ōsaka no kōjo" (Factory girls of Osaka). *Jogaku zasshi* (Women's education magazine) 469 (10 August 1898): 30.

"Japayuki-san." *Fujin minshu shinbun* (Women's democratic newspaper), no. 2018, 5 December 1986, 1.

Kagoyama Takashi. "Kaisetsu: jokō to kekkaku" (Female factory workers and tuberculosis: A commentary). In Ishihara, *Jokō to kekkaku*, 5–46.

Kajinishi Mitsuhaya. *Nihon kindai mengyō no seiritsu* (Formation of Japan's modern cotton industry). Tokyo: Kadokawa, 1950.

Kajinishi Mitsuhaya, Tatewaki Sadayo, Furushima Toshio, and Oguchi Kenzō. *Seishi rōdōsha no rekishi* (A history of silk workers). Tokyo: Iwanami, 1955.

Kanno Noriko. "Nōson josei no rōdō to seikatsu" (Labor and daily life of rural women). In *Nihon josei shi 3: kinsei*, 63–94.

Katō Kōzaburō. "Nihon shihonshugi keisei ki" (The period of formation of Japanese capitalism). In Teruoka, *Nihon nōgyō shi*, 1–48.

Katō Tomotada. *Kōjo kun* (Factory girls' lessons). N.p. 1910.

Kinugawa Taichi. *Honpō menshi bōseki shi* (A history of cotton-spinning in Japan). 8 vols. Osaka: Nihon mengyō kurabu, 1937–1944.

Kitazaki Toshiji. "Bokkō ki ni okeru waga kuni no bōseki-gyō to rōdō mondai: Meiji 22 nen no Tenma bōseki ni okeru sutoraiki o chūshin ni" (The sudden rise of the Japanese cotton-spinning industry and labor problems: The Tenma Cotton-Spinning Company strike of 1889). *Rekishi hyōron* (Historical review) 113 (January 1960): 59–73.

Kiyokawa Yukihiro. "Entrepreneurship and Innovation in Japan: An Implication of the Experience of Technological Development in the Textile Industries." *The Developing Economies* 22, no. 2 (June 1984): 211–36.

Kodansha Encyclopedia of Japan. 9 vols. Tokyo: Kodansha, 1983.

Koh, Sung Jae. *Stages of Industrial Development in Asia: A Comparative History of the Cotton Industry in Japan, India, China, Korea*. Philadelphia: University of Pennsylvania Press, 1966.

Kōzu Zenzaburō. *Kyōiku aishi* (The pitiful history of education). Nagano City: Ginka shobō, 1978.

Kublin, Hyman. "The 'Modern' Army of Early Meiji Japan." *The Far Eastern Quarterly* 9, no. 1 (November 1949): 20–40.

Lambertz, Jan. "Sexual Harassment in the Nineteenth Century English Cotton Industry." *History Workshop* 19 (Spring 1985): 29–61.

Large, Stephen S. *The Yuaikai 1912–19: The Rise of Labor in Japan*. Tokyo: Sophia University, 1972.

Levine, Lawrence W. "Slave Songs and Slave Consciousness." In *Anonymous Americans: Explorations in Nineteenth-Century Social History*, edited by Tamara K. Hareven, 99–126. Englewood Cliffs, N.J.: 1971.

Lin Yutang. "Feminist Thought in Ancient China." *Tien Hsia Monthly* (Nanking) 1, no. 2 (September 1935): 127–50.

Lockwood, William W. *The Economic Development of Japan: Growth and Structural Change*. Princeton: Princeton University Press, 1968.

———, ed. *The State and Economic Enterprise in Japan: Essays in the Political Economy of Growth*. Princeton: Princeton University Press, 1965.

Marshall, Byron K. *Capitalism and Nationalism in Prewar Japan: The Ideology of the Business Elite, 1868–1941*. Stanford, Calif.: Stanford University Press, 1967.

Matsumoto Hiroshi. "Jinushi no shihai to nōmin" (Peasants and the rule of landlords). In *Kokken to minken no sōkoku* (The struggle between state's rights and people's rights), edited by Emura Eichi and Nakamura Masanori, 355–91. Vol. 6 of *Nihon minshū no rekishi* (History of the Japanese People). Tokyo: Sanseidō, 1974.

Matsunaga Shōzō. "Shakai mondai no hassei" (Genesis of social problems). In *Nihon Rekishi*, edited by Iwanami kōza (Iwanami lectures), 16:241–80. 26 vols. Tokyo: Iwanami, 1975–1977.

Meiji shiryō kenkyū renrakukai (Meiji historical materials research committee), ed. *Meiji zenji no rōdō mondai* (Labor problems of the early Meiji period). Tokyo: Ochanomizu shōbu, 1960.

Miller, Randall M. "The Fabric of Control: Slavery in the Antebellum Southern Textile Mills." *Business History Review* 55, no. 4 (Winter 1981): 471–90.

Miura Toyohiko. *Rōdō no rekishi* (A history of labor). Tokyo: Kinokuniya, 1964.

Miyashita Michiko. "Nōson ni okeru kazoku to kon'in" (Family and marriage in the countryside). In *Nihon josei shi 3: kinsei*, 31–62.

Morisaki Kazue, *Karayuki-san*. Tokyo: Asahi shinbunsha, 1976.

———. *Makkura* (Pitch dark). Tokyo: San'ichi Shobō, 1977.

Morosawa Yōko, ed. *Onna no hataraki* (Women's work). Vol. 3 of *Dokyumento onna no hyakunen* (Documents of a century of women). Tokyo: Miraisha, 1978.

———. *Shinano no onna* (Women of Shinano). 2 vols. Tokyo: Miraisha, 1969.

Murakami Nobuhiko. *Meiji josei shi* (A history of Meiji women). 4 vols. Tokyo: Rironsha, 1971.

Murakami Hatsu. "Sangyō kakumei to josei rōdō" (The Industrial Revolution and female labor). In *Nihon josei shi 4: kindai*, 77–114.

Myers, Raymon. *The Chinese Peasant Economy*. Cambridge: Harvard University Press, 1970.

Nagashima Atsuko. "Kinsei josei no nōgyō rōdō ni okeru ichi" (The position of women in agricultural labor during the late feudal period). *Rekishi hyōron* (Historical review) 382 (March 1982): 48–65.

Nagoya josei shi kenkyū kai (Nagoya women's history research association), ed. *Haha no jidai: Aichi no josei shi* (The age of our mothers: A history of Aichi women). Nagoya: Fūbaisha, 1969.

Nakamura Masanori. *Rōdōsha to nōmin* (Laborer and peasant). Vol. 29 of *Nihon no rekishi* (History of Japan). Tokyo: Shōgakukan, 1976.

———. "Seishi-gyō no tenkai to jinushi sei" (Advance of silk reeling and the landlord system). *Shakai keizai shigaku* (Social and economic history) 32, nos. 5–6 (1967): 46–71.

Nakamura Masanori and Corrado Molteni. "Seishi gijutsu no hatten to joshi rōdō" (The development of silk-reeling technology and female labor). In *Gijutsu kakushin to joshi rōdō* (Technological innovation and female labor), edited by Nakamura Masanori, 33–70. Tokyo: Tokyo Daigaku shuppan kai, 1985.

Nakamura Takafusa. *Economic Growth in Prewar Japan* [*Sensenki Nihon keizai seichō no bunseki* (Tokyo: Iwanami, 1971)]. Translated by Robert A. Feldman. New Haven: Yale University Press, 1983.

Nawa Tōichi. *Nihon bōseki-gyō no shiteki bunseki* (A historical analysis of the Japanese cotton-spinning industry). Tokyo: Chōryūsha, 1948.

NFMSS. See *Nihon fujin mondai shiryō shūsei.*

Nihon fujin mondai shiryō shūsei (*NFMSS*) (Collected documentary materials concerning Japanese women). 10 vols. Tokyo: Domesu Shuppan, 1977–1980.

Nihon josei shi 3: kinsei (History of Japanese women 3: Late feudal period) and *Nihon josei shi 4: kindai* (History of Japanese women 4: Modern period). Vols. 3 and 4 of *Nihon josei shi* (History of Japanese women), edited by Josei shi sōgō kenkyū kai (Women's history research collective). Tokyo: Tokyo Daigaku shuppan kai, 1982.

Nihon kindai shi jiten (Dictionary of modern Japanese history). Tokyo: Kyoto daigaku bungakubu kokushi kenkyū shitsu (National history research laboratory of Kyoto University Faculty of Arts), 1958.

Nihon rekishi daijiten (Great dictionary of Japanese history). 12 vols. Tokyo: Kawade shobō, 1969.

Nishinarita Yutaka. "Joshi rōdō no shorui gata to sono hen'yō" (The various types of female labor and their transformation: 1980s to 1940s). In Nakamura Masanori, *Gijutsu kakushin to joshi rōdō,* 7–31.

———. "Nihongata chinrōdō no seiritsu" (Formation of the Japanese pattern of wage labor). In *Kindai Nihon keizai o manabu* (Studying the modern Japanese economy), edited by Ishii Kanji, Uno Fukuju, Nakamura Masanori, and Egusa Tadaatsu, 1:107–36. 2 vols. Tokyo: Yūhikaku, 1977.

Norman, E. Herbert. *Japan's Emergence as a Modern State.* New York: Institute of Pacific Relations, 1940.

Nōshōmu-shō, shōkō-kyoku (Ministry of Agriculture and Commerce, Commerce and Industry Department), ed. *Kōjō oyobi shokkō ni kan suru tsuhei ippan* (Common evils afflicting factories and factory workers). Tokyo, 1897.

———. *Shokkō jijō* (Factory workers' conditions). Vol. 4 of *Seikatsu koten sōsho* (Classics of everyday life). Tokyo: Kōseikan, 1971.

Ōe Shinobu. *Nihon no sangyō kakumei* (Japan's industrial revolution). Tokyo: Iwanami, 1975.

Ōishi Kaiichirō, ed. *Nihon sangyō kakumei kenkyū* (A study of Japan's industrial revolution). 2 vols. Tokyo: Tokyo Daigaku shuppan kai, 1975.

Ōkōchi Kazuo. *Labor in Modern Japan.* Tokyo: The Science Council of Japan, 1958.

———. *Reimei ki no Nihon rōdō undō* (The dawn of the Japanese labor movement). Tokyo: Iwanami, 1952.

Orimoto Sadayo. "Myōnichi no josei: jokō o kataru" (Women of tomorrow: Talking about factory women). *Chūō kōron* 44, no. 12 (1929). Reproduced in *NFMSS*, 3:239–43.

Ōsaka shi-yakusho (Osaka City Hall) ed. *Meiji Taishō Ōsaka shi shi* (A history of Osaka City during the Meiji and Taisho eras). 8 vols. Osaka: Seibundō, 1932.

Ōtsuka Hisao. "Modernization Reconsidered with Special Reference to Industrialization." *Developing Economies* 3, no. 4 (December 1965): 387–403.

Patrick, Hugh, ed. *Japanese Industrialization and Its Social Consequences*. Berkeley: University of California Press, 1976.

Robinson, Harriet H. *Loom and Spindle or Life among the Early Mill Girls*. Kailua, Hawaii: Press Pacifica, 1976.

Rōdō undō iin kai (Committee for historical materials pertaining to the labor movement), ed. *Nihon rōdō undō shiryō* (Historical materials pertaining to Japan's labor movement). 5 vols. Tokyo: Tokyo Daigaku shuppan kai, 1968.

Saitō Isamu. *Nagoya chihō rōdō undō shi* (History of the labor movement in the Nagoya region). Nagoya: Fubaisha, 1969.

Sakisaka Itsurō. *Nihon shihonshugi no shomondai* (Problems of Japanese capitalism). Tokyo: Ikuseisha, 1937.

Sakura Takuji. *Jokō gyakutai shi* (A history of the ill-treatment of female silk-factory workers). Nagano City: Shinano mainichi shinbunsha, 1981.

Sanpei Kōko. *Hataraki josei no rekishi* (A history of working women). Tokyo: Nihon hyōron shinsha, 1956.

———. *Nihon kigyō shi* (A history of Japan's weaving industry). Tokyo: Yūsankaku, 1961.

———. *Nihon mengyō hattatsu shi* (A history of Japan's cotton industry). Tokyo: Keio shobō, 1941.

———. "Nihon ni okeru fujin rōdō no rekishi" (History of women's labor in Japan). In *Fujin rōdō* (Female labor), edited by Ōkōchi Kazuo and Isoda Susumu, 29–55. Tokyo: Kōbundō, 1956.

Saxonhouse, Gary R. "Country Girls and Communications among Competitors in the Japanese Cotton-Spinning Industry." In Patrick, *Japanese Industrialization*, 97–125.

Segawa Kiyoko. *Mura no onnatachi* (Village women). Tokyo: Miraisha, 1970.

———. *Onna no hataraki, i-seikatsu no rekishi* (Women's work, a history of clothing customs). Tokyo: Miraisha, 1962.

Seishi orimono shinposha (Silk-Reeling and Woven Goods Press), ed. *Shūshin kunwa kōjo no kagami* (Moral discourses: A mirror for factory girls). Tokyo, 1912.

Shimonaka Kunihiko, ed. *Nihon zangoku monogatari* (Tales of Japanese cruelty). 5 vols. Tokyo: Heibonsha, 1972.

Smelser, Neil J. *Social Change in the Industrial Revolution: An Application of Theory to the Lancashire Cotton Industry, 1770–1840*. London: G. B. Routledge and Kegan Paul, 1959.

Smith, Robert J., and Ella Lury Wiswell. *The Women of Sure Mura*. Chicago: Chicago University Press, 1982.

Smith, Thomas C. *Nakahara: Family Farming in a Japanese Village, 1717–1830*. Stanford: Stanford University Press, 1977.

———. *Political Change and Industrial Development in Japan: Government Enterprise, 1868–1880*. Stanford: Stanford University Press, 1955.

———. "The Right to Benevolence: Dignity and Japanese Workers, 1890–1920." *Comparative Studies in Society and History* 26, no. 4 (October 1984): 587–613.

Strumingher, Laura. "Les canutes de Lyon (1835–1848)." *Mouvement Sociale* 105 (October–December 1978): 59–85.

Sumiya Mikio. *Nihon chinrōdō no shiteki kenkyū* (Historical studies of Japanese wage labor). Tokyo: Ochanomizu shobō, 1976.

———. *Nihon chinrōdō shi ron: Meiji zenki ni okeru rōdōsha kaikyū no keisei* (A history of wage labor in Japan: The formation of the laboring class in early Meiji). Tokyo: Tokyo Daigaku shuppan kai, 1955.

———. *Nihon rōdō undō shi* (A history of the Japanese labor movement). Tokyo: Yūshindō, 1966.

———. *Social Impact of Industrialization in Japan*. Tokyo: Japanese National Commission for UNESCO, 1963.

Suzuki Umejirō. "Osaka nago-machi hinmin kutsu shisatsu ki" (Observations of the Nago-machi Ghetto of Osaka). In *Meiji shoki no toshi kasō shakai* (Early Meiji society's urban lower classes), edited by Nishida Taketoshi, 123–52. Vol. 2 of *Seikatsu koten sōsho* (Classics of everyday life). Tokyo: Kōseikan, 1970.

Takahashi Kamekichi. *The Rise and Development of Japan's Modern Economy* [*Nihon kindai keizai keisei shi*]. Translated by John Lynch. Tokyo: Tokyo jiji tsūshinsha, 1969.

Takahashi Keiji. *Monogatari onna ichiba* (Tales of selling women). Tokyo: Tenbōsha, 1982.

Takamura Naosuke. *Nihon bōseki-gyō shi josetsu* (An introduction to the history of Japan's cotton-spinning industry). 2 vols. Tokyo: Kaku shobō, 1971.

Takase Toyoji. *Kanei Tomioka seishisho kōjo shiryō* (Historical materials regarding the factory girls of the Tomioka silk filature while under government management). Tokyo: Taimatsu-sha, 1979.

Takenobu Toshihiko, ed. *Jokō tokuhon* (Factory girls' reader). Tokyo: Jitsugyō kokumin kyōwa kai, 1911.

Takizawa Hideki. *Nihon shihonshugi to sanshi-gyō* (Japanese capitalism and the silk-reeling industry). Tokyo: Miraisha, 1978.

Tamura Tarō, ed. *Jokō in kun shiryō* (Materials for the training of female factory workers). Tokyo: Tōyō mosurin kabushiki kaisha chōsa ka, 1922.

Tanigawa Ken'ichi, ed. *Kindai minshū no kiroku 3: shōfu* (Record of the masses in the modern era: Prostitutes). Tokyo: Shinjinbutsu ōraisha, 1971.

Teruoka Shūzō, ed. *Nihon nōgyō shi: shihonshugi no tenkai to nōgyō mondai* (History of Japanese agriculture: Development of capitalism and agricultural problems). Tokyo: Yūhikaku, 1981.

Thompson, E. P. *The Making of the English Working Class*. Harmondsworth, Middlesex: Penguin Books, 1968.

Tilly, Louise A., and Joan W. Scott. *Women, Work and Family*. New York: Holt, Rinehart and Winston, 1978.

Tōyō Bōseki Kabushiki Kaisha. (Tōyō Cotton-Spinning Company). *Tōyō bōseki 70 nen shi* (A seventy-year history of Tōyō Cotton-Spinning). Tokyo, 1953.

"Tsumi serareru no wa itsumo kanojotachi: Japayuki-san" (It's always the women who are the sinners: Japayuki-san). *Fujin minshu shinbun*, no. 2018, 5 December 1986, 1.

"Tsurumi Shunsuke, Hashikawa Bunzō, Imai Seiichi, Matsumoto Sannosuke, Kamishima Jirō, and Sugai Junichi, eds. *Nihon no hyakunen* (A hundred years of Japan). 10 vols. Tokyo: Chikuma shobō, 1961–1964.

Uga Kiyoshi, ed. *Bōseki shokkō jijō chōsa gaiyō sho* (A summary report of the survey of conditions among cotton-spinning workers). Osaka: Dai Nihon menshi bōseki dōgyō rengō kai (Greater Japan Cotton-Spinning Alliance), 1898.

Ushiyama Keiji. "Nihon shihonshugi kakuritsu ki" (The period of establishment of Japanese capitalism). In Teruoka, *Nihon nōgyō shi*, 49–112.

Ushiyama Saijirō. "Kōjō junshi ki" (Records of an inspection tour of factories). In *Fujin mondai hen* (Women's problems), edited by Meiji bunka kenkyū kai (Meiji Cultural Research Association), 308–77. Vol. 16 of *Meiji bunka zenshū* (Collected documents on Meiji culture). Tokyo: Nihon hyōronsha, 1968.

Utley, Freda. *Lancashire and the Far East*. London: George Allen and Unwin, 1931.

Vlastos, Stephen. *Peasant Protests and Uprisings in Tokugawa Japan*. Berkeley: University of California Press, 1986.

Wada Ei. *Teihon Tomioka nikki* (Tomioka diary, the authentic text). Tokyo: Sōjusha, 1976.

"Watakushitachi no seikatsu" (Our lives). *Rōdō* (Labor) (April 1924). In *Rōdō*, edited by Akamatsu Ryōko, 235–36. Vol. 3 of *NFMSS*.

Watanabe Tōru. "Meiji zenki no rōdōryoku ichiba keisei o megute" (Establishment of the labor market during the early Meiji period). In Meiji shiryō kenkyū renrakukai, *Meiji zenki no rōdō mondai*, 96–136.

Yamada Moritarō. *Nihon shihonshugi bunseki* (An analysis of Japanese capitalism). Tokyo: Iwanami, 1934.

Yamakawa Kikue. *Onna nidai no ki* (A record of two generations of women). Tokyo: Heibonsha, 1972.

Yamamoto Shigemi. *Aa nomugi tōge* (Ah! The Nomugi Pass). Tokyo: Kadokawa, 1977.

———. *Zoku aa nomugi tōge* (Ah! The Nomugi Pass: The sequel). Tokyo: Kadokawa, 1982.

Yamamoto Shun'ichi. *Nihon kōshō shi* (History of licensed prostitution in Japan). Tokyo: Chūō hōki shuppan, 1983.

Yamanouchi Mina. *Yamanouchi Mina jiden: jūni sai no bōseki jokō kara no shōgai* (The autobiography of Yamanouchi Mina: My career from the time I was a twelve-year-old cotton-spinning factory girl). Tokyo: Shinjuku shobō, 1975.

Yamazaki Tomoko. *Sandakan hachiban shōkan* (Sandakan brothel number eight). Tokyo: Bungei shunjū, 1975.

———. *Sandakan no haka* (The graves of Sandakan). Tokyo: Bungei shunjū, 1977.

———. *The Story of Yamada Waka: From Prostitute to Feminist Pioneer* [Ameyuki-san no uta: Yamada Waka no sūki ni naru shōgai, 1978]. Tokyo: Kodansha International, 1985.

Yanagita Kunio. *Japanese Manners and Customs in the Meiji Era*. Translated by Charles S. Terry. Tokyo: Tokyo Bunko, 1957.

Yokoyama Gen'nosuke. *Naichi zakkyo no Nihon* (Japan since the opening of the country). Tokyo: Iwanami, 1954.

————. *Nihon no kasō shakai* (The lower classes of Japan). Tokyo: Iwanami, 1949.

Yoneda Sayoko. "Meiji 19 no Kōfu seishi jokō sōgi ni tsuite: Nihon ni okeru saisho no sutoraiki" (The Kōfu silk-factory girls' dispute of 1886: Japan's first industrial strike). *Rekishi hyōron* 105 (May 1959): 70–81.

Yoshimi Kaneko. "Baishō no jittai to haishō undō" (Actual conditions of prostitution and the movement for abolition of prostitution). In *Nihon josei shi 4: kindai*, 223–58.

Yoshisaka Shinzō. "Labor Recruitment in Japan and Its Control." *International Labor Review* (Geneva) 12 (October 1925): 484–99.

Yutani Eiji. " 'Nihon no Kasō Shakai' of Gennosuke Yokoyama, Translated and with an Introduction." Ph.D. diss., University of California, Berkeley, 1985.

Index